LIVING KINSHIP IN THE PACIFIC

Pacific Perspectives
Studies of the European Society for Oceanists

Series Editors: Christina Toren, University of St Andrews, and
Edvard Hviding, University of Bergen

Oceania is of enduring contemporary significance in global trajectories of
history, politics, economy and ecology, and has remained influential for diverse
approaches to studying and understanding human life worlds. The books
published in this series explore Oceanic values and imaginations, documenting
the unique position of the Pacific region – its cultural and linguistic diversity,
its ecological and geographical distinctness, and always fascinating experiments
with social formations. This series thus conveys the political, economic and
moral alternatives that Oceania offers the contemporary world.

Living Kinship in the Pacific

◆●◆

Edited by Christina Toren and Simonne Pauwels

berghahn
NEW YORK · OXFORD
www.berghahnbooks.com

First edition published in 2015 by
Berghahn Books
www.berghahnbooks.com

©2015, 2017 Christina Toren and Simonne Pauwels
First paperback edition published in 2017

Library of Congress Cataloging-in-Publication Data

Living kinship in the Pacific / edited by Christina Toren and Simonne
Pauwels. -- First edition.
    pages cm. -- (Pacific perspectives; Volume 4)
    Includes bibliographical references.
    ISBN 978-1-78238-577-6 (hardback) — ISBN 978-1-78533-520-4
(paperback) — ISBN 978-1-78238-578-3 (ebook) 1. Kinship--
Polynesia. 2. Kinship--Polynesia--Case studies. 3. Kinship--Pacific
Area. 4. Kinship--Pacific Area--Case studies. I. Toren, Christina,
1947- editor of compilation, author. II. Pauwels, Simonne, editor of
compilation, author.
    GN670.L48 2015
    306.830996--dc23

                                                          2014033533

British Library Cataloguing in Publication Data
A catalogue record for this book is available from the British Library

ISBN 978-1-78238-577-6 (hardback)
ISBN 978-1-78533-520-4 (paperback)
E-ISBN 978-1-78238-578-3 (ebook)

Contents

◆●◆

Figures and Tables

—————— ◆●◆ ——————

Figures

Tables

Introduction

Kinship in the Pacific as Knowledge that Counts

◆●◆

Christina Toren and Simonne Pauwels

This book has its starting point in Unaisi Nabobo-Baba's observation that, for the various peoples of the Pacific, kinship is generally understood to come under the heading of 'knowledge that counts' (Nabobo-Baba 2006). Needless to say this is also the case for the analyst, from whose perspective kinship is at once a heuristic domain and a material, historically structured reality that is lived by the people whose ideas and practices are the object of analysis. The book's objective is straightforward: to provide case studies of contemporary Pacific kinship, and in so doing arrive at an understanding of what is currently happening to kinship in an area where deep historical links provide for close and useful comparison. The ethnographic focus is on Fiji, Tonga and Samoa, with the addition of three instructive cases from Tokelau, Papua New Guinea and Taiwan.

There is no question but that kinship remains central to the anthropological project.[1] Indeed, the editors would argue that an understanding of kinship is always essential wherever anthropologists are working – whether it be 'down the road' in their own native places or somewhere far away from the land where they were themselves 'born and bred'.[2] If there was ever any doubt about this, it has certainly been laid to rest by the work of Eduardo Viveiros de Castro (2009) and others for Amazonia – Peter Gow (1989, 2000, 2001), Cecilia McCallum (2001), Vanessa Lea (1995, 2001, 2002), Laura Rival (1998, 2001), Fernando Santos-Granero (2007), Anne

Christine Taylor (2000), Aparecida Vilaça (2002, 2005) – and of numerous Pacific specialists, especially Mac Marshall (1981), Marshall and Cougghey (1989), Marilyn Strathern (1985, 1988), Jadran Mimica (1991) and, more recently, Rupert Stasch (2003), James Leach (2003), Sandra Bamford (2004) and Bamford and Leach (2009). In a recent wide-ranging review essay, Marshall Sahlins finds in certain of their works the answer to the question of what kinship is: a quality he denotes as 'mutuality of being' (Sahlins 2011). No one would disagree – after all, mutuality is precisely what characterizes human collectivities.

Sahlins' chapter ends with a celebration of Viveiros de Castro, whose 'work offers a revelation of a certain cultural order of intersubjectivity in which kinship takes a fundamental place, indeed a cosmic place' (ibid.: 239) – an observation that is, of course, as true for the Pacific as it is for Amazonia. Sahlins's ultimate objective, however, is to persuade cultural anthropologists, and perhaps especially cultural anthropologists in the USA, that Schneider (1984) did not put paid to the study of kinship; indeed, that following through the position he proposed – that kinship is 'culturally specific' – has made it possible for kinship to re-emerge as a central object of analytical concern.

At the same time, there is a fundamental problem with Sahlins's argument – one pointed out by Adam Kuper (2013) – that, because Sahlins is a committed 'cultural determinist', his argument depends on the dismissal of any idea that biology or what one might call, more broadly, physical substance has any significant part to play in the ideas and practices of kinship that feature in the lives of many peoples across the globe. Kuper's trenchant critique of the two extremes of the culture versus biology argument ends with the following observation: 'Like most of the important things in our lives, kinship is surely a matter of biology, of beliefs and concepts, and of social institutions and social pressures. Ultimately any kinship system is also constrained by brute necessity. You can't just make it up' (ibid.: 12).

One might take further the implication here that the problem for Sahlins, and for cultural anthropologists in general, resides in their taken for granted distinction between biology and culture. This distinction itself is historically constituted, and as such surely should not be used as a means of explaining the ideas and practices of the many peoples across the globe whose ideas of what it is to be human have their own historical inevitability.[3] History is, however, likewise a problem for Sahlins because he holds history to be, like culture, external to human beings and, as it were, imposed upon them – culture being a matter of 'received meanings' and history the process in which these same meanings are 'risked in action' and, possibly, trans-formed as a function of a clash between 'cultural schemes' (see Sahlins 1985;

cf. Toren 1988). If, however, we take the view that human autopoiesis is through and through itself a historical process, then it is possible to arrive at the awareness that literally every aspect of any given human being is historically constituted – from our genes to our most private thoughts – and that, from an anthropological point of view, the challenge is to derive a unified model of human being that provides a way in to understanding human uniqueness as a function of historical differentiation (see Toren 2012a, 2012b).

It is generally accepted in principle that history explains everything about us human beings. The problem is that history seems difficult to arrive at even once we have conceptualized it. What is under discussion here is not history as something external to us, confined to the past, nor history as it is known or generally understood, nor history as it is written, nor the personal history we can recollect and tell to others, but rather history as it is lived. An understanding of history as lived enables us to think about our in-all-respects-material selves as emergent, autopoietic – self-creating, self-producing – products of a past that from moment to moment evinces itself in the present in every aspect of our being and that is even now giving rise to a future we cannot surely predict even for ourselves as particular persons.

What is difficult to realize and to remain conscious of is the fact that we *are* our history, that from moment to moment, in literally every aspect of our being, we at once manifest our history and live its all-pervasive presence. Our history is not merely a part of us; it is the whole of us – we are constituted by the history that informs our entire being from conception throughout gestation in the womb, from our birth onwards throughout all our lives, to the very moment of our death. This history that continues to give rise to each of us in all our uniqueness is, at its most general, a material history of social relations that have transformed and continue to transform over the millennia that produced us as contemporary human beings in all our dynamic complexity. In other words, and to make the point as plainly as possible, social relations were always, and continue to be, fundamental to what it is to be human and like any other aspect of being human were always, and continue to be, differentiated in the course of daily life. Thus social relations at once transform and are inevitably transformed over time by we humans whose lives at any time and place may be understood to manifest a distinctive form of social relations. Any given human being's particular personal genetic profile is one dimension of this social history, and cannot properly be understood in isolation from it.

This theoretical position demands a brief consideration of how we theorize mind. Toren's formulation, discussed in detail elsewhere, is as follows: in respect of any one of us, mind is a function of the whole person that is constituted over time in intersubjective relations with others in the environing world (Toren 1999b, 2012a, 2012b). The constituting process is to be understood as at once biological, social and psychological, such that at any given time, in all aspects of our being, each one of us manifests the history of social relations that continues to make us who we are. Furthermore, like all other living things, we humans inhere in the world and, as humans, it is given to us to find out and objectify its aspects as a function of consciousness. The challenge for the human scientist – for the anthropologist in particular – is to demonstrate the historical processes that continue, over time, to give rise to salient aspects of the ontologies and entailed epistemologies that at once unite and differentiate us humans through time and across regions of the world (see Toren and Pina-Cabral 2012). In the present case, the focus is on kinship as the lived artefact of a long, long history of regional differentiation in which transformation and continuity over time are aspects of the self-same process.

The case studies collected here concern kinship as one aspect of history as lived. They are all intended to show how the study of kinship provides the analyst with a way in to understanding its fundamental importance, but also its articulation with other heuristic domains – exchange, for example, or gender or cosmology. It follows that ideas of kinship are historically variable, but given the close historical links between Pacific peoples, case studies of kinship ideas and practices across the region are bound to supply fascinating comparisons. It is worth stressing here that it is history that differentiates our case studies from one another, and history which, at the same time, provides for a perspective on Pacific kinship that recognizes that continuity and transformation are a function of the self-same process that day to day brings particular forms of kinship into being.

The essays achieve their objective through analyses of kinship as lived, with certain of them being concerned with kinship terminologies in order to provide a deeper, more nuanced understanding of their use. In most of the case studies, as is fitting for the Pacific, the focus is on the relation between brothers and sisters and its broader implications for marriage, and for differential status in the polity at large. As will be shown, this relation is a core relation, for some the starting point of kinship. Even when kinship is forgotten or yet-to-be found out, one can observe, during rituals, when the exchange of gifts is overwhelming, how kinship is made evident in gifting. People give as if they are brothers and sisters, or kin, and accordingly are seen to be kin. Thus the essays in this volume are bound together by the idea that to know about kinship and sisters and brothers is to know about political economy, and that to know about political economy is to know about kinship and sisters and brothers.

Kinship and Political Economy

Each of the chapters pays a good deal of attention to the articulation of kinship with political economy. Thus, for Fiji, Nabobo-Baba (Chapter 1) argues that *veiwekani* (kinship) is best understood as relationships that obtain within and across chiefdoms and, by virtue of their continued acknowledgement, in one movement build and constitute the continuing strength and stability not only of kinship as such, but of the *vanua* ('country', 'land', 'place') and all that it contains – chiefs, people, fauna and flora, and ancestral spirits. It is important here to note that Fijians are not making a distinction between what we designate, for heuristic purposes, 'political economy' and 'kinship'. Thus Nabobo-Baba's examination of gifts of land by one *vanua* to another shows that such gifts are always conceived of in kinship terms. Knowledge of kinship is important knowledge, and is intrinsically connected to the philosophy of *sautu* ('peace and plenty'), or what constitutes a good life. This chapter shows how deeply embedded in everyday kinship practice are ideas of *loloma* and *veilomani* (compassion and love), of *kauwai* and *veikau-waitaki* (care), and how they are understood to be essential to sustaining the *vanua* in all its manifestations.[4] Nabobo-Baba shows how it is possible to see in *i solisoli* (gifts of land) how *veiwekani* is (re)constituted in forms that emulate, extend or, in some cases, disrupt ideas concerning the nature of the *vanua*.

Ching-Hsiu Lin (Chapter 2) shows how kinship and political economy implicate one another – a finding that is the more evident in a situation where new economic arrangements are producing concomitant effects in kinship and in social organization at large. The chapter examines the implications of the monetization of exchange for relations between *sapah* (household) and *gxal* (feast group) among Truku people in Taiwan. During the pre-colonial period, Truku people lived as hunter-gatherers in the mountain areas of the island; their kinship system was bilateral. The household, based on a couple and their unmarried children, was the basic kinship, ritual and economic entity. The exogamous feast group was comprised of different households, and residence on marriage was virilocal. In terms of marriage exchange, the groom's household should pay bridewealth (pigs) to the bride's household, which was obliged to distribute a portion of the wedding gift (pork) to each household of their feast group. Thus the definition of the household and the feast group was associated with marriage. With the advent of cash crops and the imposition of land reform on Truku society in the 1960s, Truku exchange came to be mediated by the market, and bridewealth and the wedding feast were monetized. An ethnographic analysis of the wedding ritual shows how the monetization of marriage is transforming relations between Truku people in respect of the constitution of the household and the feast group and, in the process, is creating a socio-political hierarchy between richer and poorer households.

Jara Hulkenberg's argument (Chapter 3) likewise looks at the nature of ceremonial exchange, among Fijians in the United Kingdom. Her research on the uses of *masi* (Fijian barkcloth) in rural, urban and overseas settings reveals the perseverance of various forms of exchange and kinship obligations in daily and ceremonial life. Hulkenberg argues that current forms of exchange and the pressure to fulfil kinship obligations ultimately stem from pre-Christian ideas concerning sacrifice and tribute, where all forms of ceremonial exchange were directed towards the ancestor gods, from whom divine blessings were sought. With Christianity, many forms of ancestor god worship disappeared, but even so the necessity to acknowledge kinship obligations remains central to day-to-day life, as does the preference for ceremonial exchange over monetary transactions. The analysis suggests that, by virtue of reaffirming connectedness to the *vanua* – the reference here being to Fiji at large and its component *vanua* (referred to above) – these ceremonial practices provide for attendance on the ancestral gods, and facilitate the hierarchical kinship relations that structure relations between Fijians, no matter where they are located. Those Fijians who are unable to live a life 'in the manner of the land' (*i tovo vakavanua*), that is to say, fulfilling kinship obligations, risk godly repercussions and put in jeopardy their connection to their *vanua*.

Pauwels (2015) comes to the same conclusion when comparing city-dwellers to village people in Lakeba. It seems that for city-dwellers the brother–sister relation becomes even more important. The place of the eldest sister (see Pauwels, this volume) is not foreign to this, neither is the wish to be buried in the *vanua*. But a man is also eager to send his children to his brother's house in the city; a sister living in her husband's house is less comfortable doing this. Pauwels also observed that sending remittances is more active between brothers and sisters than between same-sex siblings or children and parents; note, however, that parents can be the ultimate beneficiaries of part of it.

Gender and household studies, along with studies of so-called house societies, have shown how kinship and other aspects of social formations may bear upon each other (Collier and Yanagisako 1987; Pauwels 1990, 1994; Toren 1990; Carsten 1995; Carsten and Hugh-Jones 1995; Théry, Bonnemère, Downs and Taylor 2008.) Ingjerd Hoëm (Chapter 4) shows how such an approach provides for an exploration of how kinship and gender, and political and other aspects of existence, are orchestrated through ritual practices – broadly defined as the choreography of life – into recognizable segments. The analysis shows how the process of 'making sides' is present in Tokelau kinship and social organization; it is also evident in, and arguably created by, ritual practices. Across different contexts, the pattern of 'making sides' is replicated, but the role, function and purpose of the activities involved vary. A mastery of relationships and characteristics, of people and situations, allows one to orchestrate the creation of sides through separation, and to facilitate the coming together of sides in a temporary unity – at once material and ideational. As Tokelauans describe the principle inherent in this dynamic, '*fau ma vehi*, "we put together (build, join) and we take apart (split, destroy)"'.[5]

Svenja Völkel (Chapter 5) provides a linguist's perspective on Tonga's highly stratified society with its *tu'a/'eiki* status distinction among kin. This hierarchical structure, which is of central importance to daily life, informs and is informed by kinship classification. According to Lowie (1928) and Murdock (1949), the Tongan kinship terminology can be classified as 'bifurcate merging Hawaiian type'; that is, the same term applies for father and father's brother (*tamai*), while there is another term for mother's brother (*tu'asina*), and the same term is used for siblings and cousins. A more detailed analysis reveals that the distinctive features of Tongan kinship terminology coincide broadly with those on which the relative *tu'a/'eiki* status is based.

The kinship terminology expresses this specific social stratification in an unequivocal and unambiguous way. Furthermore, Tongan makes use of two different possessive categories – where possession is inalienable (O) or alienable (A) – in reference to kin and while the idea of 'control' seems to determine the choice of O or A, the relative *tu'a/'eiki* status does not provide an explanation for all cases. Völkel's careful and fascinating analysis shows that, in respect of kinship terminology, the A/O dichotomy seems rather to be based on the idea of control over birth that is ascribed to the mother and the father's sister. Her chapter makes it clear that the subtleties of kinship terminology in use continue to have much to tell us about historical transformations already accomplished and those evidently in process.

Kinship and the Sister–Brother Relationship

The next few chapters all concentrate on the relation between sisters and brothers. They show that this relationship very often has to be considered across two generations, and even through two pairs of brothers and sisters, to get an overall view of its implications, especially where life-giving and life-taking capacities are at stake. Since the first writings on siblingship, as noted by Mac Marshall (1981), opposite-sex siblings seem to be an expression of complementarity, as if together they were one, or as a Lakeban villager formulated it, 'when I see my sister, I see me'. He would not say the same about his wife, who, on the contrary, is seen as taking him away from his sister. Different chapters in this volume (by Bonnemère, Cayrol,

Douaire-Marsaudon, Pauwels; see also Pauwels 2015) show the primordial role of the opposite-sex sibling in the procreative power of the other. Sisters intervene in their brothers' fertility, brothers play a role in their sisters'. The child of the one is also the child of the other in ways which are described in detail.

Pascale Bonnemère (Chapter 6) examines the relation between brothers and sisters among the Ankave-Anga, who hold that brothers and sisters share the same blood but that only women, therefore sisters, transmit it to their children. The brother–sister relationship is emphasized during the male ritual cycle, which transforms a young boy into an adult man, a warrior and a father. Bonnemère argues that this emphasis is related to the importance given to the position of the mother's brother and to the avuncular relationship. Among all male kinship statuses, only that of maternal uncle is endowed with the capacity to influence another person's own life and life-giving abilities. The analysis relies on diverse ethnographic materials: the actions a sister must perform, and the taboos she must respect for her brother during the various stages of his initiation; the content of the relationship between a married sister and her brother, and the exchanges that take place during her married life; the content of the relationship between a maternal uncle and his nephews and nieces.

Through the analyses of the sister–brother relationship in daily interaction and in ritual performance, Simonne Pauwels (Chapter 7) shows that, for the Fijians of the Lau islands, the *mana* and superiority of sister's children or *vasu* over their maternal uncle stems from the (eldest) sister's superiority over the brother. Her investigation of the history of the founding of the present-day chiefdom in Lau shows how the *vasu* (sister's child) doubly represents the whole *vanua*, being a synthesis of its relations both with the exterior, as *vasu levu*, and the interior, as *vasu taukei*. Sisters and daughters played an important role in the building up of the Lauan chiefdom through repetitive marriages intended to exploit politically the prerogatives of *vasu* status. Younger sisters of the high chief married minor chiefs within Lau, their sons became powerful *vasu taukei*; elder sisters of the high chief married chiefs in other major chiefdoms, their sons became powerful *vasu levu*. Together, through the taking of first fruits and artefacts and through waging war, they brought prosperity and peace (*sautu*) to the chiefdom.

Serge Tcherkézoff's (Chapter 8) penetrating analysis of social organization in contemporary Samoa provides an answer to an apparent puzzle: although the 'families' (*aiga*) that make up a 'village' (*nuu*) are generally far from 'related' (*aiga*), Samoans are unanimous in condemning marriage within a village – a principle that goes back as far as family accounts stretch, to the late nineteenth century. Why is this so? The answer comes to light in

Tcherkézoff's explanation of how it comes to be the case that, at a certain encompassing level of representation, all villagers are 'brother or sister' to each other. This kind of village organization is the most striking example of the continuing importance of the 'brother–sister relationship' (*feagaiga*) in Samoa. The brother–sister overarching link becomes evident by means of an analysis of the composition of the 'village' (*nuu*) not just as a group of 'families' (*aiga*) but as made up by three ceremonial groupings that include everyone, and that are also called *nuu*: the family (*aiga*) representatives (*sui*), also called family heads (*ulu*) or *matai* (translated in the literature as titleholders or 'chiefs'); their 'sons'; their 'daughters'. Tcherkézoff explores this configuration as it is evinced in ideas and practice to show not only why the deep meaning of the word *nuu* is 'community', but why that community continues to demand that marriage be exogamous.[6]

Françoise Douaire-Marsaudon (Chapter 9) sets out to reconsider the institution of the Tongan *fahu*, and through it the sociological and symbolic implications of opposite-sex siblingship. Her objective is to show that the brother–sister relationship acquires its full meaning when the brother and sister have produced their respective offspring: each of them is, in their own way, the true parent of the other's child. This appropriation of descendants through opposite-sex siblingship is institutionalized by the *fahu* relation, which appears to be the core of the unfolding of kinship over generations. As such (like the *vasu* in Fiji), the *fahu* position plays a crucial role at the interface between the domestic and the political spheres. Douaire-Marsaudon thus argues that the *fahu* complex of relationships continues to be the pivot of the Tongan kinship system, linking together generations, male and female lines, the living and the dead. As such, it shapes domains of domestic and ritual life, and the political sphere in particular, and creates kinship bonds between persons who are not supposed to be kin.

The kinship vocabulary of the Nasau people, who live in eastern central Viti Levu and are part of the former so called 'hill tribes', is analysed by Françoise Cayrol (Chapter 10). The structure of this vocabulary, in which opposite sex plays a determining role, leads to the distinguishing of two main categories of kin, shaped by the distinction, or not, of birth order. Cayrol's analysis focuses on the relations of principal importance expressed in this vocabulary: those of status, those between brother and sister, and between maternal uncle and the uterine nephew – this being linked to the famous *vasu* position associated with the 'heaviest' and most difficult work. These relations evoke the differentiated ties a person has with the origin gods of their mother's and father's group, for Christianity has had little impact on their importance for Nasau people. The analysis demonstrates how the structure of this vocabulary is linked to the omnipresent genera-tional distinction of 'ako/lavo and its particular expressions of temporality.

There is a beautiful analytical connection made here between the kinship logic and the constitution of a Nasau person in terms of place – *vanua, dra* (blood) and *bula* (life) – as expressed in the giving of names.

Knowledge that Counts

The overall objective of the present volume is to make evident the continuing central importance of kinship in the Pacific as 'knowledge that counts'. As Toren shows in the concluding chapter (Chapter 11) this knowledge is constituted over time in terms of life-cycle and other rituals, of pervasive ritualized behaviour, and of exegesis specifically concerned to remind people of ritual duties and obligations. The microhistorical process of constituting knowledge is one in which ideas are at once maintained and transformed. Thus the essays collected here will, it is hoped, enable the reader to understand what is happening to contemporary kinship in certain Pacific contexts, and at the same time enable them to see that change and continuity in the ideas and practices in which kinship consists are not separable processes, but rather aspects of one another.

Notes

1   For example, for an able consideration of the history of the genealogical method and its uses in contemporary anthropology, see Bamford and Leach (2009); see also Franklin and McKinnon (2001) and Schweitzer (2000).

2.   See Carsten (1995 and 2000), Carsten and Hugh-Jones(1995) and compare Strathern (1981), Edwards (2000), Edwards and Strathern (2000) and Evans (2006).

3.   This observation is explored by Viveiros de Castro (2009) in respect of the widespread focus on kinship as a 'constructed process'. In this connection, Toren has long argued that ideas of 'cultural' and/or 'social construction' are artefacts of taken-for-granted theoretical distinctions between biology and culture, and individual and society (see e.g. Toren 1999b).

4.   Toren (1999a) shows how the ontogenetic process of constituting kinship as intentionality makes any given Fijian able ideally to be kin with any other and, further, makes kinship serve at once as the expression of collective order, as the domain of relations in whose terms libidinal desire is structured, and as the ground of ideas of self and other. An understanding of kinship has to be constituted rather than merely received, and a key element in this process is a developed consciousness of one's peers as peers. To become consciously a subject of kinship, a Fijian child has to find its peers; in so doing it begins to know kinship as the inexhaustible and unifying medium of all its relations with others. This example of an analysis of a particular Fijian ontogeny

provides a method that allows access to the preoccupations of the people whose manifold relations with one another are the object of anthropological analysis.

5. In contrast, a house in an Eastern Indonesian house-based society strives for permanence in its relations. Two houses, wife-givers and wife-takers, constantly repeat marriage alliances, and tend to join in a much wider timeless circle of houses bound by marriage (Pauwels 1990, 1994).

6. Here Samoan kinship contrasts with the Fijian and Tongan variants, where a woman can be a sister and a spouse in the same community, even if her ritual role will always be that of a sister.

References

Bamford, S. 2004. 'Conceiving Relatedness: Non-substantial Relations Among the Kamea of Papua New Guinea', *Journal of the Royal Anthropological Institute* 10: 287–306.

Bamford, S., and J. Leach. 2009. 'Introduction', in S. Bamford and J. Leach (eds), *Kinship and Beyond: The Genealogical Model Reconsidered*. New York: Berghahn.

Carsten, J. 1995. 'The Substance of Kinship and the Heat of the Hearth: Feeding, Personhood and Relatedness among Malays in Pulau Langkawi', *American Ethnologist* 22(2): 223–41.

——— (ed.). 2000. *Cultures of Relatedness: New Approaches to the Study of Kinship*. Cambridge: Cambridge University Press.

Carsten, J., and S. Hugh-Jones (eds). 1995. *About the House: Lévi-Strauss and Beyond*. Cambridge: Cambridge University Press.

Collier, J.F., and S.J. Yanagisako (eds). 1987. *Gender and Kinship: Essays Toward a Unified Analysis*. Stanford: Stanford University Press.

Edwards, J. 2000. *Born and Bred: Idioms of Kinship and New Reproductive Technologies in England*. Oxford: Oxford University Press.

Edwards, J., and M. Strathern. 2000. 'Including Your Own', in J. Carsten (ed.), *Cultures of Relatedness: New Approaches to the Study of Kinship*. Cambridge: Cambridge University Press.

Evans, G. 2006. *Educational Failure and Working Class White Children in Britain*. Basingstoke: Palgrave Macmillan.

Franklin, S., and S. McKinnon (eds). 2001. *Relative Values: Reconfiguring Kinship Studies*. Durham, NC: Duke University Press.

Gow, P. 1989. 'The Perverse Child: Desire in a Native Amazonian Subsistence Economy', *Man* 24: 299–314.

——— 2000. 'Helpless: The Affective Preconditions of Piro Social Life', in J. Overing and A. Passes (eds), *The Anthropology of Love and Hate: The Aesthetics of Conviviality in Native Amazonia*. London: Routledge.

———— 2001. *An Amazonian Myth and its History*. Oxford: Oxford University Press.

Kuper, A. 2013 'Review of Marshall Sahlins *What Kinship Is – And Is Not*', *Times Literary Supplement*, 12 July, pp.12–13.

Lea, Vanessa R. 1995. 'The Houses of the Mebengokre (Kayapo) of Central Brazil: A New Door to Their Social Organization', in Stephen Hugh-Jones and Janet Carsten (eds), *About the House: Levi-Strauss and Beyond*. Cambridge: Cambridge University Press, pp.206–25.

————. 2001. 'The Composition of Mebengokre (Kayapó) Households in Central Brazil', in Laura Rival and Neil Whitehead (eds), *Beyond the Visible and the Material*. Oxford: Oxford University Press, pp.157–76.

————. 2002. 'Multiple Paternity amongst the Mêbengokre (Kayapó, Jê) of Central', in Stephen Beckerman and Paul Valentine (eds), *Cultures of Multiple Fathers: The Theory and Practice of Partible Paternity in Lowland South America*. Gainesville: University of Florida, pp.105–22.

Leach, J. 2003. *Creative Land: Place and Procreation on the Rai Coast of Papua New Guinea*. New York: Berghahn.

Lowie, R.H. 1928 'A Note on Relationship Terminologies', *American Anthropologist* 30(2): 263–67.

Marshall, M. 1981. 'Introduction', in M. Marshall (ed.), *Siblingship in Oceania: Studies in the Meaning of Kin Relations*. Ann Arbor: University of Michigan Press.

Marshall, M., and J.L. Cougghey (eds). 1989. *Culture, Kin, and Cognition in Oceania: Essays in Honor of Ward H. Goodenough*. Special Publication of the American Anthropological Association, 25.

McCallum, C. 2001. *Gender and Sociality in Amazonia: How Real People Are Made*. Oxford: Berg.

Mimica, J. 1991. 'The Incest Passions: An Outline of the Logic of Iqwaye Social Organization, Parts I and II', *Oceania* 62(1): 34–58, 62(2): 81–113.

Murdock, J.P. 1949. *Social Structure*. New York: MacMillan Company.

Nabobo-Baba, U. 2006. *Knowing and Learning: An Indigenous Fijian Approach*. Suva: Institute of Pacific Studies, University of the South Pacific.

Pauwels, S. 1990 'La relation frère–soeur et la temporalité dans une société d'Indonésie orientale', *L'Homme* 116: 7–29.

———— 1994 'Siblingship and (In)Temporality: Towards a Definition of the House (Eastern Indonesia)', in L.E. Visser (ed.), *Halmahera and Beyond: Social Science Research in the Moluccas in the 1980s*. Leiden: Koninklijk Instituut voor Land-Taal en Volkenkunde Press, pp.79–96.

———— 2015. 'Soeurs et frères dans les îles Lau (Fidji); la relation entre village et ville', *Anthropologica*.

Rival, L. 1998. 'Androgynous Parents and Guest Children: The Huaorani Couvade', *Journal of the Royal Anthropological Institute* 4(4): 619–42.

Rival, L. and N.Whitehead (eds). 2001. *Beyond the Visible and the Material*. Oxford: Oxford University Press.

Sahlins, M. 1985. *Islands of History*. London: Tavistock.

———— 2011. 'What Kinship Is, Parts I and II', *Journal of the Royal Anthropological Institute* 17: 2–19, 227–42.

Santos-Granero, F. 2000. 'The Sisyphus Syndrome, or the Struggle for Conviviality in Native Amazonia', in J. Overing and A. Passes (eds), *The Anthropology of Love and Hate: The Aesthetics of Conviviality in Native Amazonia*. London: Routledge, pp.268–87.

———— 2007. 'Of Fear and Friendship: Amazonian Sociality Beyond Kinship and Affinity', *Journal of the Royal Anthropological Institute* 13(1): 1–18.

Schneider, D.M. 1984. *A Critique of the Study of Kinship*. Ann Arbour: University of Michigan Press.

Schweitzer, P.P. (ed.). 2000. *Dividends of Kinship: Meanings and Uses of Social Relatedness*. London: Routledge.

Stasch, R. 2003. 'Separateness as a Relation: The Iconicity, Univocality and Creativity of Korowai Mother-in-Law Avoidance', *Journal of the Royal Anthropological Institute* 9(2): 317–37.

Strathern, M. 1981. *Kinship at the Core: An Anthropology of Elmdon, a Village in North-west Essex in the Nineteen-Sixties*. Cambridge: Cambridge University Press.

———— 1985. 'Kinship and Economy: Constitutive Orders of a Provisional Kind', *American Ethnologist* 12: 191–209.

———— 1988. *The Gender of the Gift. Problems with Women and Problems with Society in Melanesia*. Berkeley: University of California Press.

Taylor, A.C. 2000. 'Le sexe de la proie: Représentations jivaro du lien de parenté', *L'Homme* 154/155: 309–34.

Théry, I., P. Bonnemère, L.L. Downs and A.C. Taylor. 2008. *Ce que le genre fait aux personnes*. Paris: Ecole des Hautes Etudes en Sciences Sociales.

Toren, C. 1988. 'Review of Marshall Sahlins, *Islands of History*', *Critique of Anthropology* 8(1): 113–18.

———— 1990. *Making Sense of Hierarchy: Cognition as Social Process in Fiji*. London: Athlone.

———— 1999a. 'Compassion For One Another: Constituting Kinship as Intentionality in Fiji', *Journal of the Royal Anthropological Institute* 5: 265–80.

————1999b. *Mind, Materiality and History: Explorations in Fijian Ethnography*. London: Routledge.

———— 2009. 'Intersubjectivity as Epistemology', *Social Analysis* 53(2): 130–46.

———— 2012a. 'Anthropology and Psychology', in J. Gledhill and R. Fardon (eds), *Sage Handbook of Social Anthropology*. New York: Sage.

———— 2012b. 'Imagining the World that Warrants Our Imagination: The Revelation of Ontogeny', *Cambridge Anthropology* 30(1): 64–79.

Toren, C., and J. de Pina-Cabral (eds). 2011. *The Challenge of Epistemology: Anthropological Perspectives*. New York: Berghahn.

Vilaça, A. 2002. 'Making Kin out of Others in Amazonia', *Journal of the Royal Anthropological Institute* 8: 347–65.

——— 2005. 'Chronically Unstable Bodies: Reflections on Amazonian Corporealities', *Journal of the Royal Anthropological Institute* 11: 445–64.

Viveiros de Castro, E. 2009. 'The Gift and the Given: Three Nano-essays on Kinship and Magic', in S. Bamford and J. Leach (eds), *Kinship and Beyond: The Genealogical Model Reconsidered*. New York: Berghahn.

1

The Mutual Implication of Kinship and Chiefship in Fiji

◆●◆

Unaisi Nabobo-Baba

This chapter is intended to provide a perspective on contemporary Fijian kinship, *veiwekani* – a term which at its widest extent takes in all indigenous Fijians – and, in so doing, contribute to knowledge of the ideas and practice of *veiwekani* as lived.[1] The observations made here do not exhaust the matter, nor are they the only way of representing the multifaceted and increasingly turbulent relationships to be found in contemporary 'post-four-coups' Fiji. Kinship is a grand narrative of sorts amongst Fijians and, I dare say, a narrative not always committed to writing by 'insiders', that is to say by Fijians themselves. Nevertheless, *veiwekani* is critically analysed by Fijians in all its forms and processes, and especially in things ceremonial. The sharper commentaries are heard usually when, at one extreme, kinship ties are properly acknowledged in ceremonial exchange, and at the other when these ties are undervalued, weakened by a disregard of what is said to be customarily acceptable.

In an earlier, seminal work on Fijian kinship by an 'indigenous insider', Rusiate Nayacakalou (1955, 1957) provided a structural analysis, and noted the necessity of it being complemented by a sociological analysis. He went on to describe attitudes and behaviours associated with kinship, and the distinction between kin and non-kin. Culture contact, he observed, had an impact on kinship. He also drew attention to how the monetary economy was changing the nature of kinship as traditionally known. For example, in Draubuta, Tailevu, a more urbanized village, *sosolevaki* – the practice whereby kin groups work cooperatively on gardens, house building and suchlike – was being replaced by kin paying for labour. Money was also being used to pay for labour by kinsmen in cases of commercial farming. Later work by Griffin and Davis (1986) spoke of similar changes as Fijians increasingly moved to towns.

The present chapter extends the work by Nayacakalou (1957) to show how the gifting of land at once recognizes and values kinship (*veiwekani*), and how, for the chief, giving expresses chiefliness and empathy. The chapter argues further that *veiwekani* addresses economic and other development difficulties by virtue of providing for the (temporary) redistribution of land, which is the most valued possession among indigenous Fijians. The gifting of land is very costly, and it may be argued that kinship thus takes on what might otherwise be the duties of modern government and governance, despite it not always being valued or perceived in this manner. *Veiwekani* values include *veikauwaitaki*, showing care, concern for the welfare of kin and others, or empathy in respect of others' troubles; *veikauwaitaki* may be evinced in many ways, including the gifting of land. Also, *veisolisoli*, mutual giving and reciprocal exchange of gifts; and *veirairaici*, looking out for each other in times of need.

Matters concerning kinship and reciprocal exchange, especially in respect of the maintenance or nurturing of relationships, are likely to be discussed in oppositional terms as either good or bad. One hears talk of progress, mutual dependence, benefit, sustainable lives, putting people and relationships first as pivotal to life and development. On the other hand, there is talk of waste and economic loss, unrequited love and compassion, disrespect, exploitation, ignorance of tradition, failures of reciprocity, self-centredness and 'taking rather than giving'.

In what follows, I look at a significant marker of kinship, at what in Fijian is called *i solisoli*, the gifting in kinship of land or other material goods and knowledge within and across groups. Thus today kinship within and across *vanua* ('country', 'land', 'place' and by implication the people who live there) continues as part of the reality of a truly globalizing Pacific where rapid changes are influencing Fijian lives, including their *veiwekani*, compassion in relationships according to obligatory kinship and extra-kin based practices. The chapter explores *veiwekani* with reference to three contemporary instances of chiefly compassion as evinced in *i solisoli*.[2]

In the Manner of Kinship, in the Manner of Chiefs

Behaviour that is *vakaturaga* is that befitting a chief, irrespective of whether one is a member by birth of a chiefly clan. Persons whose behaviour is *vakaturaga* are so steeped in respect for others that they habitually act as if others were of more importance than themselves. 'Knowing their place in society [they] fulfil their obligations to those above, below and those of equal status to them' (Katz 1993: 28). The gifting of land (*i solisoli*) is an instance of *veiwekani vakaturaga*, chiefly kinship, that makes evident values that continue to be dear to Fijians, and that are evinced in all practices that are *vakaturaga vakavanua*. The gifting of land is, as Katz says, 'to do with forces of traditional kinship ties, where there is a sharing of resources . . . solidarity is the aim, caring for others the means' (ibid.: 28–29). Western-trained policy analysts in Fiji would see such gifting as wastage, and according to Katz may ask the question: 'Where is the desire for the competitive edge?' (ibid.: 28).

That kinship continues to be crucial to contemporary political economy in Fiji is evident in all the cases discussed here. Another argument might be that kinship is a safety net that provides welfare to those in need. In times of scarcity, resources given *vakaveiwekani*, in the manner of kinship, ensure, as in the first case discussed below, that land is made available to sustain one's living kin and their descendants. One might argue that this is sustainable development by means of a kind of distributive justice – a form of development not often discussed in economics classes in universities, where the emphasis is on individual accumulation of property and capital.

Fijians not only make it explicit that in kinship those who have much should make what they have available to those who are less fortunate, but they act in accordance with these values. The ideals of kinship and of chiefly obligation should inform the behaviour of Fijians such that they are guided by 'love and empathy for kin', as well as by the knowledge that God and the *Vu* (ancestral spirits) look kindly on those who are givers of land. In ceremonies where land is gifted, the speeches made by the recipients always refer to their continuing prayers that God's blessings may fall on the givers one hundred-fold, and especially on their descendants in future generations, their *kawa*.

Citing Thomson (1908), Tuwere outlines occasions where land is gifted or transferred to mark, affirm or enhance kinship: *veiwekani* (Tuwere 2002: 39–41). These transfers, according to Tuwere, are either for a period of time or for life, and today in Fiji many of these forms of gifting are still in force. In other words, people are still making such gifts and benefiting from them. The occasions on which land may be given are said by Tuwere to be the following; it will be obvious that certain of them can no longer be observed.

- *Ai covicovi ni i lou se draudrau*: land given by her clan to a woman on her marriage so that she may continue to eat from it, which also passes to her sons. According to Tuwere, if the donors want the land returned, they must perform the ceremony called *ai vakalutu ni qele* (lit. making the soil fall back).

- *Kete ni yalewa* ('woman's womb'): land forfeited if a spouse commits adultery. The wronged party's people plant reeds on the forfeited land, which can be redeemed after a period of time, with the ceremony of *vakalutu* performed by those whose land was forfeited.
- *Veitumalekake* ('defending the dead'): land given to prevent the corpse of a fallen warrior from being taken by an enemy.
- *Ai covi ni qaqa* ('reward for bravery'): land given to allies or to persons who show bravery in war.
- *Veitau ni vanua* ('land given in friendship'): land given by one person to another to mark their friendship; this is temporary and ceases when either party dies.
- *Ai curucuru ni gone* ('a child's introduction'): land given when the child of a high chief was taken at birth to houses of lesser chiefs. If there are not enough valuables in the house, land is gifted to honour the new arrival.

Two other forms of gifting or land transaction marked *veiwekani* or ensured its enhancement; they were for life and the land could not be redeemed by the giver.

- *Ai sere ni wa ni kuna* ('the loosening of the strangling cord'): when a widow of a high chief died, the widow was strangled to accompany him. In this case, the chief's people gave a piece of land to the deceased wife's people in honour of her death. On the other hand, the widow's people may present land to the chief's people to save her from strangling.
- *Ai sere ni sole ni mate* ('the unrolling of the shroud'): land given by a dying man to those kin who presented him, when he was terminally ill, with bales of *masi* (barkcloth) to be used to wrap his body when he dies. The dying man, unable to give anything in return, offers them a piece of land to thank them for their kindness.

The Gifting of Land

The first case to be discussed here concerns the gifting of land in Korotasere by the people of Ravinivatu in Vanua Levu so that it might become farmland and provide for the livelihood of people from another *vanua*, that of Tawake. The idea and project that is now Balawaviriki began with the vision (*rai votu*, lit. 'looking far into the future') of an elder who was the *vanua* representative of the people of the district of Tawake to the Cakaudrove Provincial Council.[3] He sought assistance from the council, telling of his people's need for land for development and sustenance, and his plea was heard by a man from the *vanua* Ravinivatu. In provincial council meetings, usually representatives discuss development agendas, issues and challenges in want of provincial support and/or proposals for further discussion with government bodies.

It is important to note that when land is gifted (*i solisoli*), the original owners (in this case the traditional owners of the *vanua* Ravinivatu) should continue to be recognized and blessed in all things that relate to the land that was given. As the landowners, or *i taukei*, they are to be revered, accorded respect and recognition, for the blessing conferred by their gift. The land, some ten thousand acres of virgin fertile bush, was gifted to, and continues to be used today by, the Cuku people.[4] The generosity implicit in the Fijian ideal of *loloma* (lit. love) informs the gifting of land. In return, the people of Cuku reciprocate the love and generosity afforded them by recognizing and acknowledging the gift in all things ceremonial, as well as in daily transactions. These public and private utterances ensure that the land's owners are mentioned and recognized even if they are not present, and remind all, especially those who do not know (visitors, for example), who the landowners are. This recognition places the givers in good stead among Fijians at large because to give in such a way is chiefly behaviour (*vakarau vakaturaga*), behaviour that shows concern for the welfare of kin.

The process of giving the land began when, following the provincial council meeting, the Ravinivatu elder summoned the visionary Simione Kanibuata. He told Simione to prepare *yaqona* (kava) and serve it so that they could drink together. In the process, the Ravinivatu elder sought clarification of the seeker's plight. The two men found out and established the relationship between them: their *veiwekani*. Both had traditional ties to Namuka: the mother of the elder from the landowning group was from Namuka, and the seeker also had close blood ties there. Namuka therefore was the point of convergence where, so to speak, their 'blood met'.

Once established, this kinship tie was the subject of most if not all conversation regarding the land gifting, and especially its justification by those involved on both sides. That both clans involved in the gifting were *vasu* (as it were, sisters' children) to Namuka was especially acknowledged in all ceremonies that accompanied the discussions; the *vasu* relationship obtains between a woman's children and the men of her natal clan. Since the day the gift was made, it has figured in Cuku stories (*talanoa*) as a matter of importance. The elder then affirmed that his family had land in Ravinivatu that he could offer to the people of Cuku and the district of Tawake in accordance with the request. The seeker returned to Cuku and the district of Tawake and relayed the information about the land.

The presentation of traditional wealth (*solevu*) in thanks to the people of Ravinivatu took place in 1991, five years after their land was settled and already in use by those from Cuku and Tawake. The people of Tawake travelled on foot through thickly forested areas of Vaturova to reach Sevaci – the village of the traditional owners of the gifted land – and their presentations of gifts and feast food to the landowners commemorated and gave thanks for what is understood to be a continuing gift that continues to be acknowledged.[5]

The land in Ravinivatu, called by the settlers Balawaviriki to show their origin, provides much needed income and support to the villages. The name Balawaviriki refers to the pandanus tree that stands at the end point of the Udu peninsula. In Fijian cosmology, *balawaviriki* is the tree that is passed by the sprits of the dead on their way to Bulu or the spirit world. Locals in the area say that when the *balawa* tree has scratch marks on it, this means that a spirit has just successfully jumped into the spirit world. This is why, in some parts of Fiji, as part of the funeral ceremony, people place a *tabua* (whale's tooth) on the chest of the deceased. This *tabua* is called 'stone for the balawa' (*vatu ni balawa*), and the deceased uses this *tabua* to gain entry to Naicobocobo, the spirit world. Without the *tabua*, the spirit cannot enter Naicobocobo, and therefore roams endlessly around the world or returns to life.

Today, even in the absence of the landowners, the ritual formulae of all ceremonies that take place in the farmlands that are now Balawaviriki continue to acknowledge them. Thus, in any important ceremony or other occasion such as a church service, and in prayers, the settlers from Tawake and Cuku make a point of articulating the honorific title of the people of *vanua* Ravinivatu and their act of love, the gifting of land. Indeed, on national radio stations today, one can hear a song written and recorded by a group related to the people of Tawake that pays respect to the Ravinivatu landowners.

A Case of Chiefly Concern for His People

The second case discussed here is the gifting of the land called Wailekutu to become the site of a new village. This is the new village of Namuka, situated outside Lami town on the outskirts of Suva. It is populated largely by people who came from Namuka in the Lau islands, who have built permanent homes and created a new village. The new village was an *i solisoli* by the local paramount chief, the Roko Baleni, to the displaced Lau islanders. The Roko Baleni is paramount chief of the *vanua* of Navakavu. People say that the land was gifted because the local chief had empathy for the plight of the migrants who had to find a piece of land to live on in Suva so they might send their children to secondary school there, pay the school fees and at the same time make a living. This took place in the early 1980s.

Today, Namuka has become less of a village and more of a small town, part of the *vanua* of Navakavu. A couple of houses are still a reminder of struggle and new settlement, with tell-tale signs of the sheer hardship migrants go through when settling in a new place. A number of homes, however, reflect a new class of people who are evidently doing well – those who perhaps over time have managed to better their lot. The brand of cars in a few homes and the presence of two different churches are further evidence of the rootedness that signals long term habitation. There is, however, something about the forever expanding new village that is different from the other villages on the same stretch of the Queen's Highway. Unlike nearby original villages belonging to the landowners, in the 'new' village there is always a new home being built or some old building improved. People say this is because the 'new settlers' are expected to treat the gift made to them with due diligence and, like others who have been likewise generously treated, show their continuing gratitude in the way they attend on the local chief and support him in respect of his communal obligations, as well as in any of his traditional duties (*oga*). When the gifted land is not used diligently or well, village commentaries usually are heard explaining that the receivers of the gift lack appreciation of the land (*era sega ni kauwaitaka na loloma levu*). *Sega ni kauwai* refers to neglect, ignorance of the importance of gifting, sheer laziness, ignorance of relationships or *veiwekani*, or a combination of these things.

Of course, one also comes across differing views. Some of those who are counted among the original owners of the place (*taukei ni vanua*) may voice their opposition to the idea of gifting to people who are not closely related. Such oppositional commentaries emphasize, among other things, a concern that the old chief may not have had at heart the interests of his own descendants (*kawa*) – that is, the present day descendants of the original owners – when he gifted 'prime real estate' to others. Other angry commentaries focus on the freedom assumed by the 'new settlers' and their apparent lack of concern for the chief's *lotu* ('church' or 'religion') in turning away from Methodism to become New Methodists. Here we can see the expectation that being 'a visitor' on someone else's land means one should make sure in all things, including religious practice, to pay due respect to the owners of the place. Those who have split away to join the new denomination have denounced the mother Church in Fiji for various doctrinal and other reasons. The mother Church is, however, the Church of the 'gifting' chief and his people. Among indigenous Fijians, the *vanua* (here meaning 'people' or 'tribe'), *lotu* (religion) and *matanitu* (government) are often said to be focal points of life even though their goals and expectations may at times differ. And very often they are referred to in prayer and church services. *Vanua, lotu* and *matanitu* make up what historian Deryck Scarr

(1980) referred to as the 'three legged stool' of Fijian life; David Routledge's (1985) discussion of the old Fijian nations also highlights these three tenets of Fijian life after the Second World War. This means that while the Namuka people are living on the land of the chief of Waiqanake (whose traditional title is the Rokobaleni), it is deemed appropriate that they should serve the *lotu* of the old chief as well as maintain his alliances and attend to his obligations, whether they be those of *vanua, lotu* or *matanitu*. It seems likely that a problem may arise in the future from the evident 'relative affluence' of the new village as compared to the older villages.

The matter is further complicated by intermarriage between 'new settlers' and original owners, which has taken place over the past three or so decades. The establishment of close kinship ties enhances the position of the 'new immigrants', and at the same time makes it harder for the original landowners in future to consider taking back the land in question. This becomes ever more difficult as more women from the original landowning group marry into the settler group. This is because, in former times, a gift of land was meant, ultimately, to be returned, especially if it was gifted as *i covicovi ni draudrau* (lit. the picking of leaves) or *i sagisagi ni ilou* (lit. the plucking of leaves for covering food to be baked in the earth oven). These expressions denote land that was gifted in marriage along with the woman: she came from 'a people with means' (*levu na kedratou qele*, they have a lot of land) and was marrying into a group that did not have much land; the land gifted ensured that the woman was able to eat from the gifted land till she died, when by rights the land given ought to be returned. Increasingly, however, lands given under such conditions have not been returned. This is because people's ideas about the gifting of land are not uniform and also, as people say at times, because given new values that promote greed, custom is likely to be neglected and the land not returned.

Gifting Land for the 'Public Good'

The third case is that of the gifting of land by the Tui Vugalei in about 1967 to the government of the day. I heard an account of it in a meeting of chiefs in 2003, at the Tailevu Provincial Council office in Nausori town, which I was invited to attend by a maternal uncle, Ratu Emori Latitoga, who was at the time the *roko* or provincial administrator. This case shows how Fijian ideas of gifting can easily be exploited by legal eagles of modern day Fiji.[6]

In 1967, a high chief of Cakaudrove in eastern Fiji, Ratu Penaia Ganilau, was sent by the then colonial administration to the chief of *vanua* Vugalei in Tailevu to seek land for a government mahogany plantation. Some forty or so years later, in 2003, all the important chiefs of Tailevu and all the village chiefs and the *vanua* chief of Vugalei assembled in the Tailevu Provincial

Council office in Nausori to discuss the Vugalei mahogany plantation. The land, some 17,121 acres of native prime land, was to have been leased by the government for ninety years. This land was the original site of the Vugalei *vanua*, their *delaniyavu*, at a place called Delakurukuru, a traditional site sacred to Vugalei people. It consisted of a substantial forest of native timber. The issue at hand was the disagreement between the government at the time and the people of Vugalei, on whose land the plantation stood.

In 1967, when Ratu Penaia Ganilau visited to ask for the land, he was secretary for Fijian affairs, and also possibly already a member of the cabinet; he was not yet formally installed as Tui Cakau – the title of the paramount chief of Cakaudrove – which took place much later in 1988, but he was considered as such (Lal and Fortune 2000). When he visited to ask for the land, he had brought with him the most highly prized of Fijian valuables – a *tabua* (whale tooth) – and not much else, besides a 'chiefly promise' (*veidinadinati vakavanua vakaturaga*). This pact of truth and mutual understanding obtained between two high chiefs – the putative Tui Cakau and the then Tui Vugalei. Amongst other things agreed to was the division of gains from harvesting the mahogany between the government and the Vugalei landowners. Another was the promised employment of landowners on the mahogany project in all its peripheral industries.

The ceremonial presentation of the *tabua* gained Ratu Penaia Ganilau the land for government use, and in return he gave a promise to the Tui Vugalei. In Fijian terms, this constituted a sufficient and binding agreement. There is also to be considered the *tauvu* relationship between Tailevu, by way of Verata, of which Vugalei is a part, and Vanua Levu, of which Ganilau was a chief. Both places acknowledge and revere the god Dakuwaqa, hence their *tauvu* relationship. A government official of the *mataqali matanivanua* of the Tui Vugalei – Jovilisi Tamanalevu of Naqati in Naimasimasi village – took notes of the meeting and handover of land for his own purposes. These were read at the meeting of 2003, and gave the account I have given here of the asking for land and the chiefly promise.

In 1998, when the government established the Fiji Hardwood Corporation (FHC), no direct allocations of the harvest were stipulated by Fiji's Company Act (1985) in terms similar to the promise made by Ratu Penaia Ganilau to the landowners of Vugalei. The company belonged to the Fijian government, and its formal incorporation made no reference to land gifting and the promises made on behalf of the government. The promise of land made by Tui Vugalei was taken as given, but the promise made by the chief who had spoken for the government, Tui Cakau, who had died in 1993, was ignored. The *i solisoli* made in the spirit of sharing and obligation to kin was 'silenced' in modern law as enshrined in the Company Act. From a Fijian perspective, such a fracture of chiefly *veiwekani* is not only a denial of what is *dina* (true) and *dodonu* (straight, honest), but of *veikauwaitaki* (mutual concern and empathy), the hallmark of Fijian kinship. Today the people of Vugalei still expect to see the government promise fulfilled because it was made between chiefs (*veidinadinati vakavanua vakaturaga*) in the spirit of chiefly kinship (*veiwekani vakavanua vakaturaga*) that obtained between them.

Kinship Fractured in 'New Times'

The *veiwekani* of today is evidence of its presence in history – be it the history of a village, a district, a *vanua* (place, country, people, land), or a province – and the history of kinship in Fiji evinces itself in multiple sites. In this section I discuss one such case where transformations in the nature of Fijian kinship are occurring as a function of broader political changes.

On 25 May 2010, while on a research trip with University of the South Pacific colleagues, Samu Bogitini, Sereima Naisilisili and I were invited to address a group of Fijian chiefs and provincial leaders in Yaroi village in Savusavu (Vanua Levu) on the topic of Fijian leadership. We willingly accepted the invitation as a small means of 'reciprocating the wisdom, love and protection' of the Cakaudrove people who had looked after us during our research in the field; moreover, as Fijian intellectuals, we thought it imperative that we contribute to community development if we could. The day before the workshop, we paid a courtesy call to the provincial administrator who established *veiwekani* ties with each of us separately, and gave us a tentative programme for the meetings. Each of us belonged to different provinces and tribes in Fiji: Samu to Kadavu, Sereima to Tawake in Udu, Cakaudrove, and myself to Vugalei in Tailevu as well as to Qarani in Gau, Lomaiviti, which made me *tauvu* to the assembled chiefs. Because of our various *vanua* affiliations and my ease of relationship with the people assembled, I ended up being the one who did most talking. As a woman of the *vanua*, Sereima spoke little and only in local dialect – affirming relationship as well as acknowledging local protocol. Like me, Samu was freer than Sereima to speak to the assembled chiefly meeting.

We were informed we were participating in the pre-conference programmes of information-cum-training sessions for chiefs and leaders, and we were also invited to the opening on the following day. During the opening ceremonies, the guest of honour – the deputy CEO of the Ministry for Indigenous Affairs, retired Colonel Kurusiga – acknowledged in some detail and depth the Tui Cakau, paramount chief of the province of Cakaudrove. The Tui Cakau was not present, however, having been deposed by the military government that had brought Colonel Kurusiga to his present position.

Interestingly enough, the church pastor who blessed the meeting before the opening not only spoke of *veiwekani*, which is usual, but also made a point of emphasizing 'humility in leaders'.[7] Humility is the essence of Fijian chiefship, a sign of proper breeding so to speak, but there was a certain irony to be found in the words of the pastor and of the guest of honour. It used to be that the protocols attached to *veiwekani vakavanua vakaturaga* ('chiefly kinship according to the *vanua*') precluded any meeting such as this one in Cakaudrove where Tui Cakau was chief. He was also an exceedingly important member of the Bose Levu Vakaturaga, the Great Council of Chiefs, a body with a 150 year history, recognized under the 1990 constitution as having certain rights, including that of appointing a third of the senate, which had been suspended in 2007 as a result of the military coup of 2006.[8] Along with all its other members, Tui Cakau had been thrown out of government by the military administration that had called the present meeting.[9] In calling and holding the meeting, the government centre of the provincial administration in Yaroi, Savusavu, was at once a site of subversion and a reconstitution of *veiwekani*.

It is a subversion of indigenous Fijian ideas to hold a meeting of chiefs such as this in the absence of the Tui Cakau, who was paramount chief of all those who were present. Even so, the guest of honour was bound to acknowledge the Tui Cakau in his opening speech, and could not avoid doing so, thus acknowledging the kinship between them. In general, indigenous Fijians hold that *veiwekani* connects peoples (*vanua*) to one another by virtue especially of the kinship between those who are paramount chiefs of *vanua*. So it was not surprising that Savusavu people's comments were that while the opening day of the workshop was a great event, the *vanua* was 'hurt' or 'wounded' (*mavoa*) by the absence of their paramount chief. Such comments from those who attended on the opening day show how deeply held are the values of *veiwekani* – especially, in this case, in their association with their *vanua* and, of crucial importance, the paramount chief, who himself instantiates the *vanua* in all its expressions.

The centrality of what was missed – the paramount chief – could not be occluded by the semblance of order at the meeting, by the careful and eloquent speeches or by the decorum evident on the occasion. This raises the question as to whether, in contemporary Fiji, lesser chiefs and leaders can move effectively into the future without their paramount chiefs. To do so requires what amounts to a reconstitution of the people's criteria not only of chiefship and *veiwekani* but also of land boundaries and all their complexly rendered associations and ties. It is known that power struggles in early Fiji, post European contact, distorted the existing balance of power and brought into prominence new chiefs, chiefdoms and polities amongst the *i taukei*, much of the time by dint of force of arms (see Routledge 1985.) Given the present order of things, one has to wonder how the actions of the *i taukei* soldiers of the Fijian army are currently undermining traditional allegiances and the kinship that makes them effective.

The meeting we attended in Yaroi village was the annual provincial council meeting of chiefs and elders of the province of Cakaudrove, Vanua Levu. As the address by the guest of honour began, the significance of the occasion was apparent to many.

This was a new historical moment, where all of the visitors were seated in such a way as to ignore the fact that two of them were women and all were, relatively speaking, of lower status in the traditional hierarchy than those seated opposite and facing them.

In the workshop Samu and I were outsiders to Cakaudrove, Sereima from within. All those assembled were seated on three mats under the trees on the village *rara* (ceremonial ground). As usual, the chiefs spent some time negotiating in silence their relative seating positions as given by kinship relations (*veiwekani vakavanua vakaturaga*) that govern their status with respect to each other. Tellingly, those with the highest status – from Somosomo, Vuna and Natewa – were coaxed by others to 'move up', that is to sit *i cake* ('above') in positions appropriate to their status. Italatala – the church minister – likewise and appropriately sat outside the circle of high-status chiefs in the middle and refused to move *i cake*, while the younger chief from Natewa – an educated man, Ratu Buaserau, at the time chief elect – sat at the very end. Had he been older, he probably would have moved up to the front after being coaxed by others. The circular arrangement on the village green was seen by everyone present in the village that day, and was in full view of the women of the province who were assembled in two *vakatunuloa* (temporary shelters) at the edges of the *rara*.

As the event moved on into the late afternoon, the chiefs began speaking with us about issues we had raised. In the absence of Tui Cakau as paramount chief of the province, the others kept alluding to his presence, as if he was indeed there among us – an observance dictated by Fijian custom, especially at points where salutations and speeches of welcome and farewell are made. The chiefs were seated opposite us, at a distance sufficient for comfort, in the sense that we did not encroach on them and they did not encroach on us. Significantly, there was no *tanoa* (the large bowl in which kava is mixed and from which it is served) and thus no *yaqona* (kava) which would have made unavoidable the acknowledgement of relative status, both in the seating arrangements and in the order of drinking. In other words, had those assembled been seated in relation to the *tanoa* and drinking *yaqona* according to their relative status, it would have been evident to all that here at least the status of traditional chiefs outweighed that of any government functionary or other visitor. As it was, our conversations were conducted in workshop style in accordance with the chiefs' request that the meeting take place on mats on the village green and not in the provincial council office.

The chiefs and traditional leaders were all dressed suitably for the occasion and their offices and, as is expected, were especially courteous in the manner of their deportment and speech. There was no harshness of voice, no brashness, no condescension of manner (very different from what one may encounter among business leaders). All addresses were made with the utmost respect, and preceded by due recognition of the different titles of those who were present. Among indigenous Fijians, relationships honoured according to kinship (*vakaveiwekani*) mean business is done smoothly and there is an easy reception of ideas and views put forward. It is in the manner of one's deportment that one's message is received or ignored.

The chiefs, all men, sat in the centre of the village green with us, while the chiefly women and women leaders of the province sat in a temporary shelter erected for the occasion on the right-hand side of the village green. They were conducting their own meeting and there was a 'sort of' suggestion made in passing by the male district administrator that Sereima and I should perhaps address the ladies. This suggestion was not, however, followed, and we and Samu co-addressed the male chiefs as originally planned. Sereima and I had exchanged glances at the suggestion, but of course it was quite appropriate locally. Indeed, there was some discomfort occasioned by our speaking on such an occasion. Thus Katz notes women's refusal to join men in their work and gatherings and vice versa, and observes that traditional understandings of gender differences continue to prevail in village life (Katz 1993: 40).

For me the experience was not easy, given the multiple realities and complexities of present-day Fiji. Earlier on in the day, we had been speaking to a group of teachers about career development. The conversations (*veitalanoa*) between us and the chiefs continued into the late afternoon, after which we exchanged mutual thanks, farewells and blessings. We researchers were conscious of our relatively lower traditional status, yet throughout the workshop the chiefs addressed us in terms affirming kinship, *veiwekani*. Thus, in relating to us, the chiefs made use of our different *vanua* affiliations, which not only eased our nerves but more importantly reminded us that all Fijians are related – whether directly in genealogical terms or via marriages or other relations that are marked by kinship terms. It is not usual for women to address chiefs, let alone that people from other places (in this case, myself and Samu) should do so. Sereima was nervous too, given that she was an insider and a woman at that. The chiefs were of high status, and the three of us were not high enough to be advising chiefs, but given that we were invited by the province, we proceeded as Fijians and university persons. Words of farewell acknowledged the strengthening of our kinship ties to their province, along with the continued reminders throughout of the customary and historical ties the three of us shared with the people of the *vanua*.

The house situated to the right of the chiefly gathering had a satellite disc with the words Sky Pacific on it – a reminder of the link to the world beyond Fiji. Leaving aside the noise of expensive and oversized government vehicles whizzing around the meeting centre and the occasional cry of birds in nearby trees, the workshop went on by and large undisturbed. Those coming in government Pajeros and twin-cabs were mostly commoners from elsewhere in Fiji who had come to service the meeting, or to sit in as observers, while the chiefs had either arrived in taxis or walked to the meeting on foot. The 'new times' were signalled by those who came to serve, and who might have arrived in a less obtrusive manner and perhaps parked their vehicles some distance away. It was as if chiefly *mana* and hierarchy were reduced or even edited out in the contemporary space of the government-organized workshop, especially given that the province was assembled without its paramount chief. The usual *veiwekani* understandings and uses of social space seemed to be on the wane, or perhaps what I was seeing was the manifestation of a new configuration of old established ways of the *i taukei*, indigenous Fijians. Another reading of the situation was that, while the government workers were educated, they were not educated in ways of the *vanua*, did not have *veiwekani* locally, and were thus unwittingly obtrusive. Another observer might think I was making too much of the minutiae of Fijian life, but surely such occasions evince broader issues arising in contemporary Fiji, post the 2006 coup. Some years ago, Goneyali (1986), among others, raised similar issues related to the nature of social change, saying that village institutions were under fire; he suggested that there were big, new and just questions to be asked by the villagers or by the people of the *vanua*.

Knowledge that Counts: Kinship and Indigenous Epistemology

It is important that kinship be opened up to scrutiny and analysis in all its manifestations. Thus in all three cases presented here, Fijian kinship takes in at once the narrower, genealogical relationships, those that are classificatory in the broadest sense (for example, if a woman whom I call 'mother' calls another, very distantly related woman, 'sister', then I call the latter 'mother' irrespective of the genealogical distance between us) and also the relations between *vanua*, themselves referable to founding relations of kinship. So, for instance, when one is *vasu* (sister's child) to one's mother's brother, one is by the same token *vasu* to the village of one's mother's father, and by implication to all the people there. One is *vasu* to one's mother's brothers and, more inclusively, to the tribal lineage of one's mother. A mother's people would say of me 'she is our *vasu*'. A given *vasu* relationship may be known and widely acknowledged, or it may be historical, waiting as it were to be found out, as in the Balawaviriki case.

Fijians in general hold that kinship is one of the most valuable aspects of indigenous life as it is imagined and lived. Kinship is self-evidently a good thing, despite the fact that people also talk of the 'unrequited nature of relations of care or compassion', and in some cases the 'fractures' or the 'distortions' of kinship, especially in respect of the 'disruptive tendencies of a monetized economy' where kinship runs the risk of being 'in trans-action mode', a commodity of sorts 'sold and traded for its economic use' and thus valued less and less because of money. *Sa bibi na i lavo, mamada na veiwekani*, 'money is more important than kinship'. This is the more likely to be true in urban settings such as Namuka or in situations where the practices of the military government produce distortions – as in the Cakaudrove meeting where kinship and its associated values have been dis-torted or trampled upon. Similar comments are also to be heard in the case of Balawaviriki where, for instance, younger persons forget why they have land in the first place. This is evident in behaviour that demonstrates that they undervalue the gift they were given in kinship by either not utilizing the land properly or giving up on the land and its work. Apparently a number of farmers were using the gifted land as a means of conducting transactions whereby, for a price, they farmed the land for others, some not needy and some from outside their own *vanua*.

When kinship weakens, or when one has not nurtured it in life, one is said to be a very poor person: *ni dravudravua na tamata e sega na wekana*, 'a person without kin is a poor person indeed'. Such commen-taries on life can be seen by some, perhaps especially by non-Fijians, as inward looking, uneconomic and localized, but *vakaveiwekani*, relations according to kinship, remain a strong impetus in indigenous life and how people talk about what is important to them. One of the mistakes of modern nation building is that such strongly held views and associated practices are not understood and not examined, even though, as is evident in my account here, kinship continues to be crucial to the political economy of contemporary Fiji.

The power, influence and the obligations of kinship lie at the heart of everyday life amongst indigenous Fijians; indeed, kinship has been central to the *taukei* psyche for as long as legends, oral histories and dances have recorded it. When kinship ties are ignored, people are likely to say *sa mavoa na vanua*, 'the *vanua* is hurt, wounded'. I noted above that *vanua* takes in land, ancestral spirits, chiefs, people, all fauna and flora.[10] So when people say that the *vanua* is hurt or wounded, this is a telling remark, taking in as it does everything that the *vanua* encompasses and all the entailed kinship relations – the *veiwekani* – with other *vanua*. Witness the comments made in the Cakaudrove provincial meeting of chiefs, notable for the glaring absence of the Tui Cakau, paramount chief of Cakaudrove – this being one of the highest ranking Fijian titles.

Kinship in the *vanua*, be it rural or urban, survives in the deeply held values of *veilomani* (mutual compassion and love) and *veikauwaitaki* (caring for one another) that are embedded in kinship as it is lived. Fijian epistemology informs the processes through which children learn how to look after kin (*qaravi* or *veiqaravi*).[11] This sense of duty to kin, of obligation and service, is what makes *veiwekani* meaningful and dear to people. A child learns to love and show compassion for people as kin – *wekana*, his or her relations. *Kauwai*, 'to show deep concern and love', is essential to sustaining relations between people, to ensuring the survival of all – that is, of all that exists in and is encompassed by the *vanua* where kinship is at the core. One is nurtured in and by kinship relations, and in the process one lays down a mental map of all kinds of kin relationship. Such mind maps transcend time and space in so far as they record historical ties of kinship as well as contemporary ties and one's imaginings of the future.

Veiwekani vakaViti – Fijian kinship, whether it be qualified as *vakavanua* according to *vanua* or *vakadra* according to blood – is a matter of the *yalo*, spirit or spirit-soul. This is evident in all the speeches that accompany life-cycle ceremonies, and all chiefly and traditional ceremonies, including those ceremonial distributions of wealth that are pleasing to kin (*me yalovinaka na veiwekani*) and ensure their fulfilment of present and future ceremonial and other obligations.

In the provincial meeting described above, the interplay of forces given in *vanua* kinship, in government institutions and in the church was evident to see. The pastor's authority derived from the charismatic Church of which he was a leader – at once dignified and populist. The government business leader intended to be of service; his speech recalled the missionary zeal of pre-colonial times, now in the service of development (*veivakatoroicake-taki*) and a government imposed by force. The authority of chiefs – both present and absent – was evinced in the full awareness of the relations *vakaveiwekani*, according to kinship, that obtained both between the chiefs themselves and between the chiefs and others present, including myself and my colleagues. The Church leader blessed the meeting citing sources from the Bible that emphasized humility. His speech was at once zealous and tempered, emphasizing proper decorum and service – the listener being left to deduce whether he was making reference to the lack of humility shown by the military administration or by the paramount chief, whose absence appeared to signify a lack of forgiveness and acceptance of the coup leaders who run the government, and who were conducting that provincial council meeting in Yaroi in 2010.

A Fijian eye would, I think, have easily discriminated from others the close kin – both men and women – of the absent paramount chief; they were seated in the front row of chairs and were all more beautifully clad and apparently much more at ease than the others present. In the manner of their sitting, the waving of their fans and their sterner looks, one could easily discern their chiefly pedigree and what may be termed their critical opposition to the guest of honour and the military officers who accompanied him. Likewise, the chair of the provincial council made his speech in the local dialect of the paramount chief and, in properly acknowledging him (as is always done on such occasions), emphasized the power and influence of Somosomo and that of the paramount Tui Cakau in the province of Cakaudrove and, thus, in that day's meeting of chiefs. In this fashion, one is made aware of silent opposition as it is evinced in the subtleties of speech styles and intonations, which speak to Fijians of the many complexities of kinship and of its disruption. Thus, later I heard the following remarks concerning the absence of the Tui Cakau: that this was occasioned by 'a sin of sorts by the government that had turfed him out', that it was a 'Fijian emptiness', that it constituted a 'fracture in the landscape of *vanua* life' witnessed by all who were present and who were understood to be 'silently criticizing' the proceedings, only probably to voice their criticisms later elsewhere.[12]

It appears that what remains strong is the province's allegiance to the chiefly title, even if the present holder has been put out of government office. The chief's people are present, hence the acknowledgment by the visiting government representatives. In similar meetings of the same *vanua* elsewhere, the people provide an *i dabedabe*, 'a place to sit' – usually a pile of valuables consisting of new mats and barkcloth – that remains at the centrepiece of the function or meeting as the seat of the absent chief. The *i yau* (valuables) are taken to his home afterwards and presented. Such determination of practice constitutes 'indigenous resistance to forced change' and denotes an unshifting loyalty to the title and the office, in the knowledge that as members of the *vanua* they had been a part of the installation process, and that kinship relates not only all the indigenous people of a province but also, ideally, of the country at large.

In the Manner of Kinship, in the Manner of Chiefs

Kinship in general, and in particular kinship as evident in the gifting of land, continues to be crucial to the contemporary political economy of Fiji.

The Vugalei gifting was in response to national economic development. The Balawaviriki case has resulted in a number of properties being bought in town centres, scholarships for students, village development projects and investments. The Namuka case shows the chief (and by the same token his people) taking care of housing and other development needs of the Namuka people. It may be argued that the gifting of land has here played a crucial governance role, though it may not always be recognized as such.

Kinship and chiefship roles are intertwined. Gifting is *vakaturaga* (chiefly), and behaviour that is *vakaturaga* is by definition behaviour that is *vakaveiwekani*, 'according to kinship', for in chiefship as in kinship one is bound to show compassion and love (*veilomani*) to all kin and be courteous in all dealings in such a way as to realize the ideal of a good life or *sautu*. A condition of 'peace and plenty' is held to obtain in a *vanua* whose chief is properly installed and properly acknowledged in the people's attendance on him.[13] The matter of non-installation of a good number of traditional chiefs in contemporary Fiji may have to be addressed by Fijians, given the role articulated above and what it represents. One does not, however, as is clear in the cases described here, have to belong to a chiefly clan in order to behave in a chiefly fashion, where kinship *veiwekani* is marked by *veikau-waitaki* – feelings of compassion and of obligation to look after the welfare of kin. If the sustainability of the distributive kinship economy is crucial to the overall development of the nation, then one can conclude that chiefly installations and the nurturing of good old Fijian values described earlier are important, both for Fijians and the government too.

There are connections and parallels to the three cases discussed here as they epitomise *veiwekani*. All three point to the sharing of community spaces as a 'governing' choice of sorts by the local, communal owners of land and/or the *vanua* chief, presumably on behalf of their people. In two cases, land was given for economic reasons, while the other was for settlement, hence socio-cultural reasons. One could also say that the cases of Balawaviriki and Namuka pointed to the need to rehabilitate and provide security and welfare to kin, both within the kin group and wider extensions. The case of the provincial meeting in Yaroi in my view provides a new scenario of kinship and of chiefly *mana*, and new understandings of Fijian governance as coups become entrenched in Fiji's political life. It differs from the other cases in that it demonstrates that attempts at fracturing kin-based ties are increasingly evident via new socio-political motivations.

I end this chapter with the addition to Tuwere's list, referred to above, of three newer forms of Fijian *i solisoli*, all of which have taken place in different parts of Fiji since the 1950s. I take the liberty to name them here as:

- *A i solisoli ni bula* ('a gift for living'): this denotes a clan giving a huge piece of real estate (some 10,000 acres in this case) for purposes of economic development at the request of their kinsman. All proper ritual forms are observed – the feasting, the thanksgiving presentation of *i yau* (wealth, valuables) by the recipients; no time limit is attached to the gift.
- *A i solisoli ni koro vou* ('the gift of a new village'): this is when land is given to create a new settlement or village for a displaced population. The 'rules' of *i solisoli* remain in force: the recipients for as long as they live are bound to support the donor chief and his people in all his ceremonials, and in times of strife or need will attend on him as best they can. In the past, the chiefs of Cakaudrove, for example, gifted the land of Rabi to the people of Ocean Islands when they needed 'a home'.[14] Kioa was gifted to Tuvaluans in a similar fashion. The other example is the new village of Namuka, on Waiqanake outside Suva.
- *A i solisoli ni bula torocake raraba* ('a gift of life for the good of all'): this is when land is gifted (*soli*) by a people to the state to benefit the wider community – the province or the nation. In such a situation, the spoken promises and agreements between the chiefs involved are truthful (*dina*) and binding, and disaster is likely to befall anyone who is party to a 'breaking of truth'.

Notes

1. In this chapter, the words *veiwekani* and kinship are used interchangeably throughout.
2. The data discussed here were collected between 2003 and 2010 in a number of different research projects conducted by the author (see Nabobo-Baba 2005, 2006).
3. The district of Tawake comprises the six villages of Tawake, Wainigradru, Wainika, Vatu, Yasawa and Nagasauva.
4. Cuku or Cu'u, which comprises the four villages of Wainika, Vatu, Yasawa and Nasauva, is situated along the Udu peninsula in Vanua Levu.
5. The Cuku people – those of the four villages Wainika, Vatu, Yasawa and Nagasauva – have been consistently farming and tilling the land that was given. The two other villages, in the district of Tawake – Tawake and Wainigadru – are also involved in farming but, out of choice, only in a small way.
6. For an earlier and more detailed version of the story, see Nabobo-Baba (2005: 23–24).
7. It is worth noting here that in the history of Fiji there are instances of religious leaders being used by those in power to calm down their opponents to the point where it was easy to overthrow them – the case of the missionary

Langham who was used by the Bauans to overthrow the people of Lovoni on Ovalau comes to mind here. For the full story of Langham's heinous deceit or subterfuge, see Nabobo-Baba (2004).

8. It was formally disestablished by decree of the military government in 2012. Under the 1990 constitution, the Bose Levu Vakaturaga had fifty-five members, including some specially qualified commoners as well as chiefs from chiefly clans: the president of Fiji, vice-president and prime minister (all ex officio); six members appointed by the president on the advice of the minister for Fijian affairs; forty-two provincial councillors (three chosen by each of the fourteen provincial councils); three representatives of the Council of Rotuma, and one life member (Sitiveni Rabuka).

9. The reference here is to Ratu Naiqama Lalabalavu who, in 2010 and until the time of writing, held the title of Tui Cakau; he was minister of Fijian affairs in the Qarase government that was unseated by the military coup of Baini-marama in 2006.

10. For more detail on *vanua*, see e.g. Tuwere (2002).

11. For detail and further references, see Nabobo-Baba (2006); see also Toren (1999, 2011) on Gau.

12. For a detailed discussion of the Fijian taxonomy of silences, see Nabobo-Baba (2005, 2006).

13. For details of sautu, see e.g. Nabobo-Baba (2006).

14. The original owners of Rabi (Taukei Rabi) now reside in Lovonivonu on Taveuni.

References

Goneyali, E. 1986. 'Who Wants to Stay on the Farm?' in C. Griffin and M.M. Davis (eds), *Fijians in Town*. Suva, Fiji: University of the South Pacific/Institute for Pacific Studies.

Griffin, C., and M.M. Davis (eds). 1986. *Fijians in Town*. Suva, Fiji: University of the South Pacific/Institute for Pacific Studies.

Grossberg, L., C. Nelson and P. Treichler (eds). 1992. *Cultural Studies*. London: Routledge.

Katz, R. 1993. *The Straight Path: A Study of Healing and Transformation in Fiji*. Reading, MA: Merloyd Lawrence.

Lal, B.V., and K. Fortune. 2000. *The Pacific Islands: An Encyclopedia*. Honolululu: University of Hawaii Press.

Nabobo-Baba, U. 2005. 'Vugalei: Voices and Silences of What and How we Know – Indigenous Fijian Epistemology and Implications for Education'. PhD Education, University of Auckland, NZ.

———— 2006. *Knowing and Learning: An Indigenous Fijian Approach*. Suva, Fiji: University of the South Pacific/Institute for Pacific Studies.

Nayacakalou, R. 1955. 'The Fijian System of Kinship and Marriage, Part I', *Journal of the Polynesian Society* 64: 44–55.

———— 1957. 'The Fijian System of Kinship and Marriage, Part II', *Journal of the Polynesian Society* 66: 44–59.

Routledge, D. 1985. *Matanitu: The Struggle for Power in Early Fiji*. Suva, Fiji: University of the South Pacific/Institute for Pacific Studies.

Scarr, D. 1980. *Ratu Sukuna: Soldier, Statesman, Man of Two Worlds*. London: Macmillan.

Thomson, B. 1908. *The Fijians: A Study of the Decay of Custom*. London: W. Heinemann.

Toren, C. 1999. 'Compassion for One Another: Constituting Kinship as Intentionality in Fiji', *Journal of the Royal Anthropological Institute* 5(2): 265–80.

———— 2011. 'The Stuff of Imagination: What We Can Learn from Fijian Children's Ideas about Their Lives as Adults', *Social Analysis* 55: 23–47.

Tuwere, I.S. 2002. *Vanua: Fijian Theology of Place*. Suva, Fiji: University of the South Pacific/Institute for Pacific Studies.

Vusoniwailala, L. 1986. 'Communication, Social Identity and the Rising Cost of Fijian Communalism', in C. Griffin and M.M. Davis (eds), *Fijians in Town*. Suva, Fiji: University of the South Pacific/Institute for Pacific Studies.

2

Pigs for Money

Kinship and the Monetization of Exchange among the Truku

◆●◆

Ching-Hsiu Lin

During my fieldwork in Taiwan in 2005/6, my Truku informants taught me to listen out carefully early in the morning for the shrill scream of a pig, a sure sign that somewhere close by there were Truku people involved in an important kinship practice. The action of ritually slaughtering a pig is called *pnsanq*, whereby *sanq* describes the sound of a pig's squeals; in Truku understanding, the squealing of the pigs as they are slaughtered draws the attention of ancestral spirits, summoning them to the ritual.[1]

As a member of the Hoklo-speaking mainstream in Taiwan, I experienced something akin to culture shock the first time that I witnessed a Truku ritual in which more than ten pigs were slaughtered within the compound of a Truku household. I had never seen such an event among my own people. Moreover, considering the economic position of many Truku households, it might surprise us to know that, despite widespread poverty, pigs are still an important commodity, bought and sold within the community with the help of family or bank loans. For example, during my fieldwork I partici-pated in seven weddings. At each wedding, in excess of ten pigs and twenty tables (ten people per table) were required for the wedding feast banquet. On average, the price of a pig was $275, with each wedding costing over $3,000.[2] In fact, the cost of marriage is far too high for most Truku people to afford. According to a government report in 2006, over 70 per cent of Truku households earned less than the average Taiwanese disposable income of $14,000 per year (Council of Indigenous Peoples, CIP, 2007).

In the past, Truku people would rear pigs themselves, as would members of the other Austronesian-speaking language groups in Taiwan. Since the 1960s, however, they have purchased pigs from pig farms. As the manner in which Truku acquire pigs has changed, it is reasonable to examine whether the meanings they attribute to pigs have also changed.[3] By the same token, because pigs are commoditized in the marketplace, and people use money to purchase them, it follows that to examine the meanings of pigs for the Truku is to find out the significance they attribute to money.

I noted above that many Truku are unable to afford the expense involved in the exchange of pigs. If poverty is so widespread, how do people meet the expense involved? And why they do still continue to organize weddings and other forms of kinship practices in which pigs are important objects for sharing or exchange? If people buy pigs from the market, how has the monetization of the rearing and provision of pigs influenced Truku concepts of kinship practice and social relations at large? Based on various examples of exchange between richer and poorer households, I explore below the implications for the Truku of the monetization of the ceremonial exchange of pigs.

Gift versus Commodity and Pniqan versus Siyang

Truku people divide pork into two categories. *Pniqan* is pork received from ceremonial rituals, like weddings, while *siyang* is meat purchased from butcher shops.[4] As there is no butcher shop in my field site, Truku people buy pork in nearby urban areas or villages where most of the residents are descendants of Chinese immigrants. Pigs required for ceremonial and ritual purposes are purchased from pig farms. Truku people say that, in terms of flavour, *pniqan* is much better than *siyang*, even though both of them are purchased with money. The main difference between *pniqan* and *siyang* is that the former is said to contain people's fortunes, happiness or wishes, while the latter lacks these 'extra' elements.

The distinction between *pniqan* and *siyang* underlines the complex meanings attributed to pigs and pork by Truku people. Gregory (1982) distinguishes between the commodity as alienable and the gift as inalienable. Alienable objects are not part of the 'gifts-to-man system', so the accumulation of capital usually does not occur in respect of gift exchange (Gregory 1980: 641). Gift exchange creates relationships between subjects as they exchange aspects of themselves, while commodity exchange creates prices (Gregory 1982). For the Truku, pigs are inalienable gifts in ceremonial exchange, but if we examine the entire process of their ceremonial exchange, the distinction between alienable and inalienable objects is vague. Pigs are initially purchased from pig farms as commodities and used in ceremonial exchange where, in the final stage, pigs are eaten and thus made alienable in being removed from the cycle of exchange. From the Truku point of view, pigs may be seen as both inalienable and alienable at different points in the exchange process, from which it follows that here there may be no absolute distinction between commodity and gift.

Gregory relates the commodity/gift distinction to the difference between commodity economies embedded in capitalist markets and gift economies (Gregory 1982). However, Cheal (1988) and Carrier (1992) argue that even in capitalist markets gifts are inalienable (see also Kopytoff 1986; Miller 2001), and others argue likewise that the distinction between pure gifts and pure commodities does not hold (Appadurai 1986; Parry and Bloch 1989: 8–12). Truku people purchase pigs from the market, and pigs are simultaneously commodities and gifts in ceremonial exchange. For the many Truku people who are suffering from poverty, exchanging pigs in ceremonial events is a moral necessity, but the costs involved impose a significant financial burden. The expenditure incurred is described as 'pig money' or 'money for pigs'.

The term 'pig money' forces us to take the role of money into account in respect of the ceremonial exchange of pigs by Truku people. Money does not directly become an exchangeable object in lieu of pigs (cf. Strathern 1978), but pig exchange has been effectively monetized in that Truku people have to purchase pigs in the market. It follows that here the study of pig exchange entails an examination of the role of money in ceremonial exchange.

Hart notes that a coin has two sides: 'one side is "heads" – the symbol of the political authority which minted the coin; on the other side is "tails" – the precise specification of the amount the coin is worth as payment in exchange'; moreover, 'the coin has two sides for a good reason – both are indispensable' (Hart 1986: 638). By analogy, 'pig money' also has two sides. Because pigs are bought from pig farms, Truku practices involving pigs are subject to the price fluctuations of the market and to the imposition of governmental policies relating to pig farms. In Truku terms, 'pig money' refers to and symbolizes money engaged in the process of ceremonial exchange. The value of pigs as a commodity in the market and their value in ceremonial exchange are mutually compatible. Even though people are too poor to afford the costs involved, they still do their best to hold ceremonial pig exchanges.

Parry and Bloch assert that we need to understand the ways in which 'money is symbolized and in which this symbolism relates to culturally constructed notions of production, consumption, circulation and exchange' (Parry and Bloch 1989: 2). They further suggest that monetary exchange contains an interrelationship between long-term and short-term exchange, where a cycle of short-term exchange is the legitimate domain of individual – often acquisitive – activity, and a cycle of long-term exchange is concerned with the reproduction of the social and cosmic order (ibid.: 2). In the process of Truku ceremonial exchange, long-term and short-term exchange coexist, prompting an examination of the interaction between these different orders of transaction.

Prior to the commoditization of Truku agricultural production (see below), pigs were ordinary wealth, and thus multi-functional in respect of their uses in everyday life. I argue that the monetization of pig exchanges, for all it has transformed the meanings attributed to pigs, has not inhibited their ceremonial exchange. Today many Truku people are suffering from poverty and, because exchange is an essential part of kinship practices and ancestor worship, the performance of money-dependent kinship practices can become an onerous financial burden. As a consequence, because of the expense entailed in the ceremonial exchange of pigs, it is through monetary kinship practices that the relationship between the poor and the rich is converted into a long-term relationship between debtor and creditor. The monetary exchange of pigs has thus significantly increased the potential for wealthier households to strengthen their social and political influence.

Postcolonial Transformations

The Taiwan government's ethnic classification of 2009 recognizes 14 distinct Austronesian language groups as indigenous: Amis, Atayal, Paiwan, Bunun, Truku, Rukai, Saisyiat, Puyuma, Tsou, Thao, Sediq, Yami, Sakizaya and Kavalan. Some linguists and archaeologists suggest that 'Austronesian expansion moved from Taiwan, through the coastal Philippines, into Sulawesi and towards coastal New Guinea between about 3000 and 2000 BCE'; they argue that Austronesian people in Taiwan are the descendants of these older Austronesian societies (Bellwood 1996: 27; also see Blust 1999). Austronesian people are, however, in the minority in today's Taiwan. They have to contend not only with the displacement of their languages and their way of life as a result of assimilation by mainstream society, but also with the loss of their living areas as a result of governmental policies and the seizing of Truku lands by Chinese migrants (Simon 2005; Lin 2010).

The Truku people originated from the central mountain range in the western part of Taiwan. During the Japanese colonial period, in order to take advantage of natural resources, the regime had to have dealings with those who lived in the mountain forests.[5] The colonial government set up reservations in the plains in the eastern part of Taiwan, and forced Truku people to move into these. This shift of the Truku from the highlands to the lowlands was not simply a change of geographical location; it also altered their methods of cultivation. In the lowlands, the Japanese government introduced new technologies for the farming of paddy fields. Even so, Truku people continued to use their agricultural produce primarily for the maintenance of the household (Lin 2010). Cash cropping first began under the Kuomintang (KMT, Chinese Nationalist Party) regime, with its imposition of a series of land reforms on Austronesian people in Taiwan in the 1950s.

Under the KMT regime (between 1945 and 2000), as Taiwan's economy became increasingly capitalist and industrialized from the 1950s to the 1960s, the government also sought to improve agricultural production through a series of land reforms, thereby commoditizing agricultural production among Austronesian populations (Li 1983). In 1966, the government set up the Indigenous Peoples Reservation Land Development Management Procedure. Under this initiative, the government regulated how indigenous people gained, used, transacted and inherited their land. In particular, land held by Austronesian people was effectively privatized, and their ownership of land was defined in terms of this process (Hsiao 1984).

With the introduction of private ownership and cash cropping, Austronesian people in Taiwan were integrated at once into the Taiwanese and the world economy. These changes introduced certain structural problems: a shortage of finance and mechanized production, incomplete systems of irrigation and infrastructure, and comparatively low levels of agricultural technology and knowledge are widespread (Li 1983); furthermore, privatization and cash cropping significantly increase the expenditure of each Austronesian household. Not only must people invest money to increase agricultural output, but they have also to pay taxes relating to land ownership and income from agricultural production. For many Austronesian people, the income from cash cropping is too slight to guarantee subsistence.

In order to maintain their households, from the 1970s onwards, increasing numbers of Truku people abandoned their cultivated lands in order to become wage labourers or migrant labourers. There was an increase in non-agricultural income and an accompanying decrease in agricultural income (Lin 2011). With the advent of migrant labour came the decline of agriculture. Most Truku men went alone to cities as migrant labourers, while their wives, parents and children remained at home. Their earnings constituted the major portion of household income back in the village. With male labour absent from the village, economically sustainable agriculture, which had been encouraged by the government in the 1960s and 1970s, gradually disappeared. Most of the paddy lands which were reclaimed in the 1950s became dry lands, with villagers (women and elders) growing short term crops instead. Now, most agricultural produce is not sold at market, but is used by female farmers towards the subsistence of their households or to exchange and share with their neighbours and relatives. In most Truku communities, wage labourers outnumber farmers.

These economic changes mean that, among the Truku, agriculture plays a less important role in economic development and subsistence economics than it did in the past. In view of this, how has economic change influenced the way pigs are obtained for the purposes of kinship practices? The answer to this question entails an examination of Truku concepts of kinship and sociality.

Ancestor Worship, Pigs and Social Organization

For the Truku, the distribution of pigs is associated with concepts of *gaya*. Generally, *gaya* means a complex system of social and religious norms related to supernatural beliefs and ancestor worship (e.g. Kim 1980; Lin 2010). It is closely connected to ideas of ancestor spirits, *utux*.[6] An ancestor's spirit wields great authority, having special powers to bless or curse, and to determine the well-being of living relatives. Kim (1980), who defines *gaya* as the 'natural order', indicates that when Truku people consider something to be out of the ordinary – such as sickness, accidents, and death – it is said that someone has broken *gaya*, and consequently the relationship between living householders and ancestral spirits is transformed from one of harmony to one of tension. Since the 1940s, most Truku people have converted to Christianity, but there is still a strong belief in the necessity of sacrifice to the ancestral spirits as soon as possible after an infringement of *gaya*, for people are very much afraid of the potential punishment that ancestral spirits might inflict.[7]

In trying to understand the norms and concepts of *gaya*, Japanese anthropologists found that even where a particular principle was shared by two or more Truku communities, they might have different ways of putting it into practice (Mori 1917; Sayama 1917). Yamaji concluded that there were seven categories of offences against *gaya*: stealing, murder, disruptive behaviour, beating and injuring, adultery, divorce, and employing a witch to curse someone (Yamaji 1986: 25–30). Each of these categories was further subdivided, each offence having a distinct, corresponding penalty and compensation (ibid.: 47–53). Offences against *gaya* met with serious punishment and censure, meted out by both the kin group and victim(s). Moreover, the offender was normally expected to compensate the victim with a number of pigs. The more serious the offence, the more pigs the offender had to pay, according to the negotiation between the two sides. Both those who offended and those who were offended against had to sacrifice to the ancestral spirits.

Truku people are accustomed ritually to beg for forgiveness from the ancestral spirits, and also to give thanks for their blessings. The *powda gaya* ritual is a dynamic process of worship where the living communicate with the ancestral spirits by making offerings, such as livestock, food and drinks. *Powda gaya* practices and kinship are aspects of one another, rather than axiomatically separate domains; so, for example, the number of pigs which have to be prepared for any given *powda gaya* ritual is based on the number of kin involved.

Reflecting on the process of *powda gaya* rituals, I argue that the household is the basic social and religious entity, not the individual. The household is comprised of father (*tama*), mother (*bubu*) and their unmarried children (*laqi*). Residence on marriage is virilocal; as soon as possible, however, a couple is expected to leave the husband's parents' house for their own house in the husband's community. In terms of kinship terminology, Truku people do not have a single specific term for 'sibling'; a senior brother/sister is known as *kabsulang*, while a junior brother/sister is *swayi*. To represent the household, Truku people also use the term *ruwan sapah* (lit. inside house) meaning 'people living in the same house'. The *ruwan sapah* is defined by co-residence rather than blood ties. *Sapah* and *rqdat* are synonyms, and *rqdat* means hearth; thus Truku people also define the household as *kingal rqdat* (single hearth, sharing a hearth). The household is the basic economic unit, and the parents have responsibility for its maintenance.

For Truku people, a 'proper' pig, fit to be sacrificed for the *powda gaya* ritual, must be large enough to provide twenty-five portions of pork – that is, a pig big enough to be shared between twenty-five households. For *powda gaya* rituals carried out in respect of infringements against *gaya*, it is only the offender's household and the offender's siblings' and parents' households that have a duty to conduct the ritual. Those who are obliged to participate are categorized as *mnswayi*, which means close kin group. Only one pig is usually slaughtered for the *powda gaya* ritual, and each household in *mnswayi* receives one portion of pork. In the *powda gaya* for the celebration of the ancestral spirits' blessings, such as to share the blessings which come from the ritual and from the host's good fortune, those involved include the host's household and their kin, including households of the host's siblings, parents, first (and perhaps second) cousins, and the host's spouse's kin groups. Generally, Truku people regard the people who are invited to such rituals as *lutut* ('relatives'), referring to the host's kinsmen and kinswomen. In these ceremonies, the host's household provides at least two pigs.

Powda gaya rituals evince relations between living people and between living people and their ancestors. The nature of any particular relationship is evident in the sacrifice of pigs and the distribution of their meat. It is through the *gaya* concepts that inform ancestor worship that the sharing of food and labour in both specific rituals and day to day practice, gains importance and power. Truku practices cannot be understood without reference to ideas of collective vulnerability to spiritual or otherworldly aggression, and the need to sustain a broad alliance amongst households in order to counter it.

The *powda gaya* rituals can be seen as a domain in which different households interact with each other. When a guest household receives an invitation, it is expected to send more than one adult person as its representatives, and they are not only duty bound to take along their own portions of pork, but are also required to assist in the ritual. Assisting the host during the ritual is regarded as a form of labour exchange between households.

The exchange of labour in the process of *powda gaya* ritual is entailed in the practice of *smbarux*, which means 'to get out of debt'. In receiving gifts or favours, the receiver becomes indebted to the giver. The relationship between giver and receiver does not therefore cease once the latter has made good their debt because, in this very process, the one who initially gave becomes, in turn, a receiver, and so on. In this sense, all participants in the ritual hold positions of both creditor and debtor, and must reciprocate by fulfilling their parallel obligations in the exchange of pork and labour.

Through the *powda gaya* ritual and *smbarux* we can see how the *gxal* ('feast group') is defined by Truku people as of fundamental importance for kinship and social relations at large. If they do not maintain their own *gxal*, they risk suffering a shortage of labour for *powda gaya* rituals especially, for example, in respect of wedding rituals they may wish to hold in the future. Indeed the *gxal* group is at once evinced and constituted through weddings. *Gxal* is a form of exchange, and in so far as there is an identifiable group it is constituted through the exchanges in which any given household is involved. A *gxal* includes Ego's household, and the households of its *mnswayi, lutut* ('relatives'), affines and also non-kin such as neighbours, colleagues, fellow churchgoers and friends. That is, a *gxal* can be regarded as an aggregation of each household's social and kin relations. But the way in which a *gxal* is defined relies on the practices of exchange and sharing performed for weddings and, therefore, is always person to person.

Different kinship categories are associated with different forms of *powda gaya* ritual through which Truku people shape and reshape different kin groups, *mnswayi, lutut* and *gxal*. The sharing of food and labour constitutes the group, which is bound up in complex systems involving the distribution of pigs, as either offerings or gifts. Even though most Truku people have converted to Christianity and are faced with poverty, the inner logic of *gaya* and belief in ancestral spirits compels them to continue to conduct *powda gaya* rituals.

Monetizing Pigs, Personalizing Money

Today, most Truku do not farm or hunt, and *powda gaya* rituals related to agriculture and hunting have correspondingly declined. Instead, there has been an increase in ritual offerings of pigs to the ancestral spirits in respect of car and house purchases. Truku people view new cars or houses as objects of wealth, and as the result of their efforts as migrant or wage labourers. In *powda gaya* rituals carried out to thank the ancestral spirits for their blessings in respect of a new car or house, the Truku host usually prepares in excess of three pigs. The exact number of pigs involved in such a ritual depends on the host's personal preference. People invited by the host to such rituals might be the host's *mnswayi* ('close kin group'), some close kinsmen and kinswomen among the *lutut* ('relatives') and the *gxal* ('feast group'). By examining the new forms of *powda gaya* ritual, we can see that the market economy has significantly influenced Truku concepts and practices relating to *powda gaya* rituals and kinship.

When discussing the importance of pigs prior to the 1960s, many Truku over the age of sixty associated the number of pigs that a household might possess with the extent of its wealth. In the past, Truku people raised pigs themselves; there was no clear gender division of labour here. Parents, in cooperation with their unmarried children, farmed and grew crops for the domestic pigs within their compound; they needed land to accommodate pigs and to cultivate crops for pig feed, and they put a great deal of time into rearing and caring for them. The pig was regarded as the surplus of economic production and as the principal indicator of wealth. If a household had many pigs, it meant that it was wealthy enough to afford the necessary land and labour. The pig was the most valued and important element of bridewealth and sacrifice, so it would not be consumed in the normal course of daily life. Meat eaten at feasts would include domestic chicken, wild game and pork given by the kin groups or affines in certain kinds of *powda gaya* ritual. There were two distinct kinds of pigs: domestic pigs (*babuy*) and wild boars (*bowyak*); domestic animals, including pigs, were property, while wild game including boars were seen as the gifts of ancestral spirits. Hunting (*mgaya*) was an activity in which hunters followed *gaya*: to catch wild animals in the hunt was to interact with ancestral spirits and receive their blessings. Wild animals, as gifts given by ancestral spirits, were not suitable to be offered in *powda gaya* rituals. Domestic pigs were a proper sacrifice because they were the product of people's hard work and diligence. Wild animals were not commodities, but were an important element of the complex system of reciprocity in Truku daily life.

Today, personal labour is commoditized, and so are pigs – both domestic and wild – and as most Truku now work as migrant or wage labourers rather than farm or hunt, the significance of wild game and domestic animals has changed. Most Truku hunters sell their wild game in the market rather than directly invest it in reciprocal kinship practices. Nevertheless, when they purchase wild game from Truku hunters, Truku people still tend to share this game with their close kin, neighbours and friends. Moreover, it is very common for people to buy pork for use in *powda gaya* rituals from butcher shops in the adjacent non-Austronesian villages or in town. Thus Truku people use the money they earn by their labour to acquire pigs and wild game.

Given that the acquiring of pigs has become monetized, what are the implications of the monetization of *powda gaya* rituals for Truku concepts and practices of kinship? Weddings provide a means for analysing the meanings of pigs and monetary exchanges and their implication in kinship because, for most Truku people, the wedding ritual is the most important kinship practice of all. The principal aim of many of those who became migrant and waged labourers in the 1970s was to earn enough money to invest in their own wedding or that of their siblings. In analysing the recent history of marriage in Truku society, I find that the practice of using money in bridewealth originated in the economic developments of the 1960s. None of the twenty-seven marriage stories of informants who married before 1960 included the giving of money as bridewealth. However, most of those informants who married in the 1960s and 1970s indicated that money had become part of bridewealth. During this period, Truku people had increasingly used money to buy pigs for bridewealth from the pig farm. The preparation of bridewealth has gradually been monetized since the 1960s.

The main element of the bridewealth in Truku society is the pig. Before the monetization of bridewealth in the 1960s, parents would rear at least three pigs to coincide with their son's attainment of marriageable age. Normally, the groom's household would provide one pig at betrothal, and two or three for the wedding ceremony itself. On average, it would take three years or more to rear a pig for bridewealth for the wedding. If parents wanted to indicate that their son was not old enough for marriage, or did not yet possess the requisite abilities to establish and maintain his own household, they would say 'our pigs are not big enough for the wedding'.

In examining the transformation in the ways that *powda gaya* rituals and weddings are conducted, we can see that money has become integrated into exchanges between kin. In terms of Marxist theory, under capitalist economies, money from wage labour entails the alienation of labour and is by definition impersonal. However, earnings from migrant or wage labour constitute the largest part of household income for most Truku households. It is through monetary-based kinship practices, in terms of pigs, that Truku people's earnings become personalized and socialized. Their monetary kinship practices also contain a relationship between long-term and short-term exchange. Concerning short-term exchange, in kinship practices prior to the 1960s, people would exchange pigs, goods and labour with each other. Since they have had to use money in order to purchase pigs and services in the maintenance of kinship practices, this short-term exchange came increasingly to articulate a long-term relationship of exchange, which is based on ideas of ancestor worship and on a complex system of norms (*gaya*).

Monetary Kinship Practices

As *powda gaya* rituals have become monetized, the principle of equality that traditionally underpinned the rituals is, by virtue of the commoditizing of labour and pigs, exacerbating distinctions between the 'haves' and the 'have nots'.

I was taught that the making of each bag of pork equates to one of the most important principles in the practice of *powda gaya* ritual. According to *smbarux*, people are expected to give something in return which is equal in value to that which they had received. In *powda gaya* rituals, Truku men have to acquire particular skills. When domestic pigs are brought from the pig farm to the ritual site, the ritual has officially begun. In butchering, the body of the pig is cut into twelve parts: tenderloin, chop, pig skin, rack, intestines, lung, bacon, rump, collar butt, kidney, lean meat and liver. The only principle applied to the butchery is that each portion of each kind of meat must be equal, carefully cut to size and weighed. After the butchering is finished, the twelve different types of meat cut are put into their appropriate piles. Participants, men and women, sit behind each pile and, taking a plastic bag, place one portion of each cut into a bag, then pass it on to the next pile. The upshot of this procedure is that each bag contains a cut from every one of the twelve piles, is of equal weight and size, and is considered in total to represent one 'portion'. The hosts, being the groom's parents or the bride's parents, then read from the guest list, and each guest named will pick up a bagged portion of pork. In the *powda gaya* ritual, the equal measures of pork given to each guest constitute an equality of relations between all those present.

In *powda gaya* rituals, the host is always very careful in organizing the ritual. Not only is it essential to make a respectful sacrificial offering to the ancestral spirits, but it is also necessary to pay close attention to the way that the bags of pork are distributed to members of their kin groups and social network. On the other hand, members of the host's kin groups also are expected to contribute their labour to the *powda gaya* ritual. For instance, at weddings, if the host forgets to give a bag of pork from the *powda gaya* ritual to a particular member of their *gxal*, the omission would meet with considerable disapproval. The host would then be expected to give an additional bag of pork to that person. By the same token, those members of the host's *gxal* who do not take their responsibilities seriously in respect of contributing their labour during the wedding will receive no more bags of pork from the host and will be excluded from the host's *gxal*.

Ensuring that each gift to each member of the *gxal* is equal is the most important principle of the *powda gaya* ritual. It indicates the importance of carefully maintaining equal relationships with one another. Similar principles and practices existed in the sharing of wild game when Truku people lived in the highlands. If only small game was caught, it would be used to make soup which would be shared among all the members of the community; larger game, such as wild pigs, goats or bears, would be slaughtered and divided into equal portions to be distributed to each household in the community.[8] Sharing wild game with kin groups not only enabled a hunter to maintain his network of reciprocity, but was also associated with the important virtue and practice of generosity (*mhowayi*). When Truku people lived in the highlands, the head of the community was usually the man who was the best hunter (Mabuchi 1960). This position was one of spokesman for the group, rather than representing any dominance or authority over others. Most political and economic decisions relied on a common consensus among the majority of elders in the same community.

With the monetization of Truku society from the 1960s onwards, however, many of the customs that entail equal relationships largely disappeared. Many Truku people point out that the introduction of refrigerators during the 1970s has changed the principle by which wild game is shared with others. Hunters following *gaya* practices used to share their wild game with others immediately. Now they preserve their wild game in refrigerators and sell it to kin, friends, neighbours and even strangers. Wild game has become commoditized and its main consumers are the richer households; most of the poorer Truku cannot afford wild game. If they want to consume wild game, they have to hunt or wait for the sharing conducted by richer households.

Among the Truku, richer individuals might be local politicians, government servants, teachers, policemen, ministers and full-time wage or migrant labourers. Compared to the majority who do not have a stable income, those who have a full-time job enjoy better economic conditions.[9] Most Truku people have faced poverty since the 1960s. Having experienced economic difficulties, they regard the acquisition of expensive commercial products or a house as a blessing from their ancestral spirits, for which they will usually organize a *powda gaya* ritual of thanks. These new forms of *powda gaya* ritual are associated with the individual's economic performance, rather than with concepts of kinship and *gaya*. In this sense, whether or not an individual organizes a *powda gaya* ritual depends on their personal choice. Truku people are, however, expected to hold weddings and a variety of traditional forms of other *powda gaya* rituals, even though they cannot afford their monetary cost.

As the largest and most important *powda gaya* ritual, the wedding is also the most expensive, not only because pigs are now bought rather than raised, but also owing to the increase in the Truku population. According to Japanese accounts, Truku people would offer fewer than three pigs at weddings (e.g. Sayama 1917). During my fieldwork, however, the number of pigs sacrificed at *powda gaya* rituals for weddings had increased to at least six. Hence, the number of pigs sacrificed for weddings has doubled, while the number of households potentially engaged in wedding rituals has risen from fewer than 75 to over 150 households, from the Japanese colonial period to the present.

Consider the following case. Masan is twenty-seven years old. He and his wife, Iwar, have a seven-year-old daughter and live with his parents. Although their marriage has been legally registered, they have not held a formal wedding ritual and his parents and parents-in-law do not consider the marriage to be fully 'established'. Masan and Iwar have infringed *gaya* by having sex before marriage, and eight years ago Masan's parents were obliged to pay two pigs in compensation to Iwar's parents' household. At the time, Masan and his household were too poor to afford bridewealth or the wedding rituals. Masan's parents were farmers, and he and Iwar were part-time workers. In 2005, the government bought two pieces of land from his father, and thus Masan's parents had enough money to organize the wedding. Although Masan's parents-in-law asked for six pigs rather than a monetary sum for bridewealth, the sum paid by the government was insufficient to meet the costs of a full wedding ritual. Because of this, Masan's father asked a number of his relatives to help him to pay for his son's marriage.

Rowty is one of Masan's father's cousins and a man of wealth in Fushih village. Masan's household did not own a car, but Rowty freely provided three cars for the wedding. Rowty asked me to drive one of the cars on the wedding day. After finishing the early morning wedding *powda gaya*, I took Iwar to her natal family in another Truku village. Masan was absent. On the way, Iwar told me that one of Masan's brothers had married twice, and another married brother had committed adultery. In order to organize the weddings for Masan's brothers, and compensate for the infringement of *gaya*, her parents-in-law had to completely exhaust their reserves of money and lost a great deal of land. It was unfair, she said, particularly because when Masan worked as a migrant labourer he was regularly asked by his parents to help his brothers, but his brothers did not contribute to Masan's own marriage. Iwar said: 'My parents wanted to have a wedding ritual because of *gaya*, but we were so poor, you know. Even though my parents wanted to help Masan, they were actually as poor as my parents-in-law'.

During my fieldwork, I collected many similar stories. In order to afford the payment for *powda gaya* rituals for weddings, contemporary Truku accumulate money in various ways. Often, they will work as migrant or wage labourers to enable themselves, or their brothers or sons, to meet the expense of a wedding. In the past, householders cooperated with each other to raise pigs. More recently, parents will usually ask their children, those who are working, and regardless of gender, to contribute part of their earnings towards the *powda gaya* ritual.

Even so, the amount of money raised from parents and their children is rarely enough to afford a wedding. In this situation, Truku people turn to their *gxal* ('feast group') for assistance. Normally, if a guest is invited to join a wedding feast, he or she will bring their householders and give a 'red envelope' containing over $35 to the host. The principle of delayed reciprocity operates: if you give $35 to the host, they will give you more than $35 in return, when you or your children hold a wedding ritual.

For most households, this is something of a gamble. The money collected from the wedding feast can be regarded as the 'wedding fund' to cover the cost of the ritual. Most will worry about how much they will receive in the 'red envelopes' as this is their principal source of finance for the wedding and the wedding feast. If there is any money left after expenses are met, the groom's household can use it to defray any other expenses incurred by the wedding, or to contribute towards the building or refurbishment of the new home. If insufficient money is gathered from the 'red envelopes' to cover the costs of the wedding, then the groom's household may be faced with severe economic problems.

Another way to gain the money required is to borrow money from richer relatives or from the banks. For most Truku people, borrowing from banks is the least attractive prospect, as the value of their land is usually well below the amount they are borrowing. Owing to the legal strictures placed on indigenous lands, indigenous people can only sell their land within their own indigenous communities. Furthermore, most of them do not have a full-time job, so the banks tend not to take the risk of lending them money. Therefore, in order to amass sufficient money to invest in a wedding, most people will have to ask their richer relatives for help, or borrow money from them. For most poor people, however, the amounts borrowed from their richer relatives are too great to pay back quickly, and become long-term debts. Consequently, after the expense of a wedding, the relationship between households is often transformed, in that the poorer family and its richer relatives become debtors and creditors respectively.

Many richer Truku feel they have no choice but to lend to poorer relatives, to enable them to organize *powda gaya* rituals. When I asked Rowty why he had decided to help Masan, he answered that 'we are *lutut* (relatives)'. In the past, the *powda gaya* ritual was organized on the basis of *smbarux* (reciprocal exchange obligations) among households of the same kin group, but owing to the monetization of the *powda gaya* ritual many poorer families are also forced to seek financial aid from their richer relatives to afford such rituals. For many richer people, it is very difficult to refuse to lend money to their relatives, because they are expected by others to take responsibility for helping their kin. Many richer residents complained that they sometimes feared the reproach of their kin if they failed to promise immediately to lend money to poorer relatives who needed help. Hence, kinship obligations and duties are intrinsic to the monetary character of weddings among the Truku.

Monetary Practices and Social Stratification

Given that most Truku live in some degree of poverty, we might have some sympathy for the richer relatives who are expected to lend money to relatives who most likely will be unable to meet the debt. Unable to meet the regular payments, poorer relatives are forced into long-term debt, and when the richer give their money to help their relatives to organize the weddings, they may earn a reputation for generosity. In the pre-colonial period, there was no political hierarchy among the Truku. Individuals, especially men, would show their generosity through sharing their wild game with others. The head of the community was the best hunter: his gifts of wild game enabled him to express his generosity to others (cf. Godelier 1986). Nowadays, most Truku people no longer hunt, and a man no longer augments his reputation through gifts of wild game but through lending money to his poor relatives, helping them to organize their weddings.

It is instructive here to consider Edmund Leach's analysis of Kachin and Shan communities in highland Burma: 'it surely must be the case that over a period there is a shifting of economic and political power from one geographical centre to another, along with corresponding readjustments in the total network of inter-group relations, at every level of scale, throughout the whole area' (Leach 1970: 291). The marriage exchange based on *mayu/ dama* principles, along with the strategic manipulation, distribution and sharing of wealth (such as cattle), not only shaped and reshaped the distinction between Kachin *gumsa* and Shan communities, but also maintained hierarchies, including the chief's lineages, aristocratic status, commoner status and slaves. In *gumsa* communities, *mayu* (wife-taker) was ranked above *dama* (wife-giver), from which it followed that the highest ranking lineage in a village was likely have their *mayu* lineage in another village so as to maintain their position of superiority. In Kachin *gumlao* communities, however, where lineages were all of one rank, the principle of *mayu/dama* marriage exchange was not essential, and the differences between *mayu* and *dama* were avoided. Neither *gumsa* nor *gumlao* communities were continuously stable or unchanging: 'gumlao-type communities have a general tendency to develop gumsa-type characteristics, while gumsa-type communities have a tendency to break up into sub-groups organized on gumlao principles' (ibid.: 227). Among the Kachin, most communities over time moved back and forth from hierarchical to egalitarian social relations, and marriage exchange was always involved in this dynamic process. Leach argued that: 'The reciprocities of kinship obligation are not merely symbols of alliance, they are also economic transactions, political transactions, charters to rights of domicile and land use. No useful picture of "how a kinship system works" can be provided unless these several aspects or implications of the kinship organization are considered simultaneously' (Leach 1966: 90). It will be evident to the reader that Leach's account of the relationship between marriage exchange and shifting political influence and emergent power has implications for monetary marriage exchanges and the emergence of hierarchy among Truku people.

Prior to the monetization of exchange, Truku social relations were egalitarian rather than hierarchical. At that time, marriage exchange in the form of the ceremonial exchange of pigs, shaped and reshaped equal alliance relations between affines. I argue that monetary ceremonial exchange is creating a paradox for Truku people who, whether rich or poor, are customarily expected to fulfil duties of reciprocity in terms of a principle of equality. Owing to the monetization of the ceremonial exchange of pigs, the imperative to follow the principle of equality has produced financial burdens for many poor people, and caused relations between the Truku at large to become more hierarchical.

By financially aiding their relatives to organize weddings, the richer households not only have opportunities to earn reputation, but might be also able to increase the measure of their landed property. In many cases, poor relatives would sell their land to their rich kin in order to secure enough money to organize a wedding. Hence, wealthier households increase their share of landed property, and land shortage has become a serious issue for many poor households. Thus the monetization of weddings has effectively worked in the favour of richer Truku households, in terms of land distribution, with rich families becoming increasingly influential.

The social status of richer Truku people is evident in the luxurious, large-scale weddings organized by their households. The number of people involved in slaughtering pigs, making wedding gifts and attending the wedding feast not only provide ample evidence of the wealth of richer households, but also an opportunity to evince their standing in the community and their political strength. In Masan's story, I mentioned that his household was too poor to afford the expense of a wedding, and had to ask for help and economic support from Rowty, his father's cousin. Rowty and his wife are retired schoolteachers. After retirement, Rowty became the deputy head of the local government. They have three sons; two of them are also teachers and the other is a doctor.

For his eldest son's wedding ceremony in 1998, Rowty provided twenty-two pigs and set fifty tables for the wedding feast. The wedding ritual cost almost $17,000 dollars, twice the average cost of weddings in Truku society. According to Rowty's memory of his eldest son's wedding, there were more than seventy adults involved in making the pork wedding gifts, with each pig divided into twenty-five portions; more than 550 households received gifts. Around 500 guests, including his householders' kin groups, neighbours, colleagues and friends, attended the wedding feast. For many informants, this wedding was an unforgettable event in Fushih village. The wedding was more than simply a kinship event for Rowty's many relatives; it was a public occasion for the village. According to *gxal* principles, those who had received wedding gifts from Rowty's household became members of his *gxal*. Thus the wedding ceremony not only afforded Rowty an opportunity to display his economic status, it also allowed him to extend and strengthen his household's social network.

When I asked Rowty why he had provided so many pigs for his eldest son's wedding, he replied: 'I had to; it was a matter of social expectation. Honestly, most residents from the village expected me to show my *mhowayi* (generosity). On the other hand, my daughter-in-law's household is as wealthy as my household'. In saying this, Rowty indicated the importance of this extravagant wedding for two different kin groups: his own kin and neighbours, and those of his affines.

When Truku people lived in the highlands, people would show their generosity by sharing their wild game with others. Now, however, people tend to show it through the distribution of wedding gifts and the provision of extravagant wedding feasts. Hence, the monetization of weddings has created two different social spaces for the rich to display their *mhowayi*: richer households can further their reputation for *mhowayi* by providing financial aid for their relatives' weddings; in addition, they can extend their social network through sharing feasts and pork at their own, highly expensive weddings.

Prior to the 1970s, the groom's household had to prepare pigs as bride-wealth for the bride's household. The bride's household would then distribute the pigs to the members of their *gxal*. The groom's side, however, did not distribute pork to its *gxal*. After the 1970s, though, the form of marriage exchange changed. The groom's household and the bride's household each prefer to organize their own wedding feast and ceremony. The groom's household will give pigs as bridewealth to the bride's household, but it will also prepare pigs and a feast for its own *gxal*. As well as sharing the pigs given by the groom's household, bridal households from richer families will also prepare extra pigs and organize their own feast for their kin groups, friends, neighbours and colleagues. As a result, the sharing of pork with kin group and social relations on both the groom's part and the bride's has created a sense of competition, and the number of pigs used in the wedding process has sharply increased.

The monetary aspect of weddings has not only provided richer Truku households with the opportunity to display their wealth and extend their social networks, but has also created a social space in which they can form marital alliances with other richer families. The majority of poorer households do not have the money to organize frequent *powda gaya* rituals. However, economic difficulties aside, many Truku parents have little choice but to organize a wedding, if their children have offended against *gaya* principles relating to gender. I learned that *gaya* was a major issue in terms of early marriage, in that many informants attributed their unhappy marriages to the pressure to marry under *gaya* principles. For many Truku elders, if their children or grandchildren had been in an unmarried relationship for a long time, or if they had offended *gaya* in terms of unmarried intercourse, then it was imperative that a wedding be organized as quickly as possible.

For richer families, however, the monetization of *powda gaya* rituals has enabled parents to avoid undesired marital alliances. Wealthier Truku households prefer to form marriage alliances with other wealthy Truku families. If the parents do not agree to a marriage, they will try to delay it. Often they will often articulate their reluctance to accept the marriage in terms of an infringement against *gaya* on the part of the young couple, and one or two pigs will be provided as compensation by the household of their son's or daughter's lover. Although this does not mean that they necessarily reject the marriage altogether, by delaying the wedding the parents can communicate their feelings on the suitability of the match. Most poor households, however, cannot afford such a strategy. Thus, with the monetization of *powda gaya* rituals and wedding rituals, marriage not only provides richer households with the opportunity to select and create alliances with one another, it also functions to produce and reproduce a hierarchy between wealthier households and poorer households.

Conclusion

Among the Truku, the exchange of pigs is essential to the *powda gaya* rituals relating to ancestor worship. Through the exchange of pigs, Truku people not only connect with their ancestral spirits, but also with their kin groups. The number of pigs used depends on the scale of the particular *powda gaya* ritual. Through the distribution of pork and contribution of labour for the *powda gaya* ritual, they shape and reshape their kin groups. Prior to the 1960s, when they lived in the highlands, pigs were raised by every Truku household. The introduction of the commodity economy in the 1960s transformed pig production, and pigs are now purchased from the market. The acquisition of pigs has become monetized and, as a consequence, the *powda gaya* rituals in kinship and religious practices have also become monetized.

In this chapter, I have discussed the transformations in Truku kinship that have resulted from the commoditization of the economy in general and, in particular, the monetization of the exchange of pigs. In Marxist theory, money is the instrument by which foodstuffs and services are rendered comparable by measuring their value on a shared scale. Furthermore, under capitalism, labour is alienated and money is impersonal and liable to erode social organization, and especially political relations (e.g. Taussig 1980). The pig is still the main offering made both in ancestor worship and for weddings, and people are able to use money to organize these ritual and kinship practices. In this sense, money is not always impersonal (cf. Hart 1986), but is involved in long-term and short-term exchange among Truku people who regard each other as kin. Kinship practices, norms and obligations generate two different effects in the transformation of social relations. People continue to conduct *powda gaya* and to distribute pork at weddings based on the principles of *smbarux* (reciprocal exchange obligations) and of equality, which are key to their concepts of kinship and social relations. Even though most Truku continue to live in poverty, the principles of equality which underpin the complex web of *gaya*, kinship obligations and ancestor worship create the inner logic which continues to compel Truku to exchange pigs for a variety of purposes.

Prior to the monetization of exchange, equal relations among the Truku at large were at once constituted and evinced in carefully balanced exchange and reciprocity between households. With the introduction of the market economy and the commoditization of labour and land, a hierarchy between the poor and the rich has emerged. Most Truku people are too poor to afford all of the expenses of kinship practice, so this situation engenders a long-term relationship between debtors (the poor) and creditors (the rich). Moreover, this long-term debtor–creditor relationship is not only economic but also political: monetary kinship practices enable wealthier households to display their wealth and generosity and, in so doing, to strengthen their social and political influence.

Notes

1. The Truku people are an Austronesian-speaking language group in Taiwan, most of whom live in the eastern mountains and on the east coast of the country. Mainstream society is composed of Chinese immigrants and their descendants. Those comprising Austronesian-speaking groups are in the minority; their population is just over 50,000 thousand, or 2 per cent of the population of Taiwan in 2009 (Council of Indigenous Peoples, CIP, 2009). The Truku population in 2009 was 25,286; 12,298 male and 12,988 female (ibid.).
2. All values in this chapter are given in US dollars.
3. For many Austronesian-speaking peoples in Melanesia, the pig is not only food, but also a kind of ordinary wealth (Lemonnier 1993) which figures in kinship and marriage practices (Glasse and Meggitt 1969; Strathern 1984, 1988), pig feasts (Hayden and Villeneuve 2011) and pig festivals (Boyd 1985). Besides, pigs are usually regarded as an essential component in compensation or indemnity payments (Bateson 1958; Schieffelin 1976; Modjeska 1982; Lemonnier 1993). The exchange or sharing of pigs helps people to gain prestige or accumulate wealth, and thus produces and reproduces social relations in general and political relations in particular. In so called 'big man' societies (Godelier 1982, 1986), the power of the big man is usually dependant on his 'ability to collect and manipulate wealth (pigs or shells) with an eye to large intergroup exchanges' (Lemonnier 1993: 127). The exchange, production, and consumption of pigs can also be regarded as a mechanism of production and reproduction of gender inequality (Strathern 1979; Modjeska 1982). Other studies focus on the influences of ecological conditions and agricultural technologies on pig exchange (Watson 1977; Golson 1982; Feil 1985, 1987; Lemonnier 1993) and on the implications of colonialism, Christianity and capitalism for ritual practices in which pigs are normally important (Boyd 1985; Carrier and Carrier 1989; Sillitoe 2000; Mosko 2010).
4. There is, in fact, another type of pork in Truku society, called *snahaw*. This refers to pork which is considered inedible but serves as an item of compensation in Truku society. Truku people will not share or even eat *snahaw* because to eat this type of pork is to risk incurring bad luck or some sort of unpredictable accident in the future.
5. Taiwan has been ruled by a number of regimes over the years: Ching Dynasty (1683–1895), Japanese colonial government (1896–1945), Kuomintang (1945–2000) and the Democratic Progressive Party (2000–2008).

6. The spirit, *utux*, is omnipresent and exists alongside the living. Truku people commonly offer a few drops of anything that they are about to drink – using their fingers to sprinkle a few drops on the ground while emitting a loud sibilant sound – as an invitation for the spirits to partake. When a household elder, a *rudan*, dies, they will become a spirit. The spirits of deceased elders are called *utux rudan*.

7. Christianity has recently come to play an important role in ritual and kinship practices, strongly influencing Truku norms; thus people tend to integrate their concepts of *gaya* into Christianity. For example, they describe Jesus as *Utux Barow*, which means the biggest (the most respected) spirit. Indeed, Truku people tend to invite priests to give blessings and pray for the success of *gaya* practices, and many Truku priests also conduct ancestor worship.

8. This sharing of wild game, I argue, is very similar to the immediate-return system in egalitarian societies described in Woodburn's theory of hunter-gather society (Woodburn 1982). Sather (1996) suggests that competition still exists in egalitarian societies, such as the Iban; he also argues that, through competition, individuals can earn their reputation, thereby enabling them to gain further wealth and power over others (ibid.: 74).

9. According to statistical surveys of indigenous peoples in Taiwan, only 3.1 per cent of households had a yearly income of over $59,000, while more than 59 per cent had a yearly income of less than $9,600 in 2005. The average cost of a new car is in excess of $2,000. In terms of individual monthly income in Truku society, 37.4 per cent of Truku people over the age of fifteen do not have a regular income, and 35 per cent regularly earn less than $800 per month (CIP 2005: 96).

References

Appadurai, A. 1986. 'Introduction', in A. Appadurai (ed.), *The Social Life of Things: Commodities in Cultural Perspective*. Cambridge: Cambridge University Press.

Bateson, G. 1958 [1936]. *Naven: A Survey of the Problems Suggested by a Composite Picture of the Culture of a New Guinea Tribe Drawn from Three Points of View*. Stanford: Stanford University Press.

Bellwood, P. 1996. 'Hierarchy, Founder Ideology and Austronesian Expansion', in J.J. Fox and C. Sather (eds), *Origins, Ancestry and Alliance: Explorations in Austronesian Ethnography*. Canberra: Department of Anthropology, Australian National University.

Blust, R. 1999. 'Subgrouping, Circularity and Extinction: Some Issues in Austronesian Comparative Linguistics', in E. Zeitoun and Jen-Kuei Li (eds), *Selected Papers from the Eighth International Conference on Austronesian Linguistics*. Taipei: Academia Sinica.

Boyd, D.J. 1985. 'The Commercialisation of Ritual in the Eastern Highlands of Papua New Guinea', *Man* 20(2): 325–40.

Carrier, J.G. 1992. 'Introduction', in J. G. Carrier (ed.), *History and Tradition in Melanesian Anthropology*. Berkeley: University of California Press.

———— 1995. *Gifts and Commodities: Exchange and Western Capitalism since 1700*. London: Routledge.

Carrier, J.G., and A.H. Carrier. 1989. *Wage, Trade, and Exchange in Melanesia: A Manus Society in the Modern State*. Berkeley: University of California Press.

Cheal, D. 1988. *The Gift Economy*. New York: Routledge.

Council of Indigenous Peoples, CIP. 2005. 'The Research of Economic Situation of Taiwan Indigenous Peoples'. Taipei: Council of Indigenous Peoples, Executive Yuan.

———— 2007 'The Research of Economic Situation of Taiwan Indigenous Peoples'. Taipei: Council of Indigenous Peoples, Executive Yuan.

———— 2009 'Annual Statistical Report of Indigenous Peoples: Population, Marital Status, Level of Education, and Birth and Death'. Retrieved 8 June 2011 from: www.apc.gov.tw.

Fiel, D.K. 1985. 'Configuration of Intensity in the New Guinea Highlands', *Man* 19(1): 50–76.

———— 1987. *The Evolution of Highland Papua New Guinea Societies*. Cambridge: Cambridge University Press.

Glasse, R.M., and M.J. Meggitt (eds). 1969. *Pigs, Pearlshells, and Women: Marriage in the New Guinea Highlands*. Englewood Cliffs, NJ: Prentice-Hall.

Godelier, M. 1982. 'Social Hierarchies among the Baruya of New Guinea', in A. Strathern (ed.), *Inequality in New Guinea Highlands Societies*. Cambridge: Cambridge University Press.

———— 1986. *The Making of Great Men. Male Domination and Power among the New Guinea Baruya*. Cambridge: Cambridge University Press.

Golson, J. 1982. 'The Ipomoean Revolution Revisited: Society and the Sweet Potato in the Upper Wahgi Valley', in A. Strathern (ed.) *Inequality in New Guinea Highlands Societies*. Cambridge: Cambridge University Press.

Gregory, C.A. 1980. 'Gifts to Men and Gifts to God: Gift Exchange and Capital Accumulation in Contemporary Papua', *Man* 15: 626–52.

———— 1982. *Gifts and Commodities*. London: Academic Press.

Hart, K. 1986. 'Heads or Tails? Two Sides of the Coin', *Man* 21(4): 637–56.

Hayden, B., and S. Villeneuve. 2011. 'A Century of Feasting Studies', *Annual Review of Anthropology* 40: 433–49.

Hsiao, H.-H. (蕭新煌). 1984. 'The Policies of the Mountain Economic and the Problems of Economic Development in Taiwan', *Taiwan Yinhang Jikan* 35(1): 126–61.

Kim, K.-O. 1980. 'The Taruko and Their Belief System', Ph.D. diss. Oxford: Department of Social Anthropology, Oxford University.

Kirch, P.V. 1991. 'Prehistoric Exchange in Western Melanesia', *Annual Review of Anthropology* 20: 141–65.

Kopytoff, I. 1986. 'The Cultural Biography of Things: Commoditization as Process', in A. Appadurai (ed.), *The Social Life of Things: Commodities in Cultural Perspective*. Cambridge: Cambridge University Press.

Leach E.R. 1966. 'The Structural Implications of Matrilateral Cross-cousin Marriage' in *Rethinking Anthropology*. London: Athlone Press.

——— 1970 [1954]. *Political Systems of Highland Burma: A Study of Kachin Social Structure*. London: Athlone Press.

Lemonnier, P. 1993. 'Pigs as Ordinary Wealth: Technical Logic, Exchange and Leadership in New Guinea', in P. Lemonnier (ed.), *Technological Choices: Transformation in Material Cultures since the Neolithic*. London: Routledge.

Li, Y.-Y. (李亦園) (ed.). 1983. *Shandi singjheng jhengce ji yanjiou yu pinggu baogaoshu* (Report of investigation and evaluation of the administrative policy in aboriginal societies). Nantou: Taiwan Shengjhengfu Minjhengting.

Lin, C.-H. (林靖修). 2010. 'Women and Land: Privatisation, Gender Relations and Social Change in Truku Society, Taiwan', Ph.D. diss. Edinburgh: Department of Social Anthropology, University of Edinburgh.

——— 2011. 'The Circulation of Labour and Money: Symbolic Meanings of Monetary Kinship Practices in Contemporary Truku Society', Taiwan. *Journal of Marxism and Interdisciplinary Inquiry* 5(1): 27–44.

Mabuchi, T. 1960. 'The Aboriginal Peoples of Formosa', in G.P. Murdock (ed.) *Social Structure in Southeast Asia*. Chicago: Quadrangle Books.

Modjeska, N. 1982. 'Production and Inequality: Perspectives from Central New Guinea', in A. Strathern (ed.), *Inequality in New Guinea Highlands Societies*. Cambridge: Cambridge University Press.

Mosko, M. 2010. 'Partible Penitents: Dividable Personhood and Christian Practice in Melanesia and the West', *Journal of the Royal Anthropological Institute* 16: 215–40.

Miller, D. 2001. 'Alienable Gifts and Inalienable Commodities', in F.R. Myers (ed.), *The Empire of Things: Regimes of Value and Material Culture*. Oxford: James Currey.

Mori, U. 1917. *Taiwan Banzokushi* (Ethnography of Taiwanese indigenous peoples). Taihoku: Rinji Taiwan Kyūkan Chōsaka.

Parry, J. and M. Bloch. 1989. 'Introduction: Money and the Morality of Exchange', in J. Parry and M. Bloch (eds), *Money and the Morality of Exchange*. Cambridge: Cambridge University Press.

Parry, J. and M. Bloch, 1989. *Money and the Morality of Exchange*. Cambridge University Press.

Sather, C. 1996. 'All Threads Are White: Iban Egalitarianism Reconsidered', in J.J. Fox and C. Sather (eds), *Origins, Ancestry and Alliance: Explorations in Austronesian Ethnography*. Canberra: Department of Anthropology, Australian National University.

Sayama, Y. 1917. *Rinji Taiwan Kyūkan Chōsakai dai ichi-bu banzoku chōsa hōkokusho* (Survey of Sediq people). Taihoku: Taiwan Sōtokufu Rinji Taiwan Kyūkan Chōsakai.

Schieffelin, E.L. 1976. *The Sorrow of the Lonely and the Burning of the Dancers*. New York: St Martin's Press.

Sillitoe, P. 2000. *Social Change in Melanesia: Development and History*. Cambridge: Cambridge University Press.

Simon, S. 2005. 'Scarred Landscapes and Tattooed Faces: Poverty, Identity and Land Conflict in a Taiwanese Indigenous Community', in R. Eversole, J. McNeish and A.D. Cimadamor (eds), *Indigenous Peoples and Poverty: An International Perspective*. London: Zed Books.

Strathern, A. 1978 'Tambu and Kina: "Profit", Exploitation and Reciprocity in Two New Guinea Exchange Systems', *Mankind* 11(3): 253–64.

_____ 1979. 'Gender, Ideology, and Money in Mount Hagen', *Man* 14: 530–48.

Strathern, M. 1984. 'Marriage Exchanges: A Melanesian Comment', *Annual Review of Anthropology* 13: 41–73.

_____ 1988. *The Gender of the Gift: Problems with Women and Problems with Society in Melanesia*. Berkeley: University of California Press.

Taussig, M.T. 1980. *The Devil and Commodity Fetishism in South America*. Chapel Hill: University of North Carolina Press.

Watson, J.B. 1977. 'Pigs, Fodder, and the Jones Effect in Post-ipomoean New Guinea' *Ethnology* 16: 57–70.

Woodburn, J. 1982. 'Egalitarian Societies', *Man, New Series* 17(3): 431–51.

Yamaji, K. 1986. 'Customary Laws of the Tayal in Taiwan', *Kwansei Gakuin University School of Sociology Journal* 53: 51–81.

3

Fijian Kinship

Exchange and Migration

———— ◆●◆ ————

Jara Hulkenberg

Fijian kinship is integral to all aspects of living life the 'Fijian way' (*na i vakarau ni bula vakaViti*) or 'in the manner of the land' (*i tovo vaka-vanua*). This is characterized, amongst other things, by reciprocal exchange as a means to support kin and fulfil kinship obligations. The attempt to sustain this lifestyle within an ever-growing money economy has led Fijians to talk in terms of an opposition between doing things 'in the manner of the land' (*i tovo vakavanua*) and 'in the manner of money' (*vakailavo*).[1]

This chapter discusses the maintenance of 'the Fijian way' in urban and foreign settings by means of an examination of the significance of kinship and the fulfilment of kinship obligations. As will become clear, making con-tributions in material, immaterial and financial form at once fulfils kinship obligations and sustains reciprocal relations between kin. These same recip-rocal kinship relations in turn sustain the *vanua* – that is, the land, place or country to which any indigenous Fijian belongs. *Vanua* comprehends land, sea, people, chiefs and ancestral gods; the maintenance of reciprocal kinship relations is crucial for people's spiritual connection to their *vanua*, their 'life source' (Tuwere 2002: 36).

In what follows, I focus my discussion on an example of ceremonial exchange of *masi* (decorated barkcloth) in Fiji, and on the gifting and exchange of other traditional valuables, goods, services and money in multiple forms, and with reference to relations between people that are inter-island, urban–rural or transnational. I argue that 'the Fijian way' has its roots, and finds its continuing significance, in pre-Christian sacrificial practices to the ancestral gods in the hope of receiving their blessings in return. This is not, however, an interpretation most Fijians feel comfortable with. No one would deny, however, that these practices stem from pre-Christian Fiji; what they would say is that, since the coming of Christianity, the Fijian way of life is ultimately directed towards the Christian God. Even so, the presence and powers of the ancestral gods are not denied and still respected and/or feared.

Giving, Divesting and Presenting Masi

Elsewhere I have argued that *masi* embodies all aspects of the *vanua*, and therefore *is* the *vanua*; as cloth of the *vanua*, *masi* is an important mediating agent in kinship when gifted or exchanged (Hulkenberg 2009). Moreover, *masi* is a house for the ancestor god(s) and a point of access to their power; it follows that *masi* is thus *mana* (effective) in itself. As such, *masi* has an important strengthening and protective function when used as a wrap around people and sacred objects in vulnerable states, such as during the life-cycle rituals described below.

My field research in Fiji (2003/4 and 2012), both in urban Suva, certain remote islands in southern Lau (Moce, Namuka i Lau, Oneata, Nayau and Lakeba), and subsequently in the UK (2005 to 2007 and 2011), has shown that Fijians go to great lengths to obtain *masi* to wear as ceremonial attire during rites of passage. This type of *masi* is called a *sulu* and is ideally pro-vided by a close female relative on the father's side as a means for her to nurture and bless (*vakamenemenei*) the person it is given to. After the cer-emony, this *sulu* is taken off by a female relative of the mother's side (*vasu*) who then keeps it, or who is instructed as to whom the *sulu* should be given.

Giving the *sulu* to a relative of the mother's side at once shows this person the utmost respect and acknowledges the mother's kin, despite the fact that the child is 'written to' its father and belongs to its father's lineage (*mataqali*). For example, during the celebration of a *siga ni sucu* (first birth-day of the firstborn), the *sulu* worn by the child during the ceremony is usually provided by a real or classificatory FeZ. After the ceremony, this *sulu* is divested by a female relative of the mother's side, usually a classificatory MBW, and given to her or presented to the child's biological or classifica-tory MB (*momo*). As a woman from Cicia island explained to me:

> This *sulu* is provided by the father's side because they are considered stronger than the mother's side, who are weaker. This is because the woman moves to the village of the husband after the marriage ceremony is completed. But, even though the woman

moves to the village of the husband, she still belongs to the *mataqali* of her father's side. So, when her husband dies, her father's relatives will come to present a *tabua* (*i lakovi*) to request her husband's kin to let her return to her father's house. So in ceremonies for children such as the *siga ni sucu*, but also the cutting of the hair of the child (*koti*) for the first time, *masi* is provided by the father's side and a relative of the mother's side will receive it. This is often the uncle, *momo*, or another significant relative.

The removal and/or presentation of a *sulu* as a means to show respect and confirm kinship is similar for commoners and chiefs. Historical documents illustrate that when a chief removed his fine barkcloth turban – his head having been thus protected as the site of *mana* – this was to show respect and humility in the presence of another chief or a sacred site where a god resided.[2] Not showing due respect is said to cause misfortune. In addition, as described by Hocart (1971: 67–68) and Hooper (1982: 165), when the installation of a paramount chief of Lau is completed, the new chief has to bathe in the sea and let the *masi* he has worn drift away, thus presenting the *masi* to his kin, the ancestor god(s) he now embodies.[3] The presentation of his protective wrap affirms his kinship relation to the gods, and shows respect and gratitude for their protection during the installation. Thus for both chiefs and commoners, gifting one's *sulu* upon completion of a specific phase of a rite of passage publicly acknowledges one's kinship relation to the recipient and thanks to that person for all they have done.[4]

During a Fijian wedding ceremony, the removal and presentation of one's *sulu* at once mediates and confirms the transformation in the existing kinship relations between the side of the bride and the side of the groom. That is to say, upon completion of various phases of a Fijian wedding ceremony, both bride and groom are divested of their *sulu* with the help of a female relative of the opposite side who has been chosen to receive this *sulu*. The groom's *sulu* is customarily taken off by a classificatory elder female (*na levu*, lit. 'big mother', MeZ) of the bride's side, and the bride's *sulu* is taken off by a classificatory *na levu* of the groom's side. It is only when the bride and/or groom wants to present the *sulu* to a male relative that the *sulu* is not given to the woman who assists in its divestment. In such a case, the *sulu* is taken off by a female relative of the groom's side and later given to the male relative, who will usually be one of the new in-laws, such as the eldest brother of the father-in-law who is a classificatory 'big' father (*ta levu*, FeB). In return, the person who receives the *sulu* ideally provides a new *sulu*. As a woman from Narocivo, Nayau island explained: 'The giving away of the *sulu* during a wedding and being given a new *sulu* is a form of exchange. The groom gives his *sulu* to the bride's family and the bride to the groom's family. This shows they [the two families] are connected [via the marriage] and shows they get on with each other'.

Figure 3.1: Female relatives assist the bride and groom with the removal of their *sulu* in front of the people present in a house in Suva. After the *sulu* have been removed, the bride and groom present them to an in-law.

The above is a simplified description of an element of Fijian wedding ceremonies that in fact consist of a series of ceremonial acts which, in each instance, require a form of gifting and exchange that can take days or even years to complete. These presentations and exchanges establish and confirm the kinship relations between the bride's side and the groom's side transformed by the marriage, in the presence of both the Christian God and the ancestor gods.

Gift Exchange at Wedding Ceremonies

Despite regional variations and elopements for various reasons, marriage between indigenous Fijians ideally starts with the presentation of a *tabua* (whale's tooth) by the father of the man (*i duguci*). Before this *tabua* is accepted, the woman's father will ask her three times if she is in love with the man. She will not answer until the third time she is asked; if she acknowledges she loves the man, the *tabua* is accepted by her father. Then the man's side will present another confirmatory *tabua* (*i vakadonu ni gusu*). The planning of the wedding entails meetings with kin within and across the man's and the woman's sides, always accompanied by the drinking of *yaqona* (kava).

The wedding, *vakamau*, generally starts with a Christian wedding ceremony in church (*vakamau vakalotu*), for which the bride and groom are dressed in a *sulu* and stand on a set of mats with a piece *masi* on top that is known as a *masi solofua*. These are provided by one or both families and mark out a 'sacred' area for the bridal couple.[5] After the ceremony, several presentations and counter presentations of *tabua*, other traditional valuables and imported goods take place to complete the ceremony 'in the manner of the land' at either the bride's or groom's house or village. They are followed by the *tevutevu*, the preparation of the nuptial bed.

The *tevutevu* requires the participation of female relatives and the presentation of women's valuables (*yau ni yalewa*) as an expression of *loloma*

Figure 3.2: A nuptial bed that has been created in front of one of the walls of the living room in a house in Suva. One can see a *gatu taunamu ni Viti* hanging along the wall with pillows and blankets laid out in front of it on a *gatu vakatoga* that functions as a *masi solofua* on top of a variety of mats.

(generosity, reciprocity and love) to *vakamenemenei* (bless and nurture) the bridal couple in the hope of a prosperous marriage with many children.[6] The valuables consist of *masi*, mats, scented coconut oil, food bowls and so forth, and nowadays increasingly include imported goods, such as lengths of textile, mosquito nets, bedding, pots and pans – in sum, all that a woman needs to fulfil her domestic as well as her ceremonial role as a wife. The gifts, which have been provided by both families, are presented next to each other in the same room, around the nuptial bed. The bed itself consists of layers of mats, with the top layer being *masi*, and behind or in front of it a *masi* known as a *gatu taunamu ni Viti* (Fijian mosquito net).

The mats, whether used to create a bed, a seat or an area to stand on, are always laid out according to a particular ordering principle.[7] At least one big *masi*, usually a *gatu taunamu ni Viti*, is hung along the wall behind the 'bed', or the main cross beam of a traditional Fijian house. Because the nuptial bed consists of gifts from both families, there is usually more than one *gatu taunamu ni Viti*, and sometimes there are even two 'beds' side by side. This indicates, besides its nurturing function, that the *tevutevu* is an important ceremonial presentation of gifts between the two families. They literally 'face one another' (*veiqaravi*) on the occasion of unfolding (*i tevu*) in each other's presence the mats and *masi* for the nuptial bed. These acts initiate a continuing exchange of goods and services between the relatives from that moment onwards and into the future.

The preparation of a nuptial bed can take several days, during which the elderly women do not leave the room. They eat and sleep there until the *tevutevu* is completed as a form of *vakamenemenei* (nurturing and assisting) the bridal couple, who, traditionally, would consummate their marriage in the bed created behind the *gatu taunamu ni Viti*. The mothers and close female relatives of the bride and groom are expected to make everything look as beautiful as possible. The eldest sisters of the father of the bride and the father of the groom have a particularly important role. For the female relatives of the groom, the presentation of gifts during a *tevutevu* welcomes the bride into the family, and shows that they can provide for her. It is common practice for the groom's side to present the bride's side, upon arrival, with kerosene and cloth in the ceremony of welcome called *vakamamaca* (lit. 'making dry'). After this they are the first to *tevu*, 'unfold', their *tevutevu*, which is followed by a counter presentation by the bride's side to show that she comes from a 'strong' lineage that is blessed.[8] This presentation is indicative of her life-generating capacities. Therefore, for the *tevutevu*, the bride's relatives tend to bring more gifts than the groom's kin, such as furniture and, increasingly in urban areas, a television, fridge, washing machine and so on. As a woman from Cicia island explained:

The boy's side does not care as much about the *tevutevu* as the girl's side. It is different from the past because now you have all the furniture. In the past you would only spread mats, pillows and mosquito nets. Now people want to show off and compete with one another. The girl's relatives want to show that the girl comes from a well-off family, and that is why they buy the best things for her to take to her husband's kin. For example, the contents [a *tabua*, two pillows, a mosquito net and blankets] of the wooden box (*kato kau*) the bride gets from her parents is given to the mother of the groom. When the box is placed on the mats during a *tevutevu*, the mother of the groom is asked to open it and take [out] the contents. It is important for the bride's parents there is a lot in the box to show the bride comes from a good family.

The majority of the gifts displayed at the *tevutevu*, such as the furniture and crockery, are for the bridal couple to start their new life. The mother of the bride decides what gifts presented by the bride's side are for the couple, and the mother of the groom does the same with the gifts presented by the groom's side. All the other gifts (pillows, mats, *masi*, mosquito nets and textiles) are distributed amongst contributing kin after the ceremony is over. The mothers of the bride and groom decide what is given to whom. These decisions depend on the type of kinship relation and associated obligation in combination with what a person/family has contributed (traditional valuables, goods, money and/or services) to the event. If a person or side has not presented as many gifts as would be expected or required, this is expressed in the distribution of the gifts afterwards. For example, if someone has not contributed what might be expected of them according to kinship (*vakaveiwekani*), they will receive in return an equivalent item or something of lesser quality, instead of slightly more. Although it is not considered proper (*i tovo vakavanua*), the mother of the bride or groom may hold back some gifts instead of giving them out after the ceremony if they feel the other side has not contributed enough.

Like any major ceremonial event, weddings can take years to prepare, and are becoming increasingly hard for people living in cities and overseas owing to the demands of their new lives and physical distance. As a result, certain phases in ceremonies are conducted in a slightly different form or omitted, and cannot always take place in the *vanua* (country), of the people involved.[9] Even so, weddings always involve the presentation and exchange of gifts. The following account of past and planned ceremonies of a Fijian couple based in Edinburgh illustrates such changes in more detail.

After marrying at the registry office in Fiji, Cathy and Buli migrated in 2009 to Edinburgh, where Buli serves in the British army.[10] When their first child, Ana, turned one year old it was important to organize a birthday (*siga ni sucu*) because she is the first child of the marriage, and the first grandchild of the eldest male sibling on her father's side. The event took place in the community centre of the military barracks in Edinburgh.

Figure 3.3: Seating area created with mats and *masi* for the celebration of Ana's *siga ni sucu.*

Similar to the *tevutevu* display, the area where baby Ana and her mother sat during the speeches and prayer was a material expression of Ana's female kin's blessings and nurturance. Customarily, these mats and *masi* are provided by the female relatives of the child's father's side. For this event, however, Ana's MM provided more gifts than Ana's father's parents, who live in a village in Kadavu, have little money and many grandchildren. Ana's MM lives by herself in the Fijian capital Suva and has a bit more money to spend, so she sent the following gifts with a kinsman who was returning to the UK after a visit to Fiji: two mats (one *ibe vakabati*, one *ibe davodavo*), two *masi solofua* to cover the tables where the cake and presents were laid out, also baby Ana's *sulu* and *salusalu* (garland), and several metres of textile for the *rokavata*, family clothing of the same colour and fabric.[11] A man who is Ana's father's classificatory cross-cousin and who stays at the military barracks in Glencourse near Edinburgh, contributed the following gifts: one *gatu vakatoga* for the wall, one *masi solofua* and two large mats (*i coco*) which were used to create the seating area, and one small mat (*ibe lailai*) which was laid on top of *masi* to decorate the table where the cake was to be displayed.[12]

After family and guests had sung 'Happy Birthday' for Ana, her father's classificatory *tata lailai* (lit. 'small father', FyB) made a speech in which

Ana's relation to him and others present was explained, a blessing was asked for her life, and all the family and friends were thanked for coming, for their gifts and for showing their love (*loloma*) to Ana. This was followed by a prayer, after which people were invited to eat.

The food (*magiti*) was prepared by the following women: Tinai Paulini, whom Cathy calls *nei* (classificatory in-law, *veivugoni*) because Tinai Paulini's husband is a classificatory MB to Cathy's mother; Nau, whose husband's village in Fiji is next to Buli's village; Alumita, whose HFM is classificatory sister to Buli's MF; and lastly, the wife of Ana's father's cross-cousin.[13] Together with some family friends, these women also assisted with the setting up and cleaning of the community hall afterwards. All the families who contributed to the ceremony by providing services such as cooking, cleaning, making a speech or saying prayers were given food to take home when they left to show appreciation for their contributions to the event.

Ana's mother explained that if this *siga ni sucu* had been held in Fiji it would have been much bigger: 'It is very hard to obtain all the stuff you need from Fiji. We had to use whatever we got. In Fiji *tabua* (whale's teeth) and *yaqona* (kava) would have been presented, and it would be held in my husband's family house in the village [in Kadavu]'. Also, except for food, there was no presentation afterwards of traditional valuables such as *masi* and mats. Normally a classificatory *na levu* (MeZ) or classificatory *bubu* (grandmother) would sit with Ana on the mats and *masi*, but this time it was Ana's mother because there was nobody else available who was related to Ana in a manner that allowed her to fulfil that function. That relative would have been given one of the *masi* or one of the mats used during the ceremony, such as the *masi solofua* they sat on and Ana's *sulu*. Instead, Cathy kept all of the mats and *masi* for future use.

Tata lailai, who gave the speech, is a classificatory younger brother of the grandfather (Ana's FF) and the oldest man to whom, in the UK, Ana's parents are related; he and they come from the same village. In Fiji, a male relative from Ana's father's side who is more directly related would have given the speech – a *tata levu* (FeB) or, ideally, the grandfather (*tukana*). Fijians reason that the person to give the speech needs to be an elder because he is more directly related to the ancestors than a younger person, and therefore expected to have the knowledge required to give a speech that properly acknowledges kinship relations through time between the *vanua* ('chiefdoms', 'countries') of the people present.

Also different from Fiji, particularly in rural areas, are the gifts that were presented and displayed on a table covered with *masi*. In Fiji, the gifts would consist of *waliwali* (scented coconut oil), *masi*, mats, soap, drums of kerosene, lengths of textile and so on, but in this case, by and large, people gave toys, clothes and cards with money (on average £20, £500 in total).

As several women explained to me, not as many traditional valuables are presented and exchanged in the UK as in Fiji owing to their scarcity. People hold on to the traditional valuables they have and present them sparingly because they know there is only a slim chance of receiving one in return, and you need to have enough for ceremonial events for your immediate kin, such as your children.

Inter-island and Rural–Urban Exchange

Despite the growing money economy in remote southern Lau – through money remittances and the sale of fish, lobster and bêche-de-mer to Japanese ships – annual exchange (*veisa*) between people on neighbouring islands is sustained. These exchanges are a means to obtain produce in short supply and traditional valuables that the island does not produce. More importantly, *veisa* are ceremonial events that confirm kinship relations between the people involved. For example, women from Moce island generally exchange *masi* for mats. Different groups of approximately ten to twenty women organize annual inter-island exchanges with women from other islands. After both groups have specified what is going to be exchanged, they have a year to prepare.

During my research on Moce island in 2003/4, fifteen women had organized an exchange of *masi* for mats with women from Lakeba island to take place in May 2004.[14] The preparation for these exchanges is nerve-racking for the women involved because they do not know if they have produced enough *masi* of good quality for the mats they are about to receive in return. If the mats are of a better quality, and are bigger in size than the *masi*, the women of Moce will feel ashamed as representatives of their *vanua* and will be regarded as the 'weaker' exchange partner. If it is the other way round, they will be considered the 'stronger' partner, but they will go home with lesser quality valuables.[15] Only rarely are valuables of a poor quality exchanged, but it is a possibility. Therefore, exchange partners are chosen not only because of who they are as kin, but also for their reputation. The exchanges at once confirm kinship while meeting a given island's need for specific crops, materials and traditional valuables. As well as the inter-island exchanges of traditional valuables, the exchange of such valuables for imported goods and/or money between women in rural and urban areas is becoming increasingly important.

Fijians living in urban areas need traditional valuables for weddings, funerals and other life-cycle ceremonies, but they may have difficulty obtaining them if they have neglected their kin in rural areas where valuables such as *masi* are produced. Even so, obtaining such valuables through a form of exchange remains the preferred means. To facilitate this, exchange relations (*veisa*) are set up between women who have, as yet, no existing exchange relation. Unlike exchanges that take place as part of life-cycle ceremonies, *veisa* are set up solely for practical purposes – that is, the exchange of one kind of traditional valuable for another, or for imported goods or money.

Those women in Lau who have a *veisa* relation with someone in Suva may never meet one another; what is to be exchanged and details of the shipment are organized over the phone. If women do meet, they sit down on the floor in one of their houses. To start the *veisa*, they will shake hands (*lululu*) and present one another with a small gift. The woman who made the mats or *masi* will present something from her village, such as oil, and the other woman will present in return a few cups or plates. Then they both spread out their goods and/or money and valuables (mats or *masi*) and sit down again. The woman who has made all the *masi* or mats will say: 'These are the mats/*masi* I have made for you. Do you like it?' The other woman will say 'Yes' and ask the same question: 'These are goods I have brought for you. Do you like it?' The other woman will then say 'Yes'. After this, the women embrace, look at all the valuables and goods properly, have tea or lunch, and say goodbye.

Veisa exchanges are never accompanied by acts which, during official events and life-cycle ceremonies, call upon the gods to witness the exchange of traditional valuables. For example, the official acknowledgement of the gifts by clapping with cupped hands three times (*cobo*) does not take place. Instead, one simply thanks (*vaka vina vinaka*) the exchange partner for the mats and *masi* they have made, either face to face or by phone once the valuables have arrived. Unlike established kinship relations with their associated obligations, *veisa* can be attenuated without fear of repercussions after the last agreed upon exchange is completed. They are set up to meet urban women's demand for traditional valuables to fulfil their kinship obligations ceremonially, and to provide women in rural areas with much needed money or imported goods.

Veisa are preferred over impersonal money transactions at markets and shops because they enable women to sustain a life 'in the manner of the land' that serves the *vanua* and unity amongst Fijians. When a *veisa* cannot be established in time for a ceremonial occasion, a woman has to resort to buying *masi*, with the additional insecurity she might not be able to purchase exactly what she needs. Even so, when she has to buy *masi* at the market, a woman will try to buy it from an area and stall owner she is related to. Otherwise she will be judged as not making an effort to support her kin and *vanua*. There are some shops that sell *masi*, but these are aimed at the tourist market, are expensive, and often owned by Indo-Fijians. Buying from these shops does not support kin and *vanua*, and is therefore a last resort.

According to the same principle, market-stall owners are obliged to sell handicrafts and traditional valuables from the areas to which they are related, and to refrain from selling those that originate from other areas. Finau, who rents a stall at the Curio Handicraft Market in Suva is such a woman. She is a highly respected weaver who grew up on both Ogea and Oneata islands, but she has been living in Suva since 1972. Her mother is from Ogea, her father from Namuka, and her husband from Komo island. Given these connections, Finau sells mats for women from Komo and *masi* from Moce and Namuka islands. Finau prefers the aesthetic qualities of *masi* from Moce over *masi* from Namuka, but owing to her paternal kinship relation to Namuka she is obliged to sell more *masi* for relatives from Namuka than for relatives from Moce. Neither can she sell *masi* from Vatulele island. If she did, people from Lau passing her stall would say, 'Hey you are from Lau, you should sell our *masi*!'

Kinship Obligations and Transnational Exchange

There has been a significant increase in migration of indigenous Fijians over the last twenty years (Norton 2004: 2; Voigt-Graf 2008: 22) to more affluent countries such as America, Australia, New Zealand and the UK in order to get a job and education for their children. Studies of Tongan, Samoan and Fijian migrant communities show that kinship plays a crucial role in Pacific migration processes and the formation of migrant communities: established migrants routinely sponsor visa applications, provide housing for kin who are newly arrived and help them to find a job.[16]

My current research in the UK indicates that there are approximately 2,200 Fijian soldiers (with or without their immediate families) who serve in the British army. Several hundred Fijian migrants hold multiple jobs as nurses, midwives and carers, professional rugby players and so on. As money is hard to come by in Fiji, kinship obligations to relatives back home are predominantly fulfilled by sending financial remittances. These remittances are sent on a regular basis to assist close kin, such as one's parents, with the costs of everyday living, and to make contributions towards important events such as funerals and weddings. When a presentation of gifts is to be made for a special ceremony on behalf of a Fijian family in the UK, money is sent to a relative in Fiji who will present the money for them.

Just sending money is not always considered sufficient to fulfil specific kinship obligations, especially in the case of death. For example, one who returns home from overseas after several years must make a presentation of gifts in respect of any deaths that have occurred among members of their *mataqali*. When a close relative has died, such as a brother or father, one must also make a presentation of gifts to the immediate family. These presentations are called *boka*, and consist of *yaqona*, a *tabua* and/or several drums of kerosene and bales of textiles. One is required to do this alongside sending money. As a church elder of the Fijian Methodist Church in the UK explained: 'Money is new and you need to present something that is old, you know. Money does not carry the same weight as traditional valuables such as *yaqona* and a *tabua* when you need to make a formal presentation such as a *boka*'.

It is not surprising that a Fijian will never 'just' go home to visit family. Fijians in the UK often joke that they really want to go to Fiji, but incognito, so that they do not have to make multiple presentations, visit all their relatives and play a part in postponed ceremonial events that are ideally conducted in Fiji, in the *vanua*, such as weddings or baptisms. Indeed, many migrant Fijians do not visit relatives in Fiji unless they have to for specific ceremonial events.

An important and frequent form of transnational exchange entails the supply of large quantities of *yaqona* in return for money. For example, relatives in Fiji send 30 kilograms of ground *yaqona* to the UK, where relatives exchange it for £25 or £30 per kilogram with Fijian neighbours. The money they are given for the *yaqona* is sent back to Fiji. One can buy *yaqona* more easily on the internet but, as I was told: 'This is how we do things. It is a way to help our family back home financially because it is hard for them to get money'. Another means to fulfil kinship obligations is to make financial contributions to various causes concerning one's family or one's *vanua* in Fiji and the UK through the *soli*.

The *Soli*

The *soli* is an occasion when money is contributed for a specific cause. For example, *soli ni vanua*, for a cause concerning the *vanua*; *soli ni koro*, for a cause concerning the village; *soli ni soqosoqo*, for a particular group such as a sports team; *soli ni veivuke*, to help with the cost of a visa or international flight in the case of necessity; and *soli ni lotu*, money collection in church.

A *soli ni lotu* (church *soli*) takes place in Edinburgh every first Sunday of the month, and is always conducted in the form of a competition between the people present, who are divided into groups according to gender, or their neighbourhood near the military barracks or the confederacy they belong to in Fiji (Kubuna, Tovata or Burebasaga). At the end of the *soli* competition, the winner is announced and given the trophy which they must return the next month.

Besides the monthly *soli ni lotu*, I have witnessed many others: a *soli ni koro* (village *soli*) that was organized by people from Naitasiri province living in and around Edinburgh to raise money for the renovation of the house of a Methodist pastor in one of their villages; a *soli ni soqosoqo* (association *soli*) organized by the women of the new netball team, the Edinburgh Fiji Netters, to raise money to buy netball equipment and provide for travel to tournaments; and a *soli ni veivuke* to raise money for the visa application for the new wife of a Fijian soldier.

All these events took the form of a 'curry night'. The people organizing the *soli* put money in a pot to buy the ingredients for the food, plastic plates and cups and so forth, and the women involved cooked the curry, rice and roti. Those who attend may give any amount of money, usually between £5 and £10. Each contribution is placed in a box or bowl that stands on the table with the food. At the end of the night, someone will announce how much money has been raised (on average £500 is raised from a *soli* in Edinburgh), thank the people for coming to support the cause, and finish with a prayer.

There are many more money-raising events, such as the *soli* organized in Fiji and in the UK for various causes, and some Fijians say there are too many.[17] It is hard for people to contribute to all of them, but as members of the community, they feel obliged. As Toren (1999: 31) notes, contributions are never anonymous, because they at once fulfil the giver's kinship obligations, and incur obligations on the part of the receiver. In church, a person is identified according to gender, *mataqali* (kin group), village, neighbourhood and so on, and during the other *soli*, the organizers make a mental note of who has come and how much they have contributed. A Fijian woman explained to me: 'If you don't go [to all the *soli*] you're not *kai Viti* [behaving like a Fijian person]. Even if you don't have anything you have to go . . . or, well it is up to you'. The expression 'it is up to you' is often used in reply to a question as to whether one should do something or go somewhere even though one does not feel well or, in the case of a *soli*, does not have enough money to contribute. One is responsible for one's own behaviour. As an adult, one should know what to do and behave accordingly; otherwise one will be judged for it, bear the social consequences such as gossip, and risk being cursed.

No matter where a person lives, they represent their *vanua*, and any improper behaviour reflects badly on everyone belonging to that *vanua*. As Ryle writes, 'living in the manner of the land, *vakavanua*, is based on nurturing kin' (Ryle 2010: 16). Nurturing or sustaining kinship relations by providing food, goods, services and contributing to *soli* is of great importance, and not doing so may anger the ancestral gods and cause sickness or even death. There is a constant pressure to represent ones *vanua* properly by living a life 'in the manner of the land'.

Finding and Establishing Kinship in the UK

Besides the nurturing of known relations between kin in Fiji, additional specific kinship relations and associated obligations are found out amongst Fijians in the UK who, at the time of writing, number around 6,000, many of whom serve in the British army. After they have taken their pensions, most men continue to work, for example, as a security officer in the UK or Iraq or Afghanistan, or for the railway. Women may work as nurses or as housewives. These migrant Fijians form a tight and well-organized community in which people relate to one another as kin, observing and fulfilling all the many ceremonial and other obligations that are entailed and, in many cases, elaborating ties that in Fiji may well have remained unacknowledged.

All ethnic Fijians are held ideally to be kin to one another so, whenever Fijians meet for the first time, they at once ask one another where, in Fiji, they come from. No matter where Fijians are in the world, they need this knowledge if they are to behave correctly towards one another. Once they find out how they are related, their relation may, in the migrant community, be accorded a greater degree of importance than it would perhaps have received at home in Fiji. Thus once the kinship relation is discovered, they take on all the obligations proper to that relation as it is lived in Fiji. In conversation with a group of Fijians in Edinburgh, I once referred to these kinship relations as 'distant', but was corrected by a woman who was visiting relatives in Scotland: 'You as a *kai valagi* [person who is not an indigenous Fijian] call some kinship relations "distant", such as your second cousins. You might not even know about them. To us [Fijians], distant kinship relations do not exist. We are all closely related'. Thus, kinship relations are never new, they have always existed, but the people in question were previously unaware of their specificity. Some relations have to be traced back three or four generations. As Fijian Methodist Church Minister Kaci explained to me in Derby: 'It is only when you find out how you are related that you start to feel obliged to fulfil the associated obligations. If you do not know you are excused'.

Consider the following example. Fijians in the UK perform traditional Fijian life-cycle ceremonies for first birthdays, marriages, funerals or the presentation of a *meke* (traditional Fijian dance) for the first time. When a boy from Ono island presented his traditional Fijian dance for the first time in public during Fijian Independence Day Celebrations in Stoke-on-Trent, he came on stage wrapped in a length of textile, a mat and *masi*. Though kin from the boy's father's side could not be present for the event, the father's older sister (*nei*) had sent the textile, mats and *masi* over from Fiji as their contribution. The important role of divesting and presenting the young man with new attire and a *tabua* (whale tooth) was performed by a minister of the Fijian Methodist Church and his wife who resided in England at the time.

When the minister and his wife came to Stoke in 2003, both families had found out, upon meeting each other, how they were related: they traced a kinship relation four generations back through the young man's MF that makes him and the minister classificatory brothers from the same village on Cicia island. That is to say, the boy's MFFF was classificatory brother to the minister's FFF. In addition, the minister's wife comes from the same island (Matuku) and village (Makadru) as the namesake of the boy's mother. Having the same name (*veiyacani*) is in itself an important kinship relation, irrespective of the genealogical connection between the two parties, so these two women were revealed as kin by virtue of this discovery. Based on these kinship relations, the mother of the boy calls the minister *ta* (father) and his wife *na* (mother). As classificatory grandparents of the boy on the mother's side, they consider themselves to be in the *vasu* position vis-à-vis his father's side, from which it follows that they are the appropriate kin to divest the *masi*. In return, to the surprise of the parents, as this is not customarily done, they presented the boy not only with a new *sulu*, but also a *tabua* as a form of nurturing (*vakamenemenei*).

In the UK, as in Fiji, everyday services, such as babysitting, cooking food when someone is ill or busy, providing lifts to the shops and so on are also part of the fulfilment of reciprocal kinship obligations. For example, one

Figure 3.4: Young man's classificatory grandparents are divesting the *sulu*, mat and textile, which is theirs afterwards.

family from Naitasiri province in Fiji had to move out of their house in the army barracks on retirement, and before they could leave, the house had to be cleaned and painted white. They left this to the last minute and so, despite their busy schedule and the looming deployment to Afghanistan of some soldiers, all the men from Naitasiri who stayed in Edinburgh worked in the house for several days.

The Significance of Kinship and its Obligations

Why do Fijians deem so important the finding out and elaboration of kin ties in the UK, even in the face of the pressures they experience to fulfil their already acknowledged obligations to kin at home in Fiji? I argue that it is because, by virtue of sustaining and fulfilling kinship obligations, one may know oneself to be truly part of a *vanua* – land, place, country. To understand why the *vanua* is important to Fijians a more detailed discussion of the term is needed. Ryle describes the *vanua* as:

> both land and sea, the soil, plants, trees, rocks, rivers, reefs; the birds, beasts, fish, gods and spirits that inhabit these places and the people who belong there . . . *Vanua* is a relational concept that encompasses all this, paths of relationship, nurture and mutual obligations connecting place and people with the past, the present and the future. (Ryle 2010: xxix)

For Fijians, the *vanua* is the place to which one belongs because one's ancestors either founded it or moved to live there.[18] As all the ancestors are kin to one another, all Fijians are ultimately kin, and their prohibitions and freedoms are a function of how they conceive of relations between their respective ancestors.[19] It is these hierarchical kinship relations that exist between chiefs and indigenous Fijians, as well as adhering to the associated protocols that confirm or establish the relations that tie a person to a specific *vanua*. Consequently, a Fijian's relation to the *vanua* is crucial to an understanding of Fijian ideas of personhood.

Vanua maybe translated as 'land' or 'country', but what is comprehended by these terms is literally everything that belongs to these places, the very earth and sea and also the people. Toren (2004) describes the Fijian idea of the person as a locus of relationship, given in the *vanua* as the continuing source of all fertile and productive relations. The continued ceremonial, urban–rural and transnational exchange of goods, traditional valuables, services and giving of money should not be interpreted as part of an economy of sentiment, as Arno (2005) writes in relation to the motivation for exchange. These acts are crucial to sustain kinship relations between Fijians and their *vanua*, no matter where they are located. When these relations are neglected, Fijians are at risk of losing that which makes them particular Fijian persons – the set of relations in whose terms they understand themselves and their relation to the world, specifically their spiritual connection to the *vanua*, their place of belonging. As Tuwere writes, 'To be cast out from one's *vanua* is to be cut off from one's source of life' (Tuwere 2002: 36).

Hondagneu-Sotelo and Avila (1997) describe how immigrant Latina mothers in Los Angeles continue to fulfil their role as absent mothers for their children left in their homeland, and Clifford discusses the contemporary transnational exchange of money and goods more generally: these exchanges enable migrants to remain part of 'an on-going transnational network that includes the homeland not as something simply left behind, but as a place of attachment in a contrapuntal modernity' (Clifford 1997: 256). In the case of Fijian migrants, however, it is more accurate to say that these continuing exchanges at once constitute and sustain kinship, both in the places where the migrants make their new homes and in the places elsewhere to which they continue to belong. The kin relations that are found out and elaborated by Fijian migrants in their new homes are themselves aspects of the kin relations already given to them in the *vanua* to which they belong.

Migration from the rural periphery to an urban centre within Fiji is a case in point. An increasing number of Fijians who are born in Suva have never been to their father's village, their *vanua*. Nevertheless, if there is a function, such as a *soli* concerning the village, area or island they come from, they will get involved. If they do not, eventually they will cease to be recognized as belonging to that *vanua*. For example, one woman explained that she recognized a man from Moce island on the street in Suva and asked her friend to confirm this by saying, 'Hey, is he not from Moce island?' Upon which her friend replied, 'Oh no, we never see him at any of the functions'. If you do not do what is expected of you as one who belongs to a certain *vanua*, you alienate yourself from it and from the people with whom you would otherwise be kin. This man is not and cannot be from Moce island because he is not relating to others as he would do if indeed he was from Moce. In other words, from a Fijian perspective, people are kin who behave as kin to one another; it follows that if you do not behave as kin, then you cannot be kin.

Several existing studies of Pacific migrant processes argue that the main motivation for migration is the economic improvement of one's kin through sending formal and informal (unrecorded) remittances in the form of money and goods. Brown and Leeves describe this as 'remittance motivated migration' (Brown and Leeves 2007: 17) that, according to Voigt-Graf (2008: 28) ensures closeness, or a 'safety net' (Scott 2003: 188) for future needs. As will already be apparent from the material discussed here, as well as Kai'ili (2005) and Lilomaiava-Doktor (2009), I argue that these statements should be refined. Migration may indeed be motivated by the hope of financial and material prosperity, but my current research in the UK indicates that migration is a conscious strategy of Fijians to sustain a life 'in the manner of the land' in an ever-widening monetary economy and globalizing world. As a Fijian woman from Cicia living in Stoke explained: 'Working hard [often holding two jobs] is what we are here for. With the money we earn we can support our relatives in Fiji, make contributions to ceremonial events in the UK and in Fiji, make money donations to the Methodist Church in the UK and in Fiji, and provide good education for our children'. This comment indicates that monetary remittances, such as those made possible by the money that changes hands in return for *yaqona* in the UK, should not be viewed as primarily monetary transactions. They are forms of acting out kinship and associated obligations. This is stressful and costly, however, and consciously reduced to the bare minimum by some Fijian migrants.

Kai'ili (2005) observes that Tongan migration is not motivated by money or by a rejection of Tongan traditional ways; rather, it is a means to earn money and to fulfil kinship obligations via the 'socio-spatial ties' that bind a Tongan to their land.[20] Likewise, the travel of Fijians to urban or overseas settings is better understood as a means of sustaining a life 'in the manner of the land' characterized by an exchange economy in the widest sense, that is played out within, and accommodated to, a worldwide monetary economy. Migration is a means of earning money, which can then be used to mediate kinship and stay connected to the *vanua*. Even so, the continued ceremonial presentation and exchange of traditional valuables is not only a means to sustain kinship and the *vanua*. Ceremonial presentations have an aspect that is arguably sacrificial, insofar as people expect to receive in return blessings from the ancestor gods and the Christian God.

Ceremonial Exchange as Sacrifice

Sahlins (1981) underlines the importance of sacrifice in pre-Christian Fiji. Based on his analysis of documents from the nineteenth century, he states that the quantities of foods and goods that were exchanged ceremonially between different *vanua* were presented to the gods of the recipients, not to the recipients themselves. Therefore, Sahlins writes, nearly everything we call trade and tribute was sacrifice at the time. In this connection, it is interesting to note Hocart's (1936b) observation that the surrender of possessions, as part of a ceremonial offering to a deity, is required to make something sacred, and in Fiji in particular, to make a people, the land, a person or a war *mana* ('effective'). One might thus argue, for example, that a *tevutevu* exchange makes a marriage *mana* (effective, prosperous). The actual ceremonial presentation between both sides emphasizes the form of kinship relations and mutual obligations between the people involved as a result of the marriage, while also asking the ancestor gods and Christian God for their blessings. As an elderly Fijian man from Vanua Levu, who had migrated to England, explained, 'Even though all the gifts for a *tevutevu* are given out of kinship, they are also given as a sacrificial presentation to ask for the blessing of the ancestor gods'. He based his argument on the speeches men give for the presentation and reception of gifts. 'During such a speech you open the ceremony up for the gods in order for them to be witness of it, and refer to the gifts presented in order to ask for a blessing for the couple, and the new blood relation that has been created through the marriage'.[21]

It follows that the practice of exchange itself is the preferred means of obtaining especially 'traditional' valuables, but also imported goods. It enables Fijians to attend upon their god(s) by spreading word of their strength, as well as creating unity and prosperity. As Turner (1987) writes, failing to fulfil one's obligations 'according to kinship' (*vakaveiwekani*) and 'according to the land' (*vakavanua*) can make the gods turn to vengeance, and cause harm, such as illness. He goes on to argue that the prime role of exchange is not the instantiation of 'sociality', but a means to request the ancestor gods for general well-being. I want to argue, however, that the instantiation of 'sociality' is crucial for the general well-being of Fijians. As Tomlinson (2009: 65) writes: 'Social unity [in Fiji] means everyone knows his or her place: commoners fulfil their traditional obligations in service to chiefs, and chiefs act in appropriate chiefly style [that is, providing for the people]. If chiefs are effective in these ways . . . society will be strong as a result'. This is the main reason why exchange and tribute are sustained within changing contexts. They are important aspects of living life 'in the manner of the land' (*i tovo vakavanua*) and preferred over impersonal money transactions.

Unlike 'impersonal' money transactions, exchange and tribute sustain the *vanua*, the kinship collectivity, and in so doing create unity. Nevertheless, as Tomlinson (ibid.: 74) describes, many Fijians feel properly unified relationships are broken, or are in the process of breaking down, owing to changes in society such as the growing money economy and the unstable political climate that has resulted in several coups. As a result, Fijians feel the *mana* of chiefs and gods is diminished or lost, and with it the people's communal labour power which, in turn, threatens the unity of the kinship collectivity.

Despite the arguments presented above, Fijians were reluctant to talk about pre-Christian practices in general during my research in Fiji and the UK. They say, 'we don't do these things anymore', or 'we do not attend on the ancestor gods anymore because we are Christians now'. In addition, under the influence of Christianity, and especially the Pentecostal Church that was introduced to Fiji in 1926, gradual changes in perception of the purpose of exchange and the presentation of gifts in ceremonial contexts are voiced by some Fijians. For example, members of the Pentecostal Church do not see the elaborate ceremonial presentation and exchange of gifts as all-important any more. Moreover, they condemn them as an unnecessary display of wealth that drains the family financially. As Ryle writes, this can be attributed to the fact that, unlike the Methodist Church, the Pentecostal Church does not honour and remember the ancestors. Honouring and remembering the ancestors is seen as pagan, and Pentecostals focus more on the present and future: 'While Methodism is closely interwoven with maintaining and strengthening clan ties and relations to the land, Pentecostals are first and foremost connected to God and one another and to global spiritual networks through a personal relationship with Christ' (Ryle 2010: 140).

One might therefore question to what extent the ceremonial exchange of traditional valuables in contemporary Christian Fiji is directed towards the ancestor gods and considered a sacrifice. Ravuvu (1987) argues, however, that the high degree of effort exerted in ceremonial exchange is a means of requesting blessings from both the ancestor gods and the Christian God. Indeed, a number of ethnographers have argued that the Christian God has been incorporated as the superior deity of the existing pantheon (see Toren 1990: 106; 2004; Newland 2004; Tomlinson 2009; Ryle 2010). This argument can be substantiated in speeches which accompany ceremonial exchange and which are directed to the ancestor gods of the people involved by virtue of pronouncing the names of their *vanua* and their ancestral house foundations.[22] The Christian God is also included and referred to as the greatest living God whose blessings might follow on His witnessing the exchange of gifts and hearing the speeches.

I think it reasonable, therefore, to argue that relations between contemporary Fijians continue to be characterized by sacrifice, and that it remains important to attend upon the ancestral gods and the Christian God through the fulfilment of kinship obligations by contributing, presenting and exchanging traditional valuables as constitutive parts of the bodies of these gods. Imported goods, especially money, are not attributed the same value as traditional valuables, even though money is ever more important for the fulfilment of kinship obligations, and as part of ceremonial contribution, presentation or exchange.

Parry and Bloch (1989) contains many ways in which money is incorporated into non-Western cultural systems. Toren (1989), for example, argues that the incorporation of money into Fijian ceremonial practice removes from it the alienating taint of the market and transforms it into a 'gift', which implies that a return is expected, or, as Miyazaki (2005a) argues, hoped for in the future in material or immaterial form. Thus the money that changes hands in the various forms of *veisa*, money remittances and money transactions at local markets is not properly understood as part of commodity exchange (buying and selling) but as reciprocal exchanges between people who are all ultimately kin. Thus, Miyazaki (2005b) suggests that money transactions in the market can be interpreted as a novel form of *veiqaravi* (ceremonial presentations and exchanges), which involves money 'as a means to an end' in the hope of establishing 'good' and 'strong' relations between actors.

Viewed as a gift, as part of a reciprocal exchange, money remittances, money incorporated in *veisa* exchanges and money transactions in the market are incorporated within the wider system of exchange that sustains the *vanua*. However, the incorporation of money in these contexts is not a development everybody agrees with. A woman from Vanua Levu currently living in the UK is of the opinion that the incorporation of money in these *veisa* exchanges 'belittles' the principle on which a *veisa* is based: 'You are supposed to barter your valuables to obtain what you need. Money changes this Fijian barter system completely. I don't like it, but people just need money'. This comment reinforces what has been discussed earlier. The exchanges of *i yau* (valuables) evince a Fijian person's engagement in the kinship collectivity that is the *vanua* and, at its broadest, in the collectivity that comprises all indigenous Fijians. Western goods and money are not considered a traditional valuable, and are therefore valued differently. Even so, the ever growing importance of money cannot be denied, and as a result money and imported goods have become accepted as a gift in ceremonial and non-ceremonial exchange, though not considered equal to *i yau*, and are therefore not seen as a replacement for these valuables. Thus, during a ceremonial event that requires the confirmation of kinship relations in 'the manner of the land', money is generally not presented on its own in public. Instead, it has become the accepted practice to present money wrapped in a *masi* or mat, or in an envelope together with *yaqona* and/or a *tabua*.

For example, during a welcome ceremony, the head secretary of the Methodist Church in Fiji was presented with a *tabua* and an envelope containing money by the Fijian community of the northern division of the Fijian Methodist Church in the UK. The envelope was somewhat carelessly 'tossed' towards the head secretary after the *tabua* was passed over to him. This was done to indicate that the envelope was not the most important thing presented. As several men explained, it was 'just pocket money for him during his visit, nothing much'.

This behaviour in relation to the presentation of money can be explained by Ravuvu's (1987) observation that a ceremonial presentation or exchange can only mediate kinship when a ceremonial offering (*vakacabori*) of valuables (*i yau*) such as a *tabua*, mats, *masi*, *yaqona* has taken place as part of a ceremonial presentation (*veiqaravi vakavanua*, lit. 'attendance on one another in the manner of the land'). Unlike the public donation of money in church, or explicit money raising events in the form of a *soli*, ceremonies such as the welcome for the head secretary require that money be presented in a covert or careless manner, thus ensuring that it does not become a central element during the ceremonial presentation of traditional valuables.

Conclusion

This chapter has discussed the significance of kinship, and how and why Fijians sustain a life 'in the manner of the land' (*tovo vakavanua*) by continuing to gift, exchange and fulfil kinship obligations in rural, urban and transnational contexts. All the various forms of gifting and exchange of goods, services, money and traditional valuables show *loloma* (love, reciprocity), and in doing so nurture the person(s) involved and evince kinship. Tribute, gifting and exchange confirm and/or establish transformations in reciprocal kin relations between the people involved, and in so doing nurture and sustain the wider kinship collectivity that is the *vanua* at large. If Fijians do not live accordingly, even when they have migrated overseas, they risk losing their connection to their *vanua* and fear godly repercussions.

The last section of this chapter has argued that the necessity of maintaining a life 'in the manner of the land' has its historical source in Fiji's pre-Christian religion characterized by sacrifice. That is to say, Fijians deem important the finding out and elaboration of reciprocal kinship relations through gifting, exchange and tribute; kinship is an end in itself, but the exchange practices in which kinship is engaged also constitute attendance at once on the ancestral gods and the Christian God, in the hope of their blessings in the form of general well-being, prosperity and social unity. It follows that, no matter where Fijians are located, living in the manner of the land at once sustains the *vanua* and their place there – the locus of their own personhood as one among their kin. As Tuwere says, a Fijian who loses the connection to the *vanua* is divested of their 'life source' (Tuwere 2002: 36).

Notes

1. See also Toren (1989: 142–64) and Thomas (1997: 220).
2. See MacDonald (1857: 233) and Waterhouse (1997: 301) for examples of the divestment of *masi*.
3. For an account of how the sea can be used to offer gifts to the ancestor gods Ligadua and Dakuwaqa, see St. Johnston (1918: 72, 124).
4. Such presentations have often been mistaken for behaviour of a sexual nature by explorers and missionaries throughout the Pacific region.

5. In urban areas in Fiji and overseas, many women wear a white wedding dress and many men a suit during the church ceremony. Even so, *masi* is always worn by both for the remaining ritual acts that complete the wedding 'in the manner of the land', in the presence of both the ancestor gods and the Christian God.

6. Ravuvu (1987: 268) writes that, when presented ceremonially, *yau ni yalewa* provide protection and warmth, and nurture life.

7. For more information, see Hulkenberg (2009: 183).

8. The location for these ceremonial presentations should be the village green and the house of the groom. Clearly this can vary, however, especially in urban areas and overseas.

9. See Wiliksen-Bakker (1984) for a discussion of ceremonial exchange in urban settings in Fiji.

10. Many Fijians who have migrated to the UK adopt 'English' names such as Cathy because their UK neighbours and workmates find Fijian names hard to pronounce.

11. The clothes were sewn by a Fijian woman staying in Edinburgh who is known for her sewing talent.

12. Buli could not trace for me the genealogical connections that make him classificatory cross-cousin to the man who stays in Glencourse. His parents had told him, but he had forgotten, which is he says a common problem amongst Fijians who have migrated to the UK: 'We don't know because our elders are not here who can tell us'.

13. All parents are called by teknonyms *tamai/tinai* (father/mother of) plus the name of the eldest child.

14. For a detailed list of the amount and types of *masi* the women from Moce had to prepare and present in exchange for the mats they expected to receive, see Hulkenberg (2009: 251).

15. See also Arno (1971: 13–14, 42).

16. See Small (1997), Macpherson and Macpherson (1999), Scott (2003) and Lee and Francis (2009).

17. Other forms of money raising events are *gunu sede*, where one pays money for bowls of *yaqona* for others to drink (see Toren 1989) and the *kati*, a raffle of women's home-baked cakes.

18. The Kaunitoni myth is often evoked to justify specific relations to the ancestors; see France (1966), Geraghty (1993), Tuwere (2002: 22–32) and Ryle (2010: 4).

19. For a detailed explanation, see Hocart (1913, 1936a).

20. See also Small (1997)

21. The form of ceremonial Fijian speeches is similar to the simplified scheme underlying sacrificial prayer, as presented by Valeri (1985: 53). For examples and analyses of ceremonial speeches, see Hooper (1982) and Ravuvu (1987).

22. In this context, Ravuvu defines *vanua* as 'groups of people [this can be the total Fijian population, or smaller units, such as *mataqali*] who can trace descendants agnatically to a common ancestor god' (Ravuvu 1987: 16). Ravuvu also writes: 'Reference to ancestral house platforms (*dela ni yavu*) during ceremonial presentations is common, for it is on these that the spirits dwell and watch over the affairs of their living descendants. As far as most Fijians are concerned, the *dela ni yavu*, sometimes referred to as *yavutu*, is powerful in influencing human affairs' (ibid.: 15–16).

References

Arno, A. 1971. 'Property on Moce Island, Fiji', unpublished paper.

———— 2005. 'Cobo and Tabua in Fiji: Two Forms of Cultural Currency in an Economy of Sentiment', *American Ethnologist* 32(1): 46–62.

Brown, P.C., and G. Leeves. 2007. 'Impacts of International Migration and Remittances on Source Country Household Incomes in Small Island States: Fiji and Tonga', ESA (Agricultural and Development Economics Division) Working Paper No. 07–13. University of Queensland.

Clifford, J. 1997. *Routes: Travel and Translation in the Late Twentieth Century*. Cambridge, MA: Harvard University Press.

France, P. 1966. 'The Kaunitoni Migration', *Journal of Pacific History* 1: 107–14.

Geraghty, P. 1993. 'Pulotu, Polynesian Homeland', *Journal of the Polynesian Society* 102(4): 343–84.

Hocart, A.M. 1913. 'The Fijian Custom of *Tauvu*', *Journal of the Royal Anthropological Institute* 43: 101–8.

———— 1936a. *Kings and Councillors: An Essay in the Comparative Anatomy of Human Society*. Cairo: Printing Office, Paul Barbey.

———— 1936b. 'Sacrifice', *Encyclopaedia of the Social Sciences* 13: 502–4.

———— 1971 [1929]. *Lau Islands*. New York: Kraus.

Hondagneu-Sotelo, P.A., and E. Avila. 1997. '"I'm Here, but I'm There": The Meanings of Latina Transnational Motherhood', *Gender and Society* 11(5): 548–71.

Hooper, S. 1982. 'A Study of Valuables in the Chiefdom of Lau, Fiji', Ph.D. diss. Cambridge: University of Cambridge.

Hulkenberg, J. 2009. 'Masi: Cloth of the Vanua in a Globalising World', Ph.D. diss. Norwich: University of East Anglia.

Kai'ili, T. 2005. 'Tauhi vā: Nurturing Tongan Sociospatial Ties in Maui and Beyond', *Contemporary Pacific* 17(1): 83–114.

Lee, H., and S.T. Francis. 2009. *Migration and Transnationalism: Pacific Perspectives*. Canberra: Australian National University Press.

Lilomaiava-Doktor, S. 2009. 'Beyond "Migration": Samoan Population Movement (*Malaga*) and the Geography of Social Space (*Vā*)', *Contemporary Pacific* 21(1): 1–32.

MacDonald, J.D. 1857. 'Proceedings of the Expedition for the Exploration of the Rewa River and Its Tributaries in Na Viti Levu, Fiji Islands', *Journal of the Royal Geographical Society of London* 27: 232–68.

Macpherson, C., and L. Macpherson. 1999. 'The Changing Contours of Migrant Samoan Kinship', in R. King and J. Connell (eds), *Small Worlds, Global Lives: Islands and Migration*. London: Pinter.

Miyazaki, H. 2005a. 'From Sugar Cane to "Swords": Hope and the Extensibility of the Gift in Fiji', *Journal of the Royal Anthropological Institute* 11: 277–95.

———— 2005b. 'The Materiality of Finance Theory', in D. Miller (ed.), *Materiality*. Durham, NC: Duke University Press.

Newland, L. 2004. 'Turning the Spirits into Witchcraft: Pentecostalism in Fijian Villages', *Oceania* 75(1): 1–18.

Norton, R. 2004. 'Fiji Country Study', Report on Informal Remittance Systems in Africa, Caribbean and Pacific ACP Countries. Oxford: ESRC Centre of Migration, Policy and Society, University of Oxford.

Parry, J., and M. Bloch (eds). 1989. *Money and the Morality of Exchange*. Cambridge: Cambridge University Press.

Ravuvu, A. 1987. *The Fijian Ethos*. Suva: Institute of Pacific Studies, University of the South Pacific.

Ryle, J. 2001. 'My God, My Land: Interwoven Paths of Christianity and Tradition in Fiji', Ph.D. diss. London: School of Oriental and African Studies.

———— 2010. *Interwoven Paths of Christianity and Tradition in Fiji*. Aldershot: Ashgate.

Sahlins, M. 1981. 'The Stranger King, or Dumézil among the Fijians', *Journal of Pacific History* 16: 107–32.

Scott, G.G. 2003. 'Situating Fijian Transmigrants: Towards Racialised Transnational Social Spaces of the Undocumented', *International Journal of Population Geography* 9: 181–98.

Small, C.A. 1997. *Voyages: From Tongan Villages to American Suburbs*. Ithaca, NY: Cornell University Press.

St. Johnston, T.R. 1918. *The Lau Islands Fiji and their Fairy Tales and Folk-lore*. London: Times Book Company.

Thomas, N. 1997. *In Oceania: Visions, Artefacts, Histories*. Durham, NC: Duke University Press.

Toren, C. 1989. 'Drinking Cash: The Purification of Money through Ceremonial Exchange in Fiji', in J. Parry and M. Bloch (eds), *Money and the Morality of Exchange*. Cambridge: Cambridge University Press.

———— 1990. *Making Sense of Hierarchy: Cognition as Social Process in Fiji*. London: Athlone Press.

———— 1999. *Mind, Materiality and History: Explorations in Fijian Ethnography*. New York: Routledge.

_____ 2004. 'Becoming a Christian in Fiji: An Ethnographic Study of Ontogeny', *Journal of the Royal Anthropological Institute* 10: 222–40.

Tomlinson, M. 2009. *In God's Image: The Metaculture of Fijian Christianity*. Berkeley: University of California Press.

Turner, J.W. 1987. 'Blessed to Give and Receive: Ceremonial Exchange in Fiji', *Ethnology* 26(3): 209–19.

Tuwere, I.S. 2002. *Vanua: Towards a Fijian Theology of Place*. Suva: Institute for Pacific Studies, University of the South Pacific.

Valeri, V. 1985. *Kingship and Sacrifice: Ritual and Society in Ancient Hawaii*. Chicago: University of Chicago Press.

Voight-Graf, C. 2008. 'Migration and Transnational Families in Fiji: Comparing Two Ethnic Groups', *International Migration* 46(4): 15–40.

Waterhouse, J. 1997 [1866]. *The King and People of Fiji*. Honolulu: University of Hawaii Press.

Wiliksen-Bakker, S. 1984. 'To Do and To Be: Ceremonial Exchange Under Urban Circumstances in Fiji'. PhD diss. Oslo: University of Oslo.

4

Gendered Sides and Ritual Moieties

Tokelau Kinship as Social Practice

◆●◆

Ingjerd Hoëm

The approach to kinship as social practice can bring added value to the older study of kinship seen typologically as structures of relationships and classificatory systems; this chapter explores how it can do so. From gender and household studies (Collier and Yanagisako 1987) and discussions of 'house societies' (Carsten and Hugh-Jones 1995), we are reminded of how kinship and other aspects of social formations may bear upon each other. I argue for the continuation and expansion of such approaches by means of an exploration of how kinship and gender, political institutions and other aspects of everyday existence may be given a particular direction or orientation through the exercise of particular forms of leadership. In particular, I argue for the general social significance of ritual practices, with particular reference to kinship.

Among Polynesian peoples, the exercise of leadership and legitimate authority is not confined to political arenas as commonly defined. The moral, aesthetic, religious and material spheres all fall within their domain. Day-to-day existence may be orchestrated through ritual practice, broadly defined as the choreography of life, into recognizable segments (Toren 1994a; Hoëm et al. 2012). To make things orderly in the proper fashion is the duty and prerogative of Polynesian leadership, and it is important to add that leadership in these societies is both gendered and situational.

To take the situational aspect first. As Don Handelman has described in his general model of public events (Handelman 1990), on one end of the scale we have rituals that function as vehicles of transformation and on the other we have ritualized public events that may better be described as spectacles. In Tokelau society, both ends of the spectrum are provided for. Festive and competitive activities and entertainment are classified as 'things of no importance' (*mea tauanoa*), thus falling most closely on the 'spectacle' side of Handelman's model. The political arena proper – that is to say, all meetings within kin groups and within and across villages, together with all church activities – are classified as things of importance, as serious activities; they have transformational potential in Handelman's sense.

My main point in this chapter is to demonstrate the exercise of leadership as it is evinced in a general and dominant mechanism of social organization that is called 'making sides' (*fai itu*),[1] joining (*fau, hohoko*) by separation (*va, vehi*). Some important issues follow from this premise. Firstly, while 'making sides' is equally present in the constitution of kin groups (where the sides are the *tamatane*, offspring of a brother's side, and *tamafafine*, offspring from a sister's side) and in village sides (ritual moieties called *faitu*), the way they work and the two contexts in which they operate differ markedly. The overriding distinction, however, is not one between kin groups (*kaiga*) and village organization (*nuku*), but between the two main kinds of situations: serious and non-serious. Secondly, and more importantly, when both ways of making sides are taken together, we can see that they complement each other. The activities of the sides formed by ritual moieties – competitive, festive, and by definition non-serious – serve as a commentary on and a mirror for the everyday 'sides' activities that take place in families (*kaiga*), meetings (*fono*) and villages (*nuku*). These are all 'serious', embedded in the kin group based on the brother–sister relationship; as such, they provide the raw material that is employed by the non-serious sides, which create what may be called a virtual mirror in which villagers may see themselves.[2] The two ways of making sides together constitute a whole that provides a dynamic and flexible structure to social life – one that allows room for a running commentary.

Even so, because the two kinds of sides feed into each other, the distinction made by Handelman between transformative and representative events is actually always in the process of being cancelled out. The challenges represented by an anti-structure in Victor Turner's sense – here present in 'non-serious activities' – is real. However, as we shall see towards the end of this chapter, the 'cancelling out' tendency is halted in so far as 'non-serious activities' are contained by the meeting places or *fono*, which are directly governed by the leadership.

The mechanism of making sides is present in Tokelau kinship, it is present in social organization, and it is also present in, and arguably created by, ritual practices. Across different contexts, the pattern of 'making sides' is replicated but, as noted above, the role, function and purpose of the activities involved vary.

The Challenge of Tokelau Kinship

The Tokelau kinship system is cognatic and has been described as representing a transitional state, in-between what Lévi-Strauss has described as simple and complex systems (Huntsman 1971). This means that Tokelau kinship is likely to exhibit features extraneous to kin as conceived of within so-called lineage systems, features that are absent from practices related to marriage, cooperation and the transfer of property between generations in 'simple systems'. 'House societies' (Lévi-Strauss 1982) are examples of how the tendency for a dispersal of clan property and personnel within systems of cognatic descent may be contained and managed in something 'larger' than the lineage or clan group: the house (Carsten and Hugh-Jones 1995). Thus, shifting alliances over time may gain an anchoring point, the house, allowing actual social groupings to take on qualities resembling that of a 'corporate group', which earlier research considered only possible within 'simple', lineage-based systems of descent.

Tokelau kin groups, in the period before the chiefly line of descent (*aliki*) was abolished – that is, before 1914 – were organized in houses. There were nine houses on Fakaofo, seven on Atafu and four on Nukunonu (see e.g. Huntsman and Hooper 1985). Since that time, these houses, associated with the largest encompassing kin groups – clans or 'cognatic stocks' in Hooper and Huntsman's terminology; in Tokelauan the *pui-kaiga*, a term that means 'wall, what surrounds, or covers the kin group' – has diminished in importance. Currently they serve as references to a mythical and glorious past, and as emblems of contemporary kin groups' (*kaukaiga, kaiga*) rights to particular, named land areas in the atolls.

Tokelau kinship, in its current form, and even without the existence of such 'houses', represents a unique solution to what has been labelled the cognatic dilemma. When looking at contemporary kinship practices, we learn how it is possible to achieve something akin to corporate groups, realizing both cooperation around a common estate and transfer of property and rights over time, while at the same time retaining a great amount of flexibility in actual arrangements 'on the ground' (see e.g. ibid.). What is more important however, and what has not received much attention in the literature, is how this so-called transitional state, the openness of the social organization, is precisely what has allowed for the orchestration of the whole that I described above – the constant dynamic vacillation between practice and the commentary on that practice. This social phenomenon is, as I have described elsewhere (Hoëm 2004), of general importance, not least because it shows that commonly held conceptions of oral societies as non-reflexive, caught in day-to-day, face-to-face interaction, and held hostage by the visions of their leaders, or by their mode of production, are mistaken.[3] The establishment of an arena that allows society to take itself as an object for reflection represents a compelling counter-case to these still prevalent arguments. When kinship is seen as a social practice, group formation in general and, in particular, the significance of what may be described as ritual moieties, becomes apparent.

Faka Tokelau: The Tokelau Way as Communicative Practice

When Tokelauans are invited to comment on what is typical for life in Tokelau, things that immediately spring to mind are the atoll landscape, the food, village life and in particular the relationship between brothers and sisters.[4]

E ha i te va o te tuagane ma te tuafafine . . ., 'In the relationship between brother and sister, it is forbidden to . . .' A group of schoolchildren in Nukunonu, Tokelau, all used variations on this theme as captions for drawings that they made in response to my suggestion that they should describe or illustrate the Tokelau way of life as they saw it. Furthermore, they all depicted the relationship between brother and sister, as self-evidently synonymous with Tokelau ways.

The word *va* literally means 'space between', and points in this connection to the distance, or in anthropological terms avoidance relationship, that is deemed proper for behaviour in this relationship. In the past, people have told me, a brother and sister would not communicate directly with each other, but conveyed their messages through a third party. Ideally, in a Tokelau household, the most senior sister resides in the siblings' natal household, and the brother moves out to reside in his wife's homestead upon marriage. However, brother and sister remain a working unit, holding their natal *kaiga* together after their respective marriages. The separation between the sexes begins in early childhood. It is, for example, common courtesy for a brother to take his meals elsewhere, so that he may eat away from his sister. Jokes and serious matters of a sexual nature are equally avoided in situations where people who are related as brothers and sisters are present.

I use the formulation 'related as brothers and sisters' deliberately, as the Tokelau kinship system is classificatory (within limits of ethnicity), and thus categories such as 'mother' would include an Ego's mother and the mother's sisters and female cousins. The category 'sister' most commonly includes all female relatives of Ego's generation. The *va*, or avoidance between people who are related as brothers and sisters, is bridged by a mutual obligation of complementary rights and duties called *feagaiga* (Huntsman 1971). Kinship relations are about the division of labour, conceptions of gender and many other things, but in daily life the first and foremost issue that people associate with kinship is morality (Hoëm 1993). This field of morality is gendered and stratified. Relative age is a basis for relations of command/authority (*pule*) and obedience (*uhitaki*). Proper behaviour is other-centred, outgoing and sharing, while fostering an awareness of relative statuses and division of tasks necessary to keep the social whole functioning. Elsewhere I have described these patterns of social practice as producing 'a sense of place', both in the spatial and social meaning of the term (Hoëm 1999, 2004). In Tokelauan, this sense of place is called *tulaga*, and its reference ranges from the concrete to the abstract: from denoting a mark, a notch carved in a tree, to an opportunity, a position, a place from which to speak and act. From the perspective of social organization, hierarchical structures are always kept in check by egalitarian forces setting the interests of the whole above that of any kin group or descent line (such as the *aliki* of old) or side (in the kin groups or in the villages) (see Hoëm 2009b; Besnier 2009: 76–80).

On an ideological level, it is possible to describe this system as a hierarchy of value in the Dumontian sense (see Hoëm 2009b: 245–67), in that the ultimate source of the Tokelau way of life, *faka Tokelau*, granting life, harmony and fecundity to the life-world, is God. In pre-Christian days, the ultimate source of *mana* was the light of *ao* (day, this world, light) as separate from the darkness of the *po* (night, darkness, after-world).[5] This hierarchy of value is reflected in a social structure where elders command (*pule*) and younger comply (*uhitaki*), and where status and power is achieved through strategies of what Fox (1995) has called ascent (in the Tokelau case, *tupu*). However, and as described just above, the bid for power by any group will always be matched with similar bids arising from other groups, and thus overall equilibrium and equality is ensured. That is, the whole is valued above the part, groups are sides that constitute the valued whole (such as *kaiga*, village, *nuku* or Tokelau), and it is the role of leaders, within the family and in the village institutions, to make sure that this balance is achieved.

Earlier social stratification was expressed in a system headed by chiefs or *aliki*. The *aliki* was from the offspring of brothers, *tamatane*-side of the kin group and wielded *pule* or secular power. The priest or *vakataulaitu* came from the offspring of sisters, *tamafafine*-side, and wielded spiritual power (Huntsman 1971). This social system has undergone many transformations (see e.g. Huntsman and Hooper 1985). What consistently has been retained throughout is the awareness that power and social position are dependent upon the possession of certain kinds of knowledge. In this volume Christina Toren, drawing on the work of Nabobo-Baba, proposes that kinship in the

Pacific be seen as 'knowledge that counts'. In terms of Tokelau practice, this means that certain kinds of knowledge – such as kinship terminology, not to mention knowledge of actual genealogical relationships of contemporary relevance – are highly valued. The command and ownership – that is, possession of and rights to this knowledge – are, at least in principle the prerogative of a few respected elders. In practice however, knowledge of different kinds of relationships, in the form of moral precepts and patterns of interaction, is actively used by all. The elders use their specialist knowledge in order to discuss and determine land rights, to settle marriage proposals and to adjudicate in matters of conflict concerning rights and obligations. Ordinary knowledge of kinds of relationships, in the form of moral precepts and patterns of interaction, is actively used, although in a more pragmatic manner, and with varying degrees of understanding (see also Hoëm 1995).

Reappraising Tokelau Kinship

As Tokelauans present it, the central concept of Tokelau kinship is *kaiga*, variously translated as family, extended family, kin or relations. In an intricate and sophisticated analysis, Huntsman and Hooper (1985) have reconstructed the historical kin relationships between the inhabitants of the three Tokelau atolls: Atafu, Nukunonu and Fakaofo. In brief, the inhabitants of the three Tokelau atolls together constitute three distinct communities with strong local allegiances. Historically, Fakaofo is described in the literature as a conquest state (Goldman 1970). Fakaofo was at war with Nukunonu, and is said to have caused the original inhabitants of Atafu to flee. The local interpretations of outcomes of these conflicts, as represented in narratives or 'stories from the past' (*tala mai anamua*), differ in significant ways.

The three atolls' representations of the respective statuses and kinship ties of the Fakaofo and Nukunonu *aliki* lines differ on the following central points: Fakaofo contend that Fakaofo, through the *aliki* Kava Vahefanua's status as the founding father of Fakaofo, and through his conquest of Nukunonu, be seen as older brother and senior branch (*latupou*) to Nukunonu's junior branch (*lafalala*). Nukunonu takes a different view. All atolls are in agreement that Nukunonu is affiliated with Fakaofo through the marriage of Kava to an *aliki* woman from Nukunonu called Nau. It is, however, a matter of contention whose status counts highest, the *aliki* woman's through her father's chiefly line, or the *aliki* status of the Fakaofo man. Which interpretation to support is not only a matter of atoll allegiance; it is also a matter of perspective: in anthropological terms, the question is whether descent or alliance is to be counted as more valuable. Is the brother–sister relation most significant? That is, which should count the most: Nau's status in her own *kaiga*, or her status as part of a couple?[6]

This point of difference may be raised even today, as it is expressive of underlying tensions between male/female as a (possible) couple, and the brother–sister relationship.[7] Thus Toren shows how, in the Fijian case, patrilocal residence on marriage makes the woman subordinate to her husband even while, in her natal home, she may have the highest possible status as the eldest of her sibling set (Toren 1994b). In one aspect, this is clearly different from gender as practised in Tokelau, where the preferred residence upon marriage is uxorilocal, and where the sister may thus retain her powerbase in more contexts, even when married. If she is able to follow the ideal marriage pattern and stay in her house of birth, she may eventually become a *fatupaepae*. The *fatupaepae*, the female elder who resides in her natal *kaiga*'s *fale* (house), and orchestrate the distribution of goods to her natal *kaiga*, is emblematic of the sister's (or aunt's or female elder's) power (*manana*, the power to bless and to curse). This power is complemented by the brother's (or male elder's) power (*pule*, the power to command and direct), and the etiquette regulating the brother–sister relationship is dominant in most, if not all, social situations. The brother, even if he changes residence upon marriage, is supposed to continue working, providing for and making decisions in the council of elders if he is a member there, on behalf of his natal *kaiga* (see also Huntsman 1969: 224). In other words, a central part of the social dynamic of Tokelau life, the etiquette governing the brother–sister relationship, might also be brought to bear upon contexts outside this particular relationship.[8]

Since the 'days of war', the atolls' populations have been linked through intermarriage. Today, on all the three atolls, the most significant units are the *(kau)kaiga*, extended family or family. The *kaukaiga* are described by Huntsman and Hooper (1973: 368) as corporate groups. In theory the cognatic nature of Tokelau kinship would seem to rule out the possibility of forming clans or lineages centred on an estate, which may be transferred from generation to generation. In Tokelau, members of each *kaiga* have many possible groups they may choose to connect with (*hohoko*); however, attachments always follow the gendered division of kin groups into two sides (*itu*): the *tamatane* (offspring of brothers) and the *tamafafine* (offspring of sisters). For example, a man may decide that he is better off joining his distant cousins' fishing crew, rather than working with his closer male relatives. Be that as it may, he is still working with members of his *kaiga*.

A *(kau)kaiga* (extended family group) becomes and remains a *kaiga* through common ownership and exploitation of coconut plantations (*mataniu*) on the outer islets (*utafenua*), and through association with a particular land area in the village (*fenua o kakai*) where their homestead (*fale*) is located. *Kaiga* is also the basis for the formation of fishing crews manning a *kaiga* boat, and of similar task groups, for example at weddings and funerals. This common estate also bestows on its holders the right to a seat (*tulaga, nofoaga*), giving it formal representation in the governing body of the villages, the village council of elders (*Fono o Taupulega*).[9] People who live away from Tokelau take care to maintain the rights of their *kaiga* in the atolls by, if at all possible, keeping a family member in Tokelau.

After the overlordship of Fakaofo was formally ended in 1914, the office of *aliki* was abolished on the grounds that 'there should not be a colony within a colony'. Tokelau was a British Protectorate from 1889 to 1909, part of Gilbert and Ellice Islands Colony in 1910. In 1926, it was formally handed over by Great Britain to New Zealand. Around the time of this transition, the village leadership came to be in the hands of elders, old men (*toeaina*). Huntsman and Hooper (1985) describe this form of governance as a gerontocracy. These old men (approximately aged sixty and upwards) were family heads and representatives of their *kaiga* in the village councils. It is possible to observe a gradual shift from *kaukaiga* (large extended families) being represented in the village councils to a situation where today smaller units (*kaiga*) may be represented. Also the age of the representatives has changed somewhat, as younger males also occasionally attend, and in some cases even females may represent their families. In Fakaofo the council traditionally consists of elders; in Atafu it consists of older *matai* (or 'chiefs', as they are called, derived from Samoan), the younger men being organized in the *aumaga* – the village work force of able-bodied men. In Nukunonu the council consists of younger and older *matai*.

Atafu is wholly Protestant, Nukunonu is Roman Catholic and Fakaofo is predominantly Protestant, but with a Roman Catholic contingent. Since the establishment of the churches in Tokelau in the mid nineteenth century, contact with Church institutions in Samoa and overseas has been a constant feature of village life. Upon formalization of the relationship between Tokelau and New Zealand, and becoming more frequent from the early 1950s onwards, inter-atoll meetings, or general *fono*, have been conducted for the discussion of affairs common to the three atolls. The inter-atoll relationships have been characterized by rivalry and competition, however, and issues connected with 'the days of war', and in particular the issue of Fakaofo's claim to dominance, still tend to surface occasionally.

Sides as Kin and as Ritual Moieties

A *kaiga* is in principle strictly exogamous and holds land (*fenua*) in common. In their discussion of what constitutes incest in Tokelau conceptions, Huntsman and Hooper (1976) point out that who is to count as *kaiga*, family in the sense of kin is, as a minimum defining criterion, identified as those who hold land together. Huntsman and Hooper (ibid.) further show that, in a pragmatic fashion, if an allowable marriage is proposed between a man and woman whose families hold land in common – that is, who are in a potentially incestuous relationship – the common landholdings may be dissolved. It is then said that the *kaiga* is *tatala* or *malepe*, broken up, dismantled, or dead. The principle is uxorilocal residence upon marriage, and ideally one is not supposed to marry closer than fourth, or possibly third, cousins. Marriage between second cousins or people more closely related is forbidden by law. These laws, or village rules (*tulafono o te nuku*) now exist in written form, and function as legal reference in cases of dispute.

As noted above, Huntsman and Hooper (ibid.) describe Tokelau kinship as in transition between 'simple' and 'complex', following Lévi-Strauss's terminology. In my analysis, as presented here, this transitional state is evinced not only in the classificatory nature of the nomenclature, and in the role that houses play in the formation of groups, but also in the documented fact that the moieties (*faitu*) Huntsman observed in the villages have no detectable function in respect of marriage practices. Huntsman (1969) and Huntsman and Hooper (1996: 83–92) describe *faitu* as a geographical division of villages into two competing sides, for sports and other activities associated with games and fun. Such activities are defined as *mea tauanoa*, 'things of no account', or as *tafafao*, 'wander about', 'roaming', 'playing'. By definition they are not to be taken seriously, for competitive activities often verge on becoming serious conflicts. To make sure that this does not happen is the role of the leaders of the *faitu* and, ultimately, the responsibility rests with the elders in the villages.

Huntsman and Hooper (1996) note that the *faitu* institution is described locally as always having been there, although in a different manner than its more recent form, and as having its roots in the introduction to Tokelau of cricket (*kilikiti*) in the early 1900s. Everybody is a member of one of the villages' two sides by virtue of parental residence. It is possible to change affiliation upon marriage, although some express discomfort with suddenly having to compete for the other side. Earlier, as described for Nukunonu, the sides were associated with inland and ocean, the *alatua* and the *alatai*; the function of the sides at that time is unknown.[10]

Brothers and Sisters: Different Kinds of Leadership and Power

The words of a contemporary popular song describe central tenets of Tokelau kinship in the following manner:

Fatupaepae o te kaiga   Cornerstone, foundation of the family[11]
Fatupaepae o te kaiga   The senior sister of the family

E felau fakahoa te katiga	Shares, distributes the foodstuff to go with the fish
E felau fakahoa te utuga	Shares, distributes the fishermen's catch
Tamatane o te uta fenua	Brothers of the family, of the outer islets
Tamatane o vaka o utua	Brothers of the family, of the fishing boats
Taofi ke mau	The lots and positions are founded and may
Ia kupu	Stand fast/be retained by the words
A tupuna e	Of the ancestors
Ke ola ia Tokelau	That there be life for/something to live off for Tokelau

In structural terms, the most significant kin terms and positions governing divisions of domains of responsibility and power, work tasks and the distribution of goods within the framework of extended families (*kaukaiga*) are those of *tamatane* and *tamafafine*, the offspring of brothers (*tamatane*) and the offspring of sisters (*tamafafine*) of an ancestral couple. The members of the *tamatane* side hold the right to the produce from family lands, and gather food from that land and from the sea, both the lagoon (*tai*) and open ocean (*moana*), for the kin group. The members of the *tamafafine* side have the right to reside on the family homestead, in the *kaiga* house (*fale*), and are accorded the task of dividing (*felau*) the food and other produce brought by the *tamatane*. The senior male *tamatane* is the *pule* or *ulu*, the controlling power, ruler, head, or leader of the family. The senior female, the *fatupaepae* (lit. 'the cornerstone of the house') is the overseer and divider of the family's goods. All men, regardless of *tamatane* and *tamafafine* positions in their natal family, are expected to be active providers. All women are expected to support, receive, refine and hand out the produce again to others. *Alofa* (love, compassion, generosity) and respect (*fakaaloalo*) should govern the relationships between kin.

A significant term that speaks of expectations of female gender roles is the *matua ha*, or *matua tauaitu*, father's sister, or in contemporary terms 'aunt', and, traditionally, 'sacred', or 'spirit holding mother'. The *matua ha* has a special relationship with the *tama ha*, her brother's children (father's sister/brother's child and grandchild). The sister in her capacity as a spirit-holding mother has the power (*mamana*) to curse and afflict her brother's wife with reproductive disorders, or to bless her with fertility if she wishes to do so. Moreover she has the right to adopt her brother's children, and she cannot be thwarted or refused if she wishes to do so. Jeanette Mageo (1998) in her analysis of Samoan conceptions translates the term *pule* as 'secular power'. This sets the term in contrast to the 'spiritual power' exercised by women in their role as sisters. This opposition is relevant for Tokelau as well (see Huntsman and Hooper 1975). However, as the secular and spiritual aspects of power have been intertwined historically,[12] and as 'spiritual power' (*mana*) today is explicitly associated only with the Church, in practice secular power has spiritual aspects and vice versa. Even so, differences according to gender still exist with respect to the kinds of power and control that are attributed to men and women (see also Hoëm 1995).

The relationship between *tuatina* (mother's brother) and *ilamutu* (sister's son) was important in the 'days of war'. Huntsman (1971) describes this complementary relationship. Another term for the *ilamutu* is *mate*, death; the term is no doubt related to the Tongan *mateaki*, bodyguard (see Churchward 1959: 344.) Huntsman and Hooper say that in Tokelau the mother's brother–sister's child relationship is rather different from the Tongan *fahu* and Fijian *vasu*, because, as they say, 'the onus is upon the younger of the pair' (Huntsman and Hooper 1996: 330). The practice and expectation of the sister's son to function as a human shield for his mother's brother is clearly a thing of the past. It is however common that a mother's brother expects to take some part in his sister's son's upbringing, and thereby gains his help in gardening and other tasks. That is, the mother's brother still seems to expect to benefit from the relationship.

When asked to write and draw about Tokelau kinship, the schoolchildren I referred to above thought first of the brother–sister relationship. The communication pattern that has its basis in the brother–sister relationship is replicated in the structures that characterize the relationships between the two sides (*itu*) of the kin groups (*kaukaiga*), the *tamatane* and the *tamafafine*. The patterns of cooperation, mutual dependency on the one hand, and a hierarchical division of labour (*pule*, rule and *uhitaki*, comply) between the two sides is reflected in the designation of men and women collectively as the *itu malohi* (the strong side) and the *itu vaivai* (the weak side) respectively. Between these categories that Huntsman (1971: 321) labels complementary kinsmen – that is, those who are engaged in a reciprocal relationship of mutual dependency based on their fulfilling different but equally necessary roles (such as gathering and distributing food) – there is what is called a *va*. *Va* means 'space between', and signifies a relationship characterized by reciprocity (*feagaiga*) and avoidance. Such relationships are also characterized by *ma*, commonly translated as shame, hence the reference to space or 'distance between'. Within the *kaiga*, avoidance between brothers and sisters is the norm. In addition to this dominant taboo, shame is extended to relationships that are conceptualized as having a potential sexual component, such as where the sexual nature of the relationship between an opposite sex sibling and their spouse is difficult to ignore. Hence, shame is made relevant in the relationship between Ego and the same-sex affine – between a sister and her brother's wife, between a brother and his sister's husband – that is, in relationships where the etiquette relevant to the brother–sister relationship is difficult to maintain.[13] These are situations that are characterized by what Barth (1971) has described as a propensity for producing 'role dilemmas'.

In sum, the brother–sister relationship is characterized by avoidance, in particular after the onset of puberty. This avoidance is practised by all, but to varying degrees, from transmitting verbal messages through a third party (not common nowadays) and avoidance of eye contact, to ensuring that brothers and sisters do not sleep or eat in the same house after puberty. I have, for example, observed a brother coming to his natal household and being served food that his sister has prepared, but eating it sitting on the door sill facing outwards, with his back to the interior of the house that is his sister's domain. I have, however, also come across cases that differ from the norm, for example a brother and his spouse and their children temporarily sharing the residence of his sister and her children (the sister being without a partner). Such practical exceptions are made if needs must, and care is taken so as not to offend the sensibilities of those involved and of other villagers.

Most importantly, the brother–sister relationship is or should be a relation of *alofa* (compassion, affection), and as such it is subject to *ha* (restrictions), and one is to observe *fakaaloalo* (deference, and show courtesy), *mamalu* (respect, honour) and it is a relation with a certain amount of *ma*, shame, disquiet and fear of loss of face (*mata*) attached to it (see also Hoëm 2004). In this connection, I have to point yet again to the role of females in their capacity as sisters, to a more general quality of their femaleness called *manu ha*, which makes them sacred beings who hold the power to stop conflicts, and who are expected to step in and curb violent behaviour.[14] Reciprocal bonds and obligations (*feagaiga*) demand that brothers and sisters (and all who are classified as such, including distant cousins) should honour the requests of the other. The patterns of behaviour I describe are still dominant, even though ideal conceptions and practices of the brother–sister relationship have been challenged greatly over recent decades, with more work situations – in government institutions, the Tokelau public service, and outside the atoll environment – demanding close contact and cooperation between both related and unrelated men and women, where before interaction was more easily separated into the contexts of kin (within the family) and village. Indeed, it is to these norms and ideal patterns of brother–sister behaviour that schoolchildren unanimously turn when asked to explain basic principles in Tokelau culture.

The following is an extract from school children's contributions when asked to describe Tokelau culture.[15] It was striking that in their depictions of brother and sister, they all noted what is forbidden or bad; not one phrased the relationship positively by remarking, for example, that brothers and sisters should care for each other, or that they depend on each other. Their answers fell into the following three categories:

- 'It is not Tokelau culture for the sister to lie around or sit about doing nothing (or go fishing or make wood carvings) while her brother does the washing and sweeping of the village'. Here the reference is to the gendered division of labour.
- 'It is bad for the brother and sister to say hard words to each other (or quarrel, for the sister to refuse the brother something, or answer back)'. Here the reference is to an ideal of cooperation conducive of peace and harmony, quiet and acceptance – that is, the *pule* and *uhitaki* behavioural model.
- 'It is not Tokelau culture for the girls to go to *uta* (the plantations) while the boys stay in the family house (*fale*)'. Note the connection here between gender, mobility and place; the message seems to be that each should keep to their place, lot or position (*tulaga*).

Huntsman (1971: 324) highlights this third principle in a Tokelau saying: *Ko tagata e olo i te auala, kako fafine e nonofo i te fale*, 'men go on the path, and women sit in the house'. In this way, things are good and beautiful (*gali*) according to Tokelau customs (*faka Tokelau*). None of the children referred to situations such as shops, schools and offices, where the division of tasks is not so obviously gendered. This may of course be seen as related to the framing of the task as being about the Tokelau way of life, but also as an expression of what they perceive as its central tenets.

Kinship as Practised: Sides and Ritual Moieties

In Tokelau conceptions, if relations between people are to gain the shape and order deemed necessary for tasks to be accomplished, they have to be structured as 'sides'. Only thus can life gain a desired quality of abundance. Social harmony and well-being are achieved when all sides work together for a common purpose. This state of affairs is called *maopoopo*, which means both to gather together, to congregate, and to be well ordered, harmonious (see also Huntsman and Hooper 1996). To be able to come together in this fashion, however, people and tasks must be separated and assigned an appropriate position according to the task in hand.[16]

Thus, within the atoll villages, men and women are frequently defined and function as two groups or sides, with their respective institutions: the women's committee for the female side, and the *aumaga*, men's work force, and the political institution of the council of elders for the male side. These two sides maintain a mutual distance. They differ in demeanour and in the nature of the tasks assigned to them by the council of elders. The women's side may, for example, receive instructions to weave fans and mats to be given as gifts to visiting dignitaries. The men may be ordered, for example, to clear the village channel.

The unity of the kin group (*kaiga, kaukaiga*) is at once brought about and ensured through the production and reproduction of the two sides which have mutually dependent areas of rights and obligations: the *tamatane* (offspring of sons of a founding couple) and the *tamafafine* (offspring of daughters of a founding couple). Tasks that involve all villagers – such as sports events, the building of a communal house or putting on a feast – will be ordered by the elders and carried out through the *faitu* (competing sides or ritual moieties). This institution implies that the village is spatially and arbitrarily divided into two sides, which then compete with each other to complete the task at hand. This institution of the *faitu* bears a close resemblance to the institution *akatawa* described by Borofsky from Pukapuka, which is ethnographically very close to Tokelau (Borofsky 1987). I have argued here for describing the *faitu* as ritual moieties.[17]

To recapitulate and draw out the underlying principles derived from my analysis: Firstly, gender has a quality of sidedness to it. Men and women are frequently conceptualized as two mutually dependent sides. These sides take care to remain separate for most of the weekly round of activities. Secondly, the *kaukaiga* or kin group is divided into two, again mutually dependent, sides. These sides also observe a pattern of avoidance vis-à-vis each other. When they interact, the interaction is highly circumscribed, and the one governs or directs the activities of the other, as described above.

Finally, the division of the village into two sides (*faitu*) for competitive games and suchlike is orchestrated by designated leaders of the *faitu*, and ultimately they are under the direction and control of the councils of elders. These non-serious activities – or *mea tauanoa*, as they are categorized locally – represent an arena set apart, thus creating a qualitatively different context where challenges to the existing social balance may be aired. If this contesting of relationships of authority becomes too serious, however, the elders may realign the geographical division of the village on a new axis (something they are said to have done in the past). On Fakaofo the *faitu* are named Niu Hila and Hamoa, on Nukunonu as Egelani and Amelika. On Atafu, when the power balance of what had been named Argentina and Britain got seriously skewed after the Falklands war, Argentina was renamed Puamelo, after a kind of flower (see also Huntsman and Hooper 1996: 83–90).

In order to illustrate 'making sides' and to clarify further the differences and similarities between the gendered sides of kin and the division of the villages into two competing sides, I give the following short example which illustrates how the principle of competing for political ascendancy (*tupu*) may be expressed and work within a meeting (*fono*) and a festive gathering (*fiafia*) respectively.

Early in the 1990s, in the course of inter-atoll negotiations concerning where to locate the head office of the Tokelau public service, the Fakaofo delegation walked out of a general *fono* in protest – as they expected their status as *latupou* (senior branch) to be upheld and recognized by the *fono*. The walkout put an effective end to the proceedings, and alerted the international delegates to the fact that kinship is still an active force in Pacific politics today. This claim to political ascendancy, based on their interpretation of the kinship relations between themselves and the other atolls, effectively separated Fakaofo from the others. In the arena of the general *fono*, their claim held power, and had political consequences. Outside the *fono*, however, in jest songs were sung that reiterated the same message, presenting Fakaofo as the *latupou*, and demanding that the others bow down to its power, as in the lines of the following song:

Aue Pio e, ko au ko Tevaka e,	Oh Pio, I am Tevaka,
Te laupou na tofia e Kava e.	The senior branch that was divided/allotted by Kava.
E ifo mai, e ifo mai, koe kiate au.	Bow down to me, you bow down to me.[18]

If we refer back to the divergent interpretations of the kinship relations between Fakaofo and Nukunonu described earlier, we see how the conflicting interpretations can be read as an illustration of a possibility that is always present in any Tokelau social setting, that is, the tension between the perspective from within a *kaiga* seen as constituted by a sibling pair, and from without, as created by affinal relations. Whereas to sing such a song in the company of people from the other atolls may be seen as an error of judgement or in bad taste, and while it may cause anger and bad feeling, it is highly unlikely to have any direct effect upon the actual power balance and patterns of relationship. In keeping with the overall definition of a situation, if such were to occur within a festive, competitive gathering, the incident would be hushed up by elders, and also by women in their peace-keeping capacity as sisters, the *manu ha*. Non-serious activities should be just that, non-serious, in order to allow for the expression of otherwise very serious messages in a joking and playful form of competition (Hoëm 2009a). That these two kinds of behaviour feed on each other, and provide each other with material for new political meetings and new songs and skit, is obvious to anybody who has spent some time in the atoll villages of Tokelau. That there is, however, a thin line between respect, honour and morality, as epitomized by the brother–sister relationship or *va* on the one hand, and joking, challenges and the real danger represented by loss of honour on the other, is perhaps less easy for outsiders to see and appreciate.[19]

Leadership Orchestrates Separation and Unity

The recurrent pattern in Tokelau sociality, which I refer to in general as 'making sides', produces difference by separating any social body into two, in principle, equal social groups. As should be apparent from the above, however, what kind of restraints are placed on interaction and what kind of possibilities are opened up by this 'siding' vary according to context, whether this be within the sphere of kinship or, in a village, in a restrained and formal setting, or in the 'non-serious' arenas of games and competitions. We see here, on the one hand, a continuity between the pattern of sides that emerges within the spheres of gender and kinship, and the institution of *faitu* (competitive sides, ritual moieties) that is established for playful, competitive purposes. On the other hand, and as I have argued elsewhere (Hoëm 2003), there is a qualitative difference between these kinds of groups and the nature of the activities in which they engage.

In terms of Roy Wagner's discussion of the role of reflection and self-consciousness in the process of cultural creation (e.g. Wagner 1981; see also Hoëm 1998), we may see the non-kin based *faitu* sides as constituting a mirror for reflection on common cultural principles and current issues; the sides compete in the display of this common cultural estate, and sometimes come close to tipping over into serious conflict. Marilyn Strathern's (2010) remarks on the social significance of 'mock fights', of ritual expression of competitive hostility may also be a case in point.

However, in the competitive displays characteristic of *faitu* gatherings, the representation and hence the perception of dominant kin relationships, such as that between Fakaofo and Nukunonu referred to above, may shift situationally, according to whether the relationship between brothers, or that between brother and sister, is accentuated, or whether the principle of ultimogeniture is brought to bear. Regardless of the seriousness of the claim to dominance brought forward, in situations where the whole village is gathered, the occasional humorous interlude serves to break up the formality and seriousness of the occasion.

Old women are the most brazen clowns (*faluma*), and may risk turning male/female etiquette on its head – most commonly by commanding a brother–sister pair to act as if they were a couple (see also Huntsman and Hooper 1975). Sometimes, I have observed that 'the men' (*na tamana*) – that is, all the adult men of the village present at a specific event – have felt village order threatened by the eruptive force unleashed by such events and therefore, as represented by their male elders who are the responsible conductors of such public events, have ordered the female performance to stop.[20] Even so, all know that these things are not serious, that they are *mea tauanoa*, 'things of no account', and do not represent a real challenge to the proper order.

Occasionally, however, it may not be quite clear cut what is going on, how the situation should be interpreted and according to what principles, and ultimately what kind of relationship should be seen as most important. In such situations, the stern leadership (*pule*) of the leaders present is of critical importance, in order to avoid open conflict.

A mastery of such knowledge of relationships and characteristics of people and situations allows leaders to orchestrate the creation of sides, through separation, and to facilitate the coming together of sides in a temporary and ideational unity. As Tokelauans describe the principle inherent in this dynamic: *fau ma vehi*, 'we put together (build, join) and we take apart (split, destroy)'.

Notes

1. *Fai itu* is the verbal form, that is 'to make sides'. *Faitu* is the nominal form, 'sides'.
2. See also Hoëm (2004) for a description of the mirror image as used by the theatre group Tokelau Te Ata (a play on the words 'theatre' and 'mirror' respectively).
3. See e.g. Bloch (1975) and Bourdieu (1977) for examples of such perspectives.
4. In 1986, at my request, the headmaster of Matiti School on Nukunonu gave the following task to a total of 18 pupils who were in residence at the time, mainly attending Form Four (14 to 15 years of age); they were asked to depict *Te aganuku faka Tokelau* ('the Tokelau way of life/culture') and to label their drawings with captions. Of the 18 pupils participating, 10 were boys and 8 girls. In this chapter I use this material to support the points I make about how a focus on kinship practices – as evinced in gender behaviour, spatial organization and ritual – can add to earlier literature on kinship as structures and classificatory systems.
5. See e.g. the preamble to the recently crafted Tokelau Constitution (Pasikale 2008; Angelo 2009: 224); see also Tcherkézoff (2009: 299–330) for a similar analysis of Samoa.
6. Note that this is not a case of someone who was beaten in war and received a woman as a sign of submission, but that of a conqueror taking a chiefly woman as war booty.
7. For a comparative analysis of these pairs of relationships across Oceania, see Shore (1989).
8. In order to appreciate how the etiquette associated with the brother–sister relationship may come to be so pervasive, it is important to bear in mind that the atoll environment is small (12 square kilometres altogether), and that life in the villages is very transparent.

9. For a comparative perspective, see Hviding's (2003) analysis of patterns of cognatic kinship as practised in Marovo.
10. Hooper and Huntsman speculate that the term *faituu* (the double u represents a long vowel) is a borrowing from Samoan *feituu* (Huntsman and Hooper 1996: 83). However, as the term is unattested in Samoan, but present in Tuvaluan, it may possibly be a borrowing from Tuvaluan, or a survival of an older form (Proto-Polynesian **feituqu* or **faituqu*) in Tokelauan.
11. A literal translation of *fatupaepae* is 'white stone', i.e. the foundation, the cornerstone of the house.
12. See Macgregor (1937) on the *vakataulaitu* or priest/chief.
13. In this Tokelau system, the relationship within *kaiga* between ego (male) and his brother's wife or ego (female) and her sister's husband is easygoing, and not commonly associated with shame (*ma*). They are 'family' and not possible sexual partners to each other (Huntsman and Hooper 1976).
14. A sister cannot take a brother to task for violent behaviour towards his wife – the woman as wife may be subordinate even while as sister she may be superior. However, an aunt (*matua ha*), or even in some cases a senior woman (*manu ha*) if she is a person with authority, can intervene.
15. For information about the context of this study, see note 4.
16. See Toren (1994a) for an analysis of the significance of separation as a precondition for unity, based on her material from Fiji.
17. Cf. Hooper (1968: 239), who calls them non-exogamous moieties.
18. For more on this, see Hoëm (1992).
19. However, see e.g. MacPherson and MacPherson (2005, 2006) and Hoëm (forthcoming).
20. Cf. the anti-structural quality that I referred to in the introduction to this chapter.

References

Angelo, T. 2009. 'Tokelau', in S. Levine (ed.), *Pacific Ways: Government and Politics in the Pacific Islands*. Wellington: Victoria University Press.

Barth, F. 1971. 'Role Dilemmas and Father–Son Dominance in Middle Eastern Kinship Systems', in F.L.K. Hsu (ed.), *Kinship and Structure*. Chicago: Aldine.

Besnier, N. 2009. *Gossip and the Everyday Production of Politics*. Honolulu: University of Hawaii Press.

Bloch M. (ed.). 1975. *Political Language and Oratory in Traditional Society*. London: Academic Press.

Borofsky, R. 1987. *Making History: Pukapukan and Anthropological Constructions of Knowledge*. Cambridge: Cambridge University Press.

Bourdieu, P. 1977. *Outline of a Theory of Practice*. Cambridge: Cambridge University Press.

Carsten, J., and S. Hugh-Jones (eds). 1995. *About the House: Lévi-Strauss and Beyond.* Cambridge: Cambridge University Press.

Churchward, C.M. 1959. *Tongan Dictionary.* London: Oxford University Press.

Collier, J.F., and S.J. Yanagisako (eds). 1987. *Gender and Kinship: Essays Toward a Unified Analysis.* Stanford: Stanford University Press.

Fox, J. 1995. 'Austronesian Societies and their Transformations.' In *The Austronesians: Historical and Comparative Perspectives*, ed. P. Bellwood, J. Fox and D. Tryon. Canberra: Australian National University Press.

Goldman, I. 1970. *Ancient Polynesian Society.* Chicago: University of Chicago Press.

Handelman, D. 1990. *Models and Mirrors: Towards an Anthropology of Public Events.* Cambridge: Cambridge University Press.

Hoëm, I. 1993. 'Space and Morality in Tokelau', *Pragmatics* 3(2): 137–53.

——— 1995. *A Way with Words.* Oslo/Bangkok: Institute of Comparative Research in Human Culture/White Orchid Press.

——— 1998. 'Clowns, Dignity and Desire: On the Relationship between Performance, Identity and Reflexivity', in F. Hughes-Freeland and M. Crain (eds), *Recasting Ritual: Performance, Media, Identity.* London: Routledge.

——— 1999. 'Processes of Identification and the Incipient National Level: A Tokelau Case', *Social Anthropology* 7(3): 279–95.

——— 2003. 'Making Sides: On the Relationship between Contexts and Difference in Tokelau', in I. Hoëm and S. Roalkvam (eds), *Oceanic Socialities and Cultural Forms: Ethnographies of Experience.* Oxford: Berghahn.

——— 2004. *Theatre and Political Process: Staging Identities in Tokelau and New Zealand.* Oxford: Berghahn.

——— 2005. 'Stealing the Water of Life: The Historicity of Contemporary Social Relationship Patterns', in E. Hirsch and C. Stewart (eds). *History and Anthropology.* Vol. 16 (3). Routledge.

——— 2009a. 'Ritualized Performances as Total Social Facts: The House of Multiple Spirits in Tokelau', in G. Senft and E.B. Basso (eds), *Ritual Communication.* Oxford: Berg.

——— 2009b. 'Polynesian Conceptions of Sociality: A Dynamic Field of Hierarchical Encompassment', in K.M. Rio and O. Smedal (eds), *Hierarchy: Persisting Social Formations in the Modern World.* Oxford: Berghahn

——— forthcoming. *Languages of Government in Conflict.* Amsterdam: John Benjamins.

Hoëm, I. (ed.). 1992. *Kupu mai te Tutolu: Tokelau Oral Literature.* Oslo: Scandinavian University Press.

Hoëm, I. et. al. 2012. *Anthropos and the Material: Challenges to Anthropology.* Oslo: Department of Social Anthropology, University of Oslo.

Hooper, A. 1968. 'Socio-Economic Organisation of the Tokelau Islands', in *Proceedings of the Eight Congress of Anthropological and Ethnological Sciences.* Tokyo.

Huntsman, J.W. 1969. 'Kin and Coconuts on a Polynesian Atoll', Ph.D. diss. Philadelphia: Bryn Mawr College.

———— 1971. 'Concepts of Kinship and Categories of Kinsmen in the Tokelau Islands', *Journal of the Polynesian Society* 80: 317–54.

Huntsman, J., and A. Hooper. 1975. 'Male and Female in Tokelau Culture', *Journal of the Polynesian Society* 84: 415–30.

———— 1976 'The "Desecration" of Tokelau Kinship', *Journal of the Polynesian Society* 85(2): 257–73.

———— 1985. 'Structures of Tokelau History', in A. Hooper and J. Huntsman (eds), *Transformations of Polynesian Culture*. Auckland: Polynesian Society.

———— 1996. *Tokelau: A Historical Ethnography*. Auckland: Auckland University Press.

Hviding, E. 2003. 'Disentangling the Butubutu of New Georgia: Cognatic Kinship in Thought and Action', in I. Hoëm and S. Roalkvam (eds), *Oceanic Socialities and Cultural Forms: Ethnographies of Experience*. Oxford: Berghahn.

Lévi-Strauss, C. 1982. *The Way of the Mask*. Seattle: University of Washington Press.

Macgregor, G. 1937. *Ethnology of Tokelau Islands*. Honolulu: Bernice P. Bishop Museum.

Macpherson, C., and L. Macpherson. 2005. 'The Ifoga: Establishing the Exchange Value of Social Honour in Contemporary Samoa', *Journal of the Polynesian Society* 114(2): 109–34.

———— 2006. 'The Nature and Limits of Traditional Dispute Resolution Processes in Contemporary Samoa', *Pacific Studies* 29(1/2): 128–58.

Mageo, J.M. 1998. *Theorizing Self in Samoa: Emotions, Genders, and Sexualities*. Ann Arbor: University of Michigan Press.

Pasikale, T. (ed.). 2008. *Tokelau: A Collection of Documents and References Relating to Constitutional Development*, 5th edn. Apia, Samoa: Council for the Ongoing Government of Tokelau.

Shore, B. 1989. 'Mana and Tapu', in A. Howard and R. Borofsky (eds), *Developments in Polynesian Ethnology*. Honolulu: University of Hawaii Press.

Strathern, M. 2010. 'Sir Raymond Firth Memorial Lecture', delivered at the European Society for Oceanists conference, University of St Andrews, 5 July.

Tcherkézoff, S. 2009. 'Hierarchy is not Inequality – in Polynesia, for Instance', in K.M. Rio and O. Smedal (eds), *Hierarchy: Persisting Social Formations in the Modern World*. Oxford: Berghahn.

Toren, C. 1994a. '"All Things Go in Pairs, or the Sharks Will Bite": The Antithetical Nature of Fijian Chiefship', *Oceania* 64(3): 197–216.

———— 1994b. 'Transforming Love: Representing Fijian Hierarchy', in P. Gow and P. Harvey (eds), *Sex and Violence: Issues in Representation and Experience*. London: Routledge.

Wagner. R. 1981. *The Invention of Culture*. Chicago: University of Chicago Press.

5

Tongan Kinship Terminology and Social Stratification

◆●◆

Svenja Völkel

From an ethnolinguistic perspective, kinship terminology provides an excellent example to demonstrate the co-constitution and operation of linguistic structures, cognitive features, biological concepts and socio-cultural ideas (cf. e.g. Foley 1997; Lynch 1998). My aim here is to analyse Tongan kinship terminology and relational kinship descriptions with respect to central ideas of how people (more precisely, kin) relate to one another.

Tonga has a highly stratified society with a relative inferior/superior (*tuʻa*/*ʻeiki*) status distinction among relatives (*kāinga*). This hierarchical structure, of central importance to Tongans, corresponds with their kinship classification as expressed by kinship terminology. According to Lowie (1928) and Murdock (1949), Tongan kinship terminology can be classified as 'bifurcate merging Hawaiian type' – that is, the same term applies to father and father's brother (*tamai*), while there is another term for mother's brother (*tuʻasina*); furthermore, siblings and cousins are subsumed under the same terms. A more detailed analysis presented here reveals that the distinctive semantic features of Tongan kinship terminology coincide broadly with those on which the relative status of *tuʻa* and *ʻeiki* is based. It follows that the kinship terminology is a perfect means at once to express and constitute this social distinction in an unequivocal and unambiguous way.

In descriptions of kinship relations, the Tongan language makes use of two different possessive categories (A and O). To date, earlier research has demonstrated that the idea of 'control' seems to be the underlying semantic concept determining the choice of A- or O-possessives in Polynesian languages (see e.g. Wilson 1982; Lichtenberk 1983; Bauer 1997; Völkel 2010). While A is defined by the possessor's control over the initiation of the possessive relationship or over the possessum, O is used as the default case. In relational kinship descriptions, the possessor's control is closely linked to the idea of social stratification (cf. Mulloy and Rapu 1977; Thornton 1998). However, Polynesian languages vary somewhat in the use of A- or O-possessives in descriptions of kinship relations. My aim here is to demonstrate which ideas of power and control (i.e. the *tuʻa/ʻeiki* hierarchy and/or the impact on birth) are encoded by the possessive category in Tongan.

Tongan kinship terminology and relational kinship descriptions provide an instructive example of the way that the linguistic classification of kinship reaches into and is bound up in social relations at large. While the hierarchical structure within the *kāinga* (extended family) is evinced in kinship terminology, the idea of impact on birth seems to determine the choice of the possessive category in most relational kinship descriptions.

Tongan Kinship Terminology

My account here of the Tongan kinship terminology is followed by a description of the *tuʻa/ʻeiki* hierarchy. The analysis that follows demonstrates that the classification of kinship terms and *tuʻa/ʻeiki* stratification have the same underlying features – such as sex of Ego versus sex of referent, and relative age among same-sex relatives in Ego's generation. Thus the kinship terminology evinces status differences within the *kāinga*. For example, *tuofefine* (♂Z) are superior/higher ranked, that is to say *ʻeiki* to Ego, while *tuongaʻane* (♀B) are inferior/lower ranked, that is to say *tuʻa* to Ego. Likewise, *taʻokete* (♂eB/♀eZ) are *ʻeiki*, and *tehina* (♂yB/♀yZ) are *tuʻa* vis-à-vis Ego.

I noted above that the Tongan kinship terminology is classified as 'Hawaiian type' (Murdock 1949, in Jonsson 2001: 120, see also Biersack 1982: 184), which means that in Ego's own generation (G0) the same terms are used for siblings as for cousins. This becomes apparent in the definitions of *tokoua* (same-sex siblings and cousins), *tuofefine* (sisters and female cousins of a male Ego) and *tuongaʻane* (brothers and male cousins of a female Ego) (see Table 5.1). Lowie's characterization of the terminology as 'bifurcate merging' focuses on the kinship classification within the first ascending generation (G+1); it means that the same term is used for F and FB (*tamai*), while there is a separate term for MB (*tuʻasina*) (Lowie 1928, in Jonsson 2001: 1207). By the same token, M and MZ are both subsumed under the term *faʻē*, while FZ is termed differently (*mehekitanga*).

Table 5.1: Tongan kinship terminology

Generation	Kin term	Description
G+2 etc.	*kui*	all male and female kin two or more generations above Ego (i.e. FM, FF, MF, MM, etc.)
G+1	*tamai*	father (F) and all patrilateral male kin one generation above Ego (i.e. FB)
	fa'ē	mother (M) and all matrilateral female kin one generation above Ego (i.e. MZ)
	mātu'a	parents: *fa'ē* and *tamai*
	tu'asina	all matrilateral male kin one generation above Ego (i.e. MB); *fa'ē tangata* (lit. 'male mother') is a synonym for *tu'asina*
	meheki-tanga	all patrilateral female kin one generation above Ego (i.e. FZ, especially the eldest one)
	mali	spouse (H, W) and other affinal kin (i.e. HB, WZ)
G0	*tokoua*	kin of the same sex and the same generation (i.e. ♂B, ♀Z, etc.)
	ta'okete	*tokoua* older than Ego (i.e. ♂eB, ♂MeZS, ♂FeBS, ♀eZ, ♀MeZD, ♀FeBD)
	tehina	*tokoua* younger than Ego (i.e. ♂yB, ♂MyZS, ♂FyBS, ♀yZ, ♀MyZD, ♀FyBD)
	tuofefine	from male Ego's perspective, all female kin of the same generation (i.e. ♂Z, ♂FBD, ♂FZD, ♂MBD, MZD)
	tuonga'ane	from female Ego's perspective, all male kin of the same generation (i.e. ♀B, ♀FBS, ♀FZS, ♀MBS, ♀MZS)
G-1	*'ofefine*	from male Ego's perspective, daughters of himself and *tokoua* (i.e. ♂D, ♂BD)
	foha	from male Ego's perspective, sons of himself and *tokoua* (i.e. ♂S, ♂BS)
	tama	from female Ego's perspective, children of herself and *tokoua* (i.e. ♀S, ♀D, ♀ZS, ♀ZD)
	'ilamutu	from male Ego's perspective, children of *tuofefine* (i.e. ♂ZD, ♂ZS, etc.)
	fakafotu	from female Ego's perspective, children of *tuonga'ane* (i.e. ♀BS, ♀BD, etc.)
G-2 etc.	*mokopuna*	all male and female kin two or more generations below ego (i.e. DD, DS, SD, SS, etc.)

It is worth noting here that most kinship terms (such as *tamai*) subsume close relatives, that is, focal members who are part of the nuclear family (e.g. F), as well as more remote relatives or non-focal members (e.g. FB). However, there is the possibility of distinguishing non-focal members from focal ones by adding the suffix –*'aki* to the corresponding kinship term (such as *tamai* for F versus *tamai'aki* for FB). So compared to English and other non-Polynesian languages, Tongan kinship terms are structured along different combinations of social criteria or semantic features, as the descriptions in Table 5.1 illustrate (see also Kaeppler 1971: 175–76; Biersack 1982: 184–85, van der Grijp 1993: 167). Apart from generation, other distinctive features are sex (of referent as well as speaker or relating/connecting relative) and relative age. The distinction between consanguineous versus affinal kinship is hardly of relevance. With the exception of *mali* (a non-traditional term which is derived from the English word 'marry'), all kinship terms describe consanguineous relatives of Ego. These relatives form Ego's *kāinga*, extended family. Collateral versus lineal kinship is barely a distinctive feature either (apart from the possible affixation of –*'aki* as noted above). Most kinship terms (such as *tamai*) subsume collateral (e.g. FB) and lineal kin (e.g. F). Apart from Ego's generation, only the terms *mehekitanga*, *tu'asina*, *'ilamutu* and *fakafotu* denote exclusively collateral kin.

Within generations closer to Ego, there is conspicuously more terminological differentiation and a greater number of semantic distinctions than within generations at a greater distance from Ego. This is a typical pattern of kinship terminologies (Foley 1997: 136). Relative age between referent and Ego, for instance, is only a distinctive feature in Ego's generation (*ta'okete* versus *tehina*), and the kin terms of the second ascending and descending generation (G+2 and G–2) do not even make a distinction according to sex of referent. This does not mean, however, that it is impossible to make further distinctions; these are made not by separate genuine kin terms, but by additive descriptive terms, such as 'male/man' or 'female/woman', as in the example of *kui tangata* (lit. 'male *kui*') and *kui fefine* (lit. 'female *kui*').

Table 5.2 shows for each kin term the distinctive semantic features that determine the relationship. For purposes of simplification, the table lists only those kin types subsumed under one kin term who relate to Ego through not more than one connecting relative.

Social Structure: The Hierarchy of *Tu'a* and *'Eiki*

In Tonga, nobody is of equal rank and status to anybody else. Apart from the overarching hierarchy of kingly, chiefly and common ranks, there is a relative hierarchy within the extended family (*kāinga*). In other words, Ego's status is defined in relation to other members of their kin group.

Table 5.2: Underlying semantic features of Tongan kinship terminology

Kin term	Kin type(s)	Distinctive semantic features
kui	FF/FM/MF/ MM	generation
tamai	F	generation, sex of referent
	FB	generation, sex of referent, sex of connecting relative
faʻē	M	generation, sex of referent
	MZ	generation, sex of referent, sex of connecting relative
tuʻasina	MB	generation, sex of referent, sex of connecting relative
meheki-tanga	FZ	generation, sex of referent, sex of connecting relative
tokoua:	♂B/♀Z	generation, sex of ego, sex of referent
- *taʻokete*	♂eB/♀eZ	generation, sex of ego, sex of referent, relative age
- *tehina*	♂yB/♀yZ	generation, sex of ego, sex of referent, relative age
tuofefine	♂Z	generation, sex of ego, sex of referent
tuongaʻane	♀B	generation, sex of ego, sex of referent
ʻofefine	♂D	generation, sex of ego, sex of referent
	♂BD	generation, sex of ego, sex of referent, sex of connecting relative
foha	♂S	generation, sex of ego, sex of referent
	♂BS	generation, sex of ego, sex of referent, sex of connecting relative
tama	♀S/♀D	generation, sex of ego
	♀ZS/♀ZD	generation, sex of ego, sex of connecting relative
ʻilamutu	♂ZS/♂ZD	generation, sex of ego, sex of connecting relative
fakafotu	♀BS/♀BD	generation, sex of ego, sex of connecting relative
mokopuna	SS/SD/DS/DD	generation

While certain relatives are superior or higher ranked than Ego (*ʻeiki*), others are considered as inferior or lower ranked (*tuʻa*). Any particular *tuʻa/ʻeiki* distinction (see Table 5.3) is informed by one or more of the following principles (Kaeppler 1971: 176; van der Grijp 1993: 164–65).

First, in Ego's generation (G0), sisters have higher status than brothers; elder same-sex siblings are superior to younger ones, and the status of Ego's cousins is identical with that of the relating parent. Second, in respect of the generation above Ego (G+1), patrilateral kin have higher status than Ego, while matrilateral kin have lower status than Ego, and parents (especially F) have a higher status than their children. Third, in respect of the generation below Ego (G–1), the status of children of Ego's siblings is identical with the status of their relating parent; the children of FZD and FBD are *'eiki* (higher), and all other cousins' children are *tu'a* (lower). Fourth, in respect of the two generations above and below Ego (G+2, G–2), there is little or no status difference between grandparents and grandchildren.

From these principles – more precisely in G0 and G+1 – it follows that the most superior relative is the FZ (*mehekitanga*), especially the eldest one, while the MB (*tu'asina*) is extremely low in status. He is also called 'male mother' (*fa'ē tangata*).

These status inequalities among relatives entail different behaviour, such as reserve and obedience with respect to the *mehekitanga*, demand and freedom from restraint vis-à-vis the *tu'asina*, and reciprocal respect and avoidance of contact between siblings of opposite sex, that is, *tuonga'ane* and *tuofefine* (Kaeppler 1971: 177; van der Grijp 1993: 167; Douaire-Marsaudon 1996; Morton 1996; Völkel 2010: 36–41). This behaviour becomes particularly clear at special occasions (such as funerals and weddings) when certain kin are assigned privileged tasks while others fulfil those of serving the rest, but they are also apparent in daily life. Different taboos (*tapu*) are linked with those kinship relations that are characterized by respect, for instance the avoidance of bodily contact between siblings of opposite sex or the prohibition on touching the father's head or his personal belongings.

Like the terminology for the classification of kin, the *tu'a/'eiki* distinction is determined by the features of sex and relative age – chronological as well as genealogical.

Kinship Terminology and the Hierarchy of *Tu'a* and *'Eiki*

The distinctive semantic features found in the kinship terminology coincide broadly with the distinctions that determine the *tu'a/'eiki* status within the *kāinga*. This demonstrates how deeply the semantic structure of kinship terminology entails and is entailed by the system of social relations of the corresponding society. Thus Lynch remarks that, although there are a finite number of possible kinship classifications in the languages of the world (referring to typological findings, such as Murdock's and Lowie's set of actually documented types; see Murdock 1970), each kinship terminology serves as a specific means to express a particular complex network of social relations and socio-cultural organization (Lynch 1998: 251–56).

The fact that, for relatives linked through not more than one connecting relative, each kinship term unequivocally subsumes relatives with identical

Table 5.3: Tongan kinship terms and corresponding status

Kin term	Kin type(s)	Status (towards ego)
kui	FF/FM/MF/MM	hardly a difference in status
tamai	F/FB	*'eiki*
fa'ē	M/MZ	hardly a difference in status
tu'asina	MB	extremely *tu'a*
mehekitanga	FZ	extremely *'eiki*
tokoua:	♂B/♀Z	*'eiki* and *tu'a*
- *ta'okete*	♂eB/♀eZ	*'eiki*
- *tehina*	♂yB/♀yZ	*tu'a*
tuofefine	♂Z	*'eiki*
tuonga'ane	♀B	*tu'a*
'ofefine	♂D/♂BD	*tu'a*
foha	♂S/♂BS	*tu'a*
tama	♀S/♀D/♀ZS/♀ZD	hardly a difference in status
'ilamutu	♂ZS/♂ZD	extremely *'eiki*
fakafotu	♀BS/♀BD	extremely *tu'a*
mokopuna	SS/SD/DS/DD	hardly a difference in status

or at least similar status vis-à-vis Ego, makes the mutual implication of kinship terminology and social structure, namely the *tu'a/'eiki* status, particularly clear (see Table 5.3.) It follows that, from the perspective of any given Tongan person, kinship as lived is at one with social stratification at large.

Among siblings first of all, Ego's sex is important in relation to the referent's sex. From a male's perspective, all sisters (*tuofefine*) are *'eiki*, and from a female's perspective all brothers (*tuonga'ane*) are *tu'a*. The second feature, which is of relevance within the group of same-sex siblings (*tokoua*), is relative age. From a male's perspective, older brothers (*ta'okete*) are *'eiki*, and younger brothers (*tehina*) are *tu'a* just as, from a female's perspective, older sisters (*ta'okete*) are *'eiki* and younger sisters (*tehina*) are *tu'a*. The fact that the same term applies to a male's older brother and a female's older sister is explicable by redundancy and economy: the two relationships do not overlap and they express the same status – *ta'okete* are *'eiki* towards Ego. By the same token, the term *tehina* describes all younger same-sex siblings. This demonstrates that the hierarchical principles of Ego's generation (G0) as noted above are considered in the terminological classification of

◆

siblings. The stratified relationships are thus described in unequivocal terms by means of the same semantic features.

Within the first ascending generation (G+1), the distinctive status features are the sex of referent and the sex of connecting relative, that is, matrilateral versus patrilateral kinship. The most *'eiki* relative is FZ (*mehekitanga*) and the most *tu'a* is MB (*tu'asina*). FB has the same status as F, and they are both called *tamai* (or *tamai'aki* for the FB, as noted above). Likewise, the same term (*fa'ē* or also *fa'ē'aki* for the MZ) applies to MZ and M, who also have similar status.

Within the first descending generation (G−1) from a female's perspective, her brother's children (*fakafotu*) are *tu'a* as she is their *mehekitanga*.[1] From a male's perspective, his sister's children, who are in a *fahu*[2] or *'eiki* position (vis-à-vis their *tu'asina*), are also described by a special term: *'ilamutu*. Between a female Ego and her own children or her sister's children (all *tama*), there is hardly any difference in status. The marginal status differences result from the less relevant feature of relative age (that is, children of older same-sex siblings are slightly *'eiki* towards Ego, while children of younger same-sex siblings are rather *tu'a*) compared to the much more important feature of Ego's sex in relation to the sex of the connecting relative (that is, the above described status differences between a female Ego and her brother's children). Regarding his own children and his brother's children to whom the same kin terms apply, a male Ego is always *'eiki*. However, in contrast to the terminology of one's own children and those of *tokoua* from a female's perspective, from a male's perspective a further terminological distinction is made according to the referent's sex: *foha* (sons of a male Ego and his brothers) and *'ofefine* (daughters of male Ego and his brothers). This terminological differentiation is not based on a difference in status (as *foha* and *'ofefine* are both *tu'a* vis-à-vis Ego), but it is explicable by the system of inheritance in which gender is an important factor. A man generally passes on his land and title to his oldest son, a *foha*.

The relationship between Ego and Ego's grandparents or Ego's grandchildren (G+2 and G−2) is one of nearly equal status. Apart from generation, there is no necessity for further terminological distinctions among kin within these generations, not even in respect of sex of referent. All kin of the second ascending generation are called *kui*, and those of the second descending one *mokopuna*.

Figure 5.1 illustrates for male and female Ego respectively that there are different kinship terms for the reciprocal relations associated with status inequalities: *tu'a* kin are shaded black, *'eiki* kin are non-shaded and those with only marginal status inequalities are shaded grey. The major and most important *'eiki/tu'a* relationships are those between *mehekitanga* and *fakafotu*, as well as between *'ilamutu* and *tu'asina* respectively. *'Eiki/tu'a*

a.

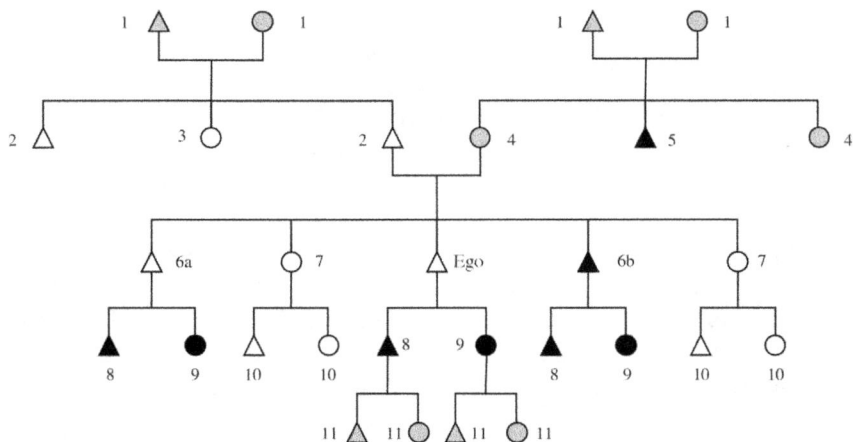

b.

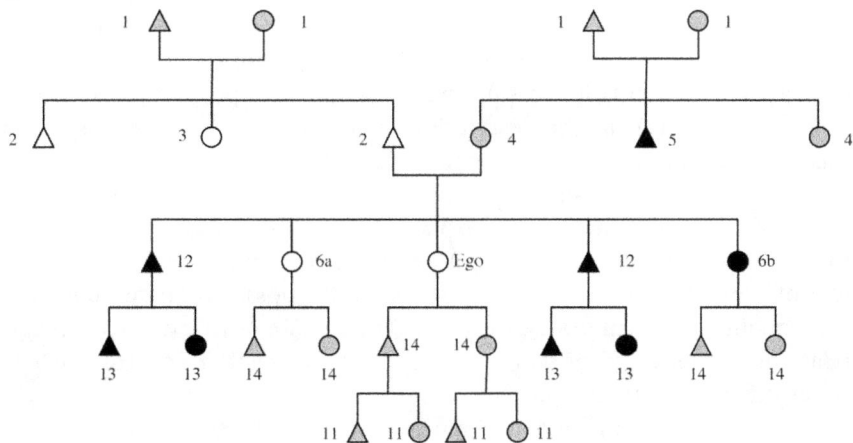

Reciprocal kinship relations:
1 (*kui*) – 11 (*mokopuna*)
2 (*tamai*) – 8 (*foha*), 9 (*'ofefine*)
3 (*mehekitanga*) – 13 (*fakafotu*)
4 (*fa'ē*) – 14 (*tama*)
5 (*tu'asina*) – 10 (*'ilamutu*)
6 (*tokoua*): 6a (*ta'okete*) – 6b (*tehina*)
7 (*tuofefine*) – 12 (*tuonga'ane*)

Figure 5.1: Kin terms and social status within the *kāinga* (a. from a male perspective; b. from a female perspective)

stratification is further associated with the *tamai–foha* and *tamai–ʻofefine* relationship, as well as those of *tuofefine–tuongaʻane* and *taʻokete–tehina*. By contrast, the *faʻē–tama* and the *kui–mokopuna* relationships are hardly characterized by a difference in status. This analysis reveals a co-variation between the classification of relatives given by Tongan kinship terminology and status differentiation, especially the *tuʻa/ʻeiki* status (but also by other practices such as inheritance of land). From the analyst's perspective, while kinship terminology and status differentiation can apparently be differentiated from the other, they have the same underlying features: generation, sex (of Ego, referent and connecting relative) and relative age, in this order of relevance. In this way, Tongan kinship terminology and the differences given by *tuʻa/ʻeiki* stratification may be seen to be refractions of one another, subsuming only kin with similar social status under each kin term.[3]

Tongan Descriptions of Kinship Relations

In expressing kinship relations between anchor (e.g. Ego) and referent, languages make use of possessive constructions, such as 'my father' – the anchor being the possessor (Ego) and the referent the possessum (father). Polynesian languages generally use different possessive categories (namely A and O) for the description of distinct kinship relations.[4] This raises the question of which semantic features or which underlying idea (relative status, for instance) govern the choice of the possessive category. Addressing this question, I first explain A- and O-possession and present the common approaches defining A and O in Polynesian languages. As the idea of 'control' seems to be the basic idea for the possessive dichotomy, the subsequent analysis of the use of A and O in Tongan descriptions of kinship relations focuses on ideas that are linked to the concept of 'control', such as status differentiation and power.

The possessor's control over the possessum (i.e. the *tuʻa/ʻeiki* hierarchy) only partially provides an explanation for the choice of the possessive category in Tongan descriptions of kinship relations. A more relevant feature is the possessor's control over the initiation of the possessive relationship, i.e. over the possessum's birth. Nevertheless, there are exceptions to this semantic definition, that is, instances in which the use of A and O is not explicable by an idea of control. This does not, however, invalidate the basic finding that the possessive category used in descriptions of kinship relations co-varies with ideas linked to the concept of 'control'. The exceptional cases are likely to be due to language change, which is supported by the fact that the Polynesian languages differ slightly concerning the use of A and O in relational kinship descriptions, but diachronic Tongan language data are needed to verify this idea.

Relational Classifiers: A-Possession and O-Possession

The Tongan language distinguishes two possessive categories (A and O) to describe different kinds of possessive relationships, including kinship relations. Example 1 shows A-possessed constructions (a. possessive preposition; b. possessive pronoun), while O-possessed ones (a. possessive preposition; b. possessive pronoun) occur in Example 2.

(1)	*a.*	*(Ko e) meʻalele ʻa Sione.*	– (It is) the vehicle **of-A** Sione.
	b.	*ʻeku meʻalele*	– **my-A** vehicle
(2)	*a.*	*(Ko e) ʻulu ʻo Sione.*	– (It is) the head **of-O** Sione.
	b.	*hoku ʻulu*	– **my-O** head

Most current Polynesian grammars show that this possessive dichotomy is based on semantic features. While A-possessive forms are generally used for alienable relationships, that means the possessor can acquire the possessum (e.g. *ʻeku meʻalele* 'my-A vehicle'), O-possession occurs with inalienable relationships, that means the possessum is inherent, partitive or closely connected with the possessor (e.g. *hoko ʻulu* 'my-O head'). More detailed approaches (Wilson 1982; Lichtenberk 1983) have shown that the choice of A- or O-possession is not determined by noun class of the possessor or the possessum respectively, but that it is based on the quality of the possessive relationship between both entities.[5] Hence Lichtenberk calls A and O 'relational classifiers' (Lichtenberk 1983: 148). The majority of possessum entities can occur in A- as well as in O-possessed contexts with a difference in meaning (so called 'minimal pairs'), as illustrated in Examples 3 and 4 (Völkel 2010: 177, 179).

(3)	*a.*	*ʻeku talanoa*	– my-A story (i.e. a story that I have written/ told)
	b.	*hoku talanoa*	– my-O story (i.e. a story that is about me)
(4)	*a.*	*ʻeku hingoa*	– my-A name (i.e. the name that I give to someone)
	b.	*hoku hingoa*	– my-O name (i.e. the name that is given to me)

Taking these minimal pairs into consideration, the most prominent and appropriate approaches providing a semantic definition of A and O in Polynesian languages are the 'control theories' (Wilson 1982; Fischer 2000). While A-possession is characterized by presence of control, such control is absent in the case of O-possession. More precisely, O-possession is the default case, that is to say it is not only used in the case of absence of control but whenever control is not explicit (Bauer 1997: 390–91; Völkel 2010:

168–69, 178). There are two control theories, the 'simple control theory' and the 'initial control theory' – the latter being the more relevant (Wilson 1982: 16; Völkel 2010: 176–82). According to the simple control theory, the possessor has (no) control over the possessum. By contrast, the initial control theory proposes a different subject matter of control: the determining factor is not the presence of the possessor's control over the possessum, but over the initiation of the possessive relationship (Wilson 1982: 15–16).

In the A-possessed examples (3a and 4a), the possessor (i.e. Ego) has control over the possessum (i.e. the story or the name), or even more precisely, over the initiation of the possessive relationship. In these cases, the possessum would not even exist without the possessor's agency. The use of O-possession (3b and 4b) instead indicates that such control of the possessor is absent or at least unspecified. In Example 3b, for instance, the storyteller or storywriter is not explicitly mentioned, and thus it could be the possessor or somebody else.

A-Possession, O-Possession and Descriptions of Kinship Relations

Generally, the semantic category of kin is described as inalienable (Heine 1997: 10–11) and thus O-possessed; yet, in Tongan as well as in other Polynesian languages, some kinship relations are O-possessed while others require A-constructions, as indicated in Table 5.4.[6] From this perspective, it is interesting to reveal the underlying semantic criteria that determine the choice of the respective possessive category.

Table 5.4: A-possession and O-possession used with Tongan descriptions of kinship relations

A-possessed kinship relations	O-possessed kinship relations
kui	kāinga
motuʻa: tamai and faʻē	tuʻasina
tama	mehekitanga
fakafotu	tokoua: taʻokete and tehina
	tuofefine
	tuongaʻane
	foha
	ʻofefine
	ʻilamutu
	mokopuna
	mali

The simple control theory leads to the prediction that the use of A- or O-possession in descriptions of kinship relations is determined by the relative hierarchy. As superior status is associated with the concept of control, ʻeiki relatives (as possessors) are supposed to have control over tuʻa kin (as possessum), and consequently this relationship would be expressed by A-possession (as in Example 5). Accordingly, O-possession would be used to describe the opposite relationship, i.e. tuʻa possessor and ʻeiki possessum (as in Example 6).[7]

(5) ʻeku   *fakafotu*   – my-A *fakafotu*
                                                            (MBC)

     POSSESSOR (i.e. ego)   POSSESSUM

(6) *hoku*   *mehekitanga*   – my-O *mehekitanga*
                                                            (FZ)

     POSSESSOR (i.e. ego)   POSSESSUM

There are, however, several exceptions to the simple control theory, as Table 5.5 illustrates. It fails as explanation in the majority of cases for which

Table 5.5: Tongan descriptions of kinship relations and 'simple control theory'

Status of possessum (towards an Ego-possessor)	Possessum (kin term)	Possessive category	
		according to 'simple control theory'	actual occurrence
ʻeiki	*mehekitanga*	O-possession	O-possession
	ʻilamutu		O-possession
	tuofefine		O-possession
	taʻokete		O-possession
	tamai		A-possession
tuʻa	tuʻasina	A-possession	O-possession
	fakafotu		A-possession
	tuongaʻane		O-possession
	tehina		O-possession
	foha		O-possession
	ʻofefine		O-possession
hardly a difference in status	faʻē		A-possession
	tama		A-possession
	kui		A-possession
	mokopuna		O-possession
	tokoua		O-possession

A-possession would be expected, for instance the case of *hoku tuʻasina* 'my-O *tuʻasina* (MB)' which actually occurs with O-possession, even though Ego is *ʻeiki* vis-à-vis his MB. And in the opposite case of *ʻeku tamai* 'my-A *tamai* (F, FB)', the simple control theory would predict O- instead of A-possession because of Ego's *tuʻa* position vis-à-vis F and FB.

The initial control theory seems indeed to provide a more appropriate explanation for the use of A and O in descriptions of Tongan kinship relations. In most Polynesian languages, generally offspring (especially from a female possessor's perspective) and spouses are the only A-possessed kin (Wilson 1982: 30–40; Völkel 2010: 257–60). These are kinship relations which the possessor 'enters voluntarily' or which they 'have chosen' or 'created' (e.g. Cook 2000: 346; Hooper 2000: 299–300). All these descriptions imply the idea of the possessor's deliberate control over the initiation of the kinship relation as defined by the initial control theory.

Given that Polynesian languages differ slightly concerning the use of A and O in relational kinship descriptions,[8] my analysis of Tongan should take other Polynesian languages into consideration. In contrast to eastern Polynesian languages (such as Maori, Hawaiian and Rapanui), that use A-possession for the relationship between a possessor and their offspring (Cook 2000: 346; Fischer 2000: 339–40; Harlow 2000: 363–64), Tongan and several Polynesian languages of the Samoic outlier branch (such as Samoan, Tokelauan, Pilani and East Uvean) make a distinction between offspring from a male's and a female's perspective (Mosel and Hovdhaugen 1992: 285; Hooper 2000: 299–300; Moyse-Faurie 2000: 321–22; Næss 2000: 313; Völkel 2010: 183). While only terms for mother's children are A-possessed (e.g. *tama* in Tongan), terms for father's children (e.g. *foha* and *ʻofefine* in Tongan) are actually O-possessed. This leads to the conclusion that in Tonga a mother is regarded as having control over the initiation of the relationship in a way the father is not. She is the one conceiving, being pregnant and giving birth. This underlying socio-cultural idea seems to be widespread in western Polynesia (Næss 2000: 313).

Apart from the mother, the *mehekitanga* is also ascribed control over the initiation of the relationship with her brother's children, which is indeed expressed by an A-possessive construction in Tongan (*ʻene fakafotu*, 'her-A *fakafotu*'). She has the power to curse a newborn to death or to provide a healthy birth, and it is mostly the *mehekitanga* who symbolically introduces the child into the *kāinga* by giving them a name (Douaire-Marsaudon 1996; Morton 1996: 50–51).[9] The mother's brother's children are also A-possessed in other western Polynesian languages, such as East Uvean (Moyse-Faurie 2000: 321–22).[10]

In contrast to eastern Polynesian languages (such as Hawaiian, Maori and Rapanui), which use A-possession with spouses (Elbert and Pukui

1979: 137–38; Fischer 2000: 339–40; Harlow 2000: 363–64), in Tongan *mali* (husband/wife) as well as *hoa* (mate) are O-possessed (Völkel 2010: 183), just as some terms denoting affinal kinship relations in other western Polynesian languages.[11] In Tongan, this is explicable from a traditional chiefly perspective, where the spouse was not freely chosen but matrimonial bonds were arranged in order to strengthen chiefly lines (Bott 1981: 20–21, 55–58). Accordingly, O-possession indicates that spouses are not regarded as having control over the initiation of their relationship. Even commoners are not entirely free to choose their marriage partner in a modern Western sense. The *mehekitanga* is the one who finally controls matrimonial destinies, that is, she has the power either to prohibit a marriage or to mediate between the *kāinga* of both spouses (Douaire-Marsaudon 1996: 147–51).

So far, the initial control theory reveals some interesting encodings of specifically Tongan ideas of control and power over the initiation of kin relationships. A mother (Example 8) and the father's sister (Example 7) are ascribed initial control over the kinship relation, which is encoded in the use of A-possession in the following cases:

(7) 'eku   *fakafotu*   – my-A *fakafotu*
                                                    (♀BS/♀BD)

     POSSESSOR (i.e. FZ)   POSSESSUM

(8) 'eku   *tama*   – my-A *tama* (♀S/♀D)

     POSSESSOR (i.e. M)   POSSESSUM

Almost all other kinship relations (including the relationship between spouses) are not initially controlled by the possessor; this is expressed by O-possession (cf. Table 5.4). Thus the 'initial control theory' generally seems to be more appropriate than the 'simple control theory' to describe the distinction of A- and O-possession in respect of Tongan kinship relations. However, there are still some problematic cases: *'eku faʻē* 'my-A *faʻē* (M, MZ)', *'eku tamai* 'my-A *tamai* (F, FB)' and *'eku kui* 'my-A *kui* (FF, FM, MF, MM)'.[12] They raise the question as to why these relationships are A-possessed even though the possessor controls neither the possessum (*faʻē, tamai* or *kui*) nor the initiation of the relationship. First of all, it is conspicuous that this use of the A-category is extremely unusual in Polynesian languages. Apart from Tongan and East Uvean (which was strongly influenced by Tongan), these relationships are generally O-possessed in eastern Polynesian as well as in western Polynesian languages of the Samoic outlier branch. Even lexical cognates, such as *whaea* (M, MZ) or *kuia* (FM, MM) in Maori and *tama* (F, FB) in Samoan, are O-possessed (Wilson 1982: 33; Thornton 1998: 389). Consequently, the use of A-possessives with parents and grandparents in Tongan is likely to be due to language change and should be regarded as irregular and exceptional (Wilson 1982: 35).[13] These exceptions to the semantic definition given by the initial control theory do not, however, invalidate the basic finding that the possessive category used in descriptions of kinship relations (and other possessive relationships) is determined by ideas linked to the concept of the possessor's initial control or power over the possessive relationship (Lichtenberk 1983: 168; Völkel 2010: 182–94).[14]

Finally, because the distinction between A- and O-possessed kinship relations does not map neatly onto the *tuʻa/ʻeiki* hierarchy within the *kāinga*, the simple control theory cannot provide an appropriate explanation. The A/O dichotomy seems rather to be based on the concept of control over one's birth (as expressed by the initial control theory), which is ascribed to M and FZ.

Conclusion

Kinship systems are expressed in their terminology and associated ideas and practices. Their constitution – their continuity and transformation in use – is necessarily bound up with what may be called political economy. In other words, any given kinship terminology is, from the analyst's perspective, going to express precisely (and at the same time to constitute) specific ideas of kinship and social relations at large. In Tongan, kinship relationships are expressed in kinship terminology and in possessive constructions – linguistic means that I have shown to be clearly implicated in the principles of differentiation that structure relations in the polity at large. First, my analysis of Tongan kinship terminology reveals that it classifies relatives in terms of the same semantic features as the *tuʻa/ʻeiki* stratification within the extended family. Thus each kin term is associated with a certain status subsuming only relatives with identical or at least similar status vis-à-vis Ego. Second, the possessive category (A or O) used in Tongan relational kinship descriptions likewise encodes hierarchical differentiation. While *tuʻa/ʻeiki* status is obviously not the main underlying concept for the use of A- versus O-possession, the idea of control over birth seems to be more relevant in the majority of cases.

It follows that any given analyst of kinship systems – linguist or ethnographer – has much to gain from an analysis that considers at once the linguistic features of a kinship terminology and the ideas and practices that have a bearing on it in the polity at large.

Notes

 1. The meaning and importance of this extremely stratified relationship is expressed in the terminology. The term *fakafotu* means 'making someone

apparent or manifest or prominent' (Helu, in Douaire-Marsaudon 1996: 149). This describes the father's sister's privileged task or function regarding her brother's children. Upon birth, she is ascribed the power to control her *fakafotu*'s destiny, that is, either to provoke the death of a newborn or to effect a healthy birth (cf. Douaire-Marsaudon 1996). In case of a successful birth, this means that the *mehekitanga* accepts her brother's child as new member of the *kāinga*. This existential function also becomes apparent in her privileged task of bestowing a name on the newborn.

2. Apart from the *mehekitanga*'s superior position of honour at special occasions ('above the law'), *fahu* also describes the special status or power of her children (Gifford 1929: 22–24; Douaire-Marsaudon 1996: 150–56).

3. As English kinship terminology is based on different classificatory criteria, it does not provide a comparably adequate system to express Tongan social structure. Thus, it is interesting to observe what happens in the situation of language contact – English being the official language besides Tongan. Mostly, Tongans make use of English kin terms according to the Tongan kinship classification. For instance, cousins as well as siblings are called 'brother' or 'sister', and the term 'father' is also used for uncles (i.e. FB). This demonstrates that the Tongan kinship classification is not only deeply anchored in the socio-cultural system, but it also represents the cognitive frame of its speakers. This raises the question whether ongoing language and culture contact will provoke a change in favour of the English classificatory and cognitive structure, and whether this change may be accompanied by a destabilisation of the Tongan *tuʻa/ʻeiki* hierarchy within the *kāinga* (similar to already observable changes in favour for the Western concept of the 'core family', *fāmili*).

4. In linguistic terms, a possessive construction expresses a relationship between the two entities 'possessor' and 'possessum' (also called 'possessee' or 'possessed entity') in which the possessum belongs to the possessor, not only in the sense of ownership but different kinds of relationship, such as kinship relations, part-whole relations, etc. (Heine 1997). The distinction between A- and O-possession is characteristic of most Polynesian languages (Clark 2000). The terminology A- versus O-possession is considered more neutral (compared to alienable versus inalienable or other terminologies), as it is based on the formal criteria of the distinctive vowels 'a' versus 'o' instead of semantic criteria (Völkel 2010), which still have to be defined below in more detail.

5. In early descriptions of Polynesian languages, A and O have often been treated as noun-class systems. This means that each possessum was categorized as either A- or O-possessed. This categorization into two noun classes implies that the use of A or O is only determined by the nature of the possessum. The inappropriateness of this noun-class theory becomes

evident by so-called minimal pairs (see Examples 3 and 4) in which a possessum can occur in A- as well as in O-possessed contexts. This is taken
into consideration by control theories (Wilson 1982; Clark 2000; Völkel
2010: 165–70).

6. Taumoefolau (1996) postulates that each possessum can be A- as well as
O-possessed, including kinship terms (*'eku fa'ē*, 'my-A mother', versus *fa'ē
'o e ta'u*, 'mother of-O the year'). Nevertheless, in descriptions of kinship
relations ('my mother' in contrast to the metaphorical use in 'mother of the
year'), each kinship term can only occur either as A- or as O-possessed entity
(Völkel 2010: 182–83).

7. For Rapanui and Maori, Mulloy and Rapu (1977: 11–13) and Thornton (1998:
382–89) also trace the idea of control back to hierarchical relationships
among members of Polynesian societies, and finally the concepts of *mana*
and *tapu*. A-possession is used with social inferiors and indicates the superior *mana* of the possessor, while O-possession occurs with social superiors
who have more *mana* than the possessor, and who are surrounded by more
tapu. However, there are exceptions to this theory, e.g. *irāmutu* (ZC), who is
A-possessed, although it is a person of great *mana* in Maori culture (Thornton 1998: 385–86); by contrast, in Tongan, *'ilamutu* (ZC) is O-possessed, and
thus no contradiction to the rule (see Table 5.5).

8. See note 7 for example.

9. See note 1.

10. Unfortunately, there is a lack of information concerning the possessive category of the relationship vis-à-vis a woman's brother's children in most Polynesian studies (e.g. Mulloy and Rapu 1977; Elbert and Pukui 1979; Mosel and
Hovdhaugen 1992; Hooper 2000).

11. While East Uvean also describes the relationship between spouses (*'ohoana*)
as O-possessed (Moyse-Faurie 2000: 321–22), in other Polynesian languages
of the Samoic outlier branch, the possessive category used with spouses is
ambivalent. The two Tokelauan terms for 'spouse' take different possessive
categories: *āvaga* (A) and *tokalua* (O) (Hooper 2000: 300). Similarly, the
Samoan terms *āvā* (wife) and *tāne* (husband) are A-possessed, whereas *to'alua*
(spouse) and *faletua* (wife of a chief) are O-possessed (Mosel and Hovdhaugen 1992: 286). This raises the question whether in Samoan the commoners
could freely choose their wives while the chiefs could not.

12. In most Oceanic languages, kinship relations are described by the use of
direct possessive constructions. Proto-Polynesian lost this construction type,
and kinship relations were consequently assigned to one of the two remaining indirect construction types, i.e. either the A- or the O-category. During
this process, or at later stages of language change, different semantic criteria
might have been taken into consideration or emphasized. Therefore, it is not
surprising that there are discrepancies and irregularities concerning the use

of A- and O-possession in the descriptions of kinship relations in Polynesian languages (Wilson 1982: 30; Lynch 1998: 122–30; 2000; see also note 7).

13. Wilson (1982: 34–35) proceeds from the assumption that a change of the possessive category occurred in these exceptional Tongan cases. Such a shift from O to A might have happened in connection with lexical changes (the terms *fa'ē* and *kui* are lexically quite distinct from Proto-Polynesian **tinana* 'M, MZ' and **tupuna* 'FF, FM, MF, MM'; Marck 1996) or it might be due to a general gradual change from O- to A-possession in Polynesian languages. In Niuean, for instance, this shift resulted in a complete loss of the A/O distinction with only A forms remaining (Lynch 1998: 130; Clark 2000: 267). Hingano (in Völkel 2010: 1993) has also currently observed a tendency towards A-possession in Tongan, e.g. children (mis)using *mehekitanga* and other O-possessed kin terms with A-possessives in the context of derision (though not in the presence of FZ, which would be regarded as too offensive and disrespectful). He presumes that such linguistic changes are caused by the spreading Western idea of having influence or control over nearly everything. In connection with the increasing importance of the core family, which is also based on Western influence (see note 3), it is quite striking that *'eku fa'ē*, *'eku tamai* and *'eku kui* describe all lineal kinship relations of ascending generations. However, diachronic data is needed to make definite statements about whether, when and which linguistic changes have occurred, and which (if any) socio-cultural ideas provoked the changes at that time.

14. The initial control theory has proved to be the general underlying semantic feature of possessive relationships in Tongan (see above; Völkel 2010: 164–82). Even other personal relationships than kinship ones express the idea of initial control of the possessor over the possessive relationship: *'eku taha ngāue* (my-A employee) versus *hoku taki ngāue* (my-O employer) (ibid.: 183). While the possessor has initial control over the relationship with their employee (i.e. the employer is free to choose and hire their employees), the possessor generally lacks such initial control over the possessive relationship with their employer.

References

Bauer, W. 1997. *The Reed Reference Grammar of Maori*. Auckland: Reed.

Biersack, A. 1982. 'Tongan Exchange Structures: Beyond Descent and Alliance', *Journal of the Polynesian Society* 91: 181–212.

Bott, E. 1981. 'Power and Rank in the Kingdom of Tonga', *Journal of the Polynesian Society* 90(1): 7–81.

Clark, R. 2000. 'Possessive Markers in Polynesian Languages', *Language Typology and Universals*, special issue, 53(3/4): 258–68.

Cook, K.W. 2000. 'Possessive Markers in Hawaiian', *Language Typology and Universals*, special issue, 53(3/4): 345–56.

Douaire-Marsaudon, F. 1996. 'Neither Black nor White: The Father's Sister in Tonga', *Journal of the Polynesian Society* 105(2): 139–64.

Elbert, S., and M.K Pukui. 1979. *Hawaiian Grammar*. Honolulu: University of Hawaii Press.

Fischer, S.R. 2000. 'Possessive Markers in Rapanui', *Language Typology and Universals*, special issue, 53(3/4): 333–44.

Foley, W. 1997. *Anthropological Linguistics: An Introduction*. Oxford: Blackwell.

Gifford, E.W. 1929. *Tongan Society*. Honolulu: Bernice P. Bishop Museum.

Harlow, R. 2000. 'Possessive Markers in Māori', *Language Typology and Universals*, special issue, 53(3/4): 357–70.

Heine, B. 1997. *Possession: Cognitive Sources, Forces, and Grammaticalization*. Cambridge: Cambridge University Press.

Hooper, R. 2000. 'Possessive Markers in Tokelauan', *Language Typology and Universals*, special issue, 53(3/4): 293–307.

Jonsson, N. 2001. 'Kin Terms in Grammar', in M. Haspelmath et al. (eds), *Language Typology and Language Universals: An International Handbook*, Vol. 2. Berlin: de Gruyter.

Kaeppler, A.L. 1971. 'Rank in Tonga', *Ethnology* 10(2): 174–93.

Lichtenberk, F. 1983. 'Relational Classifiers', *Lingua* 60: 147–76.

Lowie, R. 1928. 'A Note on Relationship Terminologies', *American Anthropologist* 30: 263–68.

Lynch, J. 1998. *Pacific Languages: An Introduction*. Honolulu: University of Hawaii Press.

———— 2000. 'Historical Overview of Central Pacific Possessive Markers', *Language Typology and Universals*, special issue, 53(3/4): 233–42.

Marck, J. 1996. 'Kin Terms in the Polynesian Protolanguages', *Oceanic Linguistics* 35(2): 195–257.

Morton, H. 1996. *Becoming Tongan: An Ethnography of Childhood*. Honolulu: University of Hawaii Press.

Mosel, U., and E. Hovdhaugen. 1992. *Samoan Reference Grammar*. Oslo: Scandinavian University Press.

Moyse-Faurie, C. 2000. 'Possessive Markers in East Uvean', *Language Typology and Universals*, special issue, 53(3/4): 319–32.

Mulloy, E.R., and S.A. Rapu. 1977. 'Possession, Dependence and Responsibility in the Rapanui Language', *Journal of the Polynesian Society* 86(1): 7–25.

Murdock, G. 1949. *Social Structure*. New York: Macmillan.

———— 1970. 'Kin Term Patterns and Their Distribution', *Ethnology* 9(2): 165–208.

Næss, Å. 2000. 'Possessive Marking in Pilani', *Language Typology and Universals*, special issue, 53(3/4): 308–18.

Taumoefolau, M. 1996. 'Nominal Possessive Classification in Tonga', in J. Lynch and F. Pat (eds), *Oceanic Studies: Proceedings of the First International Conference on Oceanic Linguistics*. Canberra: Australian National University.

Thornton, A. 1998. 'Do A and O Categories of Possession in Maori Express Degrees of *Tapu?' Journal of the Polynesian Society* 107(4): 381–93.

van der Grijp, P. 1993. *Islanders of the South. Production, Kinship and Ideology in the Polynesian Kingdom of Tonga.* Leiden: KITLV Press.

Völkel, S. 2010. *Social Structure, Space and Possession in Tongan Culture and Language: An Ethnolinguistic Research.* Amsterdam: Benjamins.

Wilson, W.H. 1982. *Proto-Polynesian Possessive Marking.* Canberra: Australian National University.

6

'I Suffered When My Sister Gave Birth'

Transformations of the Brother–Sister Bond among the Ankave-Anga of Papua New Guinea

◆●◆

Pascale Bonnemère

One day in October 2006, a young woman brought her small daughter to the house where we lived because she had a fever and her mother wanted us to give her some medication. The woman's brother, Michael, who was a few years older than she, accompanied them. The eighteen-month-old girl would not take the syrup from me or even from her mother, but when her maternal uncle took the spoon and presented it to her, she drank it all. Michael commented, saying: 'I suffered when my sister gave birth. I gave birth to her too'. His sister agreed vigorously, and her brother added: 'And that's why I received the *Simo'e* and *tuage*' gifts'.[1] The aim of this chapter is to explain this statement, in which a man says that he felt pain when his sister gave birth to her daughter, as if giving birth to her himself.[2] To understand it requires having some information about the brother–sister relationship from which the avuncular relation derives as time goes on, adding a new generation to the existing one.

The Ankave occupy three densely forested valleys to the southwest of a mountain chain running the width, from east to west, of the island of New Guinea. Some 1,500 in number, they belong to a set of twelve Anga linguistic groups, which speak related languages, share certain cultural features – male initiation, gender asymmetry, the absence of inequality among the men and the absence of big men – and have an oral history that attests to a common origin. As horticulturalists in the main, the Ankave grow taro, bananas, sugar cane and sweet potatoes in gardens cleared in the forest. They also raise a few pigs, hunt, trap eels for ceremonial purposes, and gather a wide variety of leaves and fruits in the forest. Accordingly, each family regularly builds a temporary shelter several hours' walk from the hamlet containing their main house, and so Ankave hamlets are occupied only intermittently throughout the year. The population is divided into exogamous patrilineal clans, and residence is usually patrivirilocal, but affinal relations provide the possibility of access to additional lands and enable Ankave people to satisfy their penchant for mobility. Marriage rules are expressed in the form of prohibitions, the most strict being that of marriage between a man and a woman related in the maternal line, by virtue of the belief that blood is transmitted exclusively by the mother.[3]

Brothers, Sisters and Maternal Uncles

The brother–sister relationship is important in the life of an Ankave, in large part because it is a driving force in the long process whereby a boy becomes a father. In effect, a sister who ideally has not yet borne children assists her brother through the different phases of his initiation, the last stage of which comes when his wife is delivered of his first child.[4] My analysis reveals, however, that becoming a father is not considered to close the initiation cycle. Being a maternal uncle is the status that is the most valued in Ankave men's lives, and this depends, of course, on their sisters becoming mothers. Having a sister who bears a child is not, however, a sufficient condition for a man to become a maternal uncle; he has also to be endowed with a specific capacity that is acquired gradually through ritual. The necessary presence of one of his sisters at all phases of the initiation of her brother makes this process clear.

It is not possible, therefore, to consider the brother–sister bond and the avuncular relationship independently of each other. They are closely linked, since the latter continues the former as time goes on and a new generation appears. The brother–sister relationship then expands to become a tie that relates groups and determines people's paternal and maternal affiliations. Among the Ankave, the ritual manifestations of this relationship are characterized by asymmetry, since a sister acts for her brother when he goes through initiation, while a brother never does the same for his sister. When he takes action, it is as a maternal uncle, not as a brother. In point of fact, he is an essential figure in his nephews' and nieces' lives.

Some anthropologists working in places where the main categories of filiation and alliance do not exhaust the universe of kinship have found that the brother–sister relationship has a structuring role as well. In northern India, for example, Jamous (2003) has shown terminological characteristics linked to marriage through sister exchange. A specific relation of affinity, which links two brother–sister pairs is thus emphasized. In other studies as well, the importance of the brother–sister relationship has been related primarily to marriage practices (Pauwels 1990; Beneï 1997) and to ritual. Among the Ankave, this relationship does not seem to be relevant so much to marriage as to the constitution of male personhood and locally valued social statuses.

In the 1950s, Kenelm Burridge, an anthropologist working in what was not yet Papua New Guinea, had already pointed out the importance of the brother–sister bond for social organization: 'men and women have sisters and brothers irrespective of marriage and descent', he wrote (Burridge 1959: 136). Kinship was the major topic of his work, and he devoted a number of articles to its different facets among the Tangu, who live on the northern coast of the country. In a long and detailed essay dealing in particular with siblingship, he wrote: 'one might say that in Tangu social life is possible, and individuals reach maturity, in terms of adequately resolving the sibling to marital relationship' (ibid.: 131). In this sense, 'the relationship between brother and sister could be said to be the pivot of Tangu social life and culture' (ibid.: 130). And he concludes his essay with what could serve as a general statement: 'So long as the basic unit remains the household and not a corporate descent group, siblingship provides a sufficiently flexible principle on which to base marriage and the consequent relations between households' (ibid.: 154).

Rituals linked to marriage have been analysed by both Jamous in northern India and Burridge in New Guinea, and both show the essential role of the paternal aunt and the maternal uncle respectively. Jamous has revealed the 'double movement entailed in this marriage, which separates a sister from her brother and then returns her to his family to ensure, by ritual means, the continuation of the generations' (Jamous 2003: 186). In Tangu, the maternal uncle of a man who just married gave him a special mixture to drink in what we may call a fertility rite since, 'unless it was done the couple would be childless and unable to make good gardens' (Burridge 1958: 50). A similar interpretation could be made: a brother separated from his sister when she marries becomes responsible for the fertility of her son. Whatever the case, here too, temporality is an essential aspect of the relation between a brother and a sister, which makes impossible an analysis that does not simultaneously take account of the avuncular relationship.

Among the Ankave, the link to maternal kin is grounded in representations about procreation and intra-uterine growth that attribute an essential role to the mother. She is the only one who provides blood to the foetus, which makes it grow and generates its own blood. Throughout her pregnancy she therefore has to consume great amounts of red-pandanus juice – the main vegetal substitute for human blood – in order to increase the quantity of blood in her body.[5] These ideas imply that children have the same blood as their mother and maternal uncle, and that he does not transmit it to his own progeny.[6] That is why, when blood accidentally spills out, in ritual context or during a fight, the victim's mother's brother has to be compensated.

During infancy, brothers and sisters live together close to their mothers, as breastfeeding lasts around three years, but their activities soon diverge. Little girls join their mothers when they go to work in the gardens, helping them weed, collecting greens and sugar cane, and carrying small bamboo containers filled with water. Boys stay in the village by themselves and play. Compared to their sisters' lives, theirs are idle and carefree. Rather than being an effect of cross-siblingship, however, this situation conforms to the local sexual division of labour. Although there is some restriction in the expression of their mutual attachment, caring and fondness character-ize the relationship between brother and sister, and these sentiments are expressed symmetrically in daily life, which, as we shall see, is not the case at ritual moments.

During the 1994 initiation rituals, when her younger brother returned from a long stay in town, the old Maadzi welcomed him with a nostalgic song, and they stayed a long time with their heads bent over next to each other, holding hands. 'Affection names' may be used to address each other, and a sister may tease her brother that he has taken areca nuts from her netbag without asking, but she never gets annoyed with him.[7] Their respec-tive houses are always open to each other, and sisters regularly visit their brothers, staying with them as long as they want. If her brother visits her, she will serve him food before her husband. When, in 1990, Wia Kara had an attack of cerebral malaria, it was his sister rather than his wife who spent nights and days at his side until he recovered. A married woman beaten by her husband will find refuge at her brother's house, and to take his wife back home a violent man will have to give compensation of pork, game or even money to his brother-in-law. One day in June 1987, a man broke one of his wife's teeth after a violent quarrel and, following a village court, he had to give money to her brother who 'washed her blood'. Brothers are thus helping figures for women, and they are the ones who must be compensated when their sisters have been physically assaulted. Sisters also assist their brothers, but in quite another manner.

In order to marry, Ankave men must give bridewealth. This sum of money is given to the woman's parents, but is used for her brother to take a wife. For a man, then, having a sister, especially an older one, is a precious advan-tage since he has at his disposal the money (or at least part of it) given by a man to marry her. Conversely, a man who has only sons is in an awkward position because he cannot count on receiving bridewealth when a daughter marries to help his son take a wife. Similarly, a man with no sisters cannot dispose of the money he would have if he had one. He usually marries much later than those who do have sisters. Daughters are thus very welcome because, when they marry, money is brought into the family, which in turn redistributes it to help sons in their quest for a spouse. The contribution of sisters to the life of their brothers is not, however, limited to marriage; sisters also play an essential role at moments that are considered crucial for the growth and social maturation of men, and which are marked by rituals.

Rituals in a Man's Life

In effect, a man's life is punctuated by ritualized moments during which one of his sisters is deeply involved. The Ankave ritual cycle involves three phases: two are collective and are generally organized separately (at an interval of several months), but may also be performed immediately after one another, a proceeding that corroborates the impression that they are one and the same rite. Although each phase is given a different name, which designates the main ritual act to which the boys are subjected – 'perforation of the septum' (*itchema'a*) for the first phase, and 'rubbing with red-pandanus seeds' (*chemazi'ne*) for the second – these ceremonies, organized for a group of from twenty to thirty male children between the ages of 8 and 12, form a whole and are clearly different from the third and final rite.

In explanation of the two first stages of this ritual cycle, the Ankave say that it is, essentially, to allow boys to grow up – since they are not as lucky as girls, who mature without any outside help – and to make them strong and brave. We would tend to label these initiations 'rites of passage', during which children pass on to another phase of their development or into adulthood. In short, during the few weeks of men's ritual activity, a series of actions, behaviours and ways of living can be observed. They include action on the body (perforation of the septum, hitting, anointing, stretching, heating, cooling); physical ordeals (climbing a big tree, crossing a stream on a slippery log, going down narrow corridors lined with branches, running as fast as possible); psychological ordeals (sleep deprivation, death threats, lies, revelation of secrets); living in a group (sharing meals and nights in a small shelter, hunting in parties, fetching wood and water); instruction (on sharing, mutual aid, the code of ethics, proper behaviour for adult men – not crying, self-control, self-restraint, overcoming one's fear – and taboos); scenes to be watched (theatrical miming of primeval scenes, ritualized fights between men); and imposed behaviour and attitudes (crouching in line, keeping silent, keeping the head bowed).

The third and last stage revolves around one young man whose first child has just been born, and who has spent the entire period of his wife's pregnancy preparing for the event (respecting dietary taboos, being relatively inactive, wearing unusual clothing and looking different, and so on). It is called *tsewange'*, from the name of the head ornament he will be wearing on the day of the ritual. The people involved are specialists in the rituals, the young fathers who serve as ritual sponsors for the novice, and those men who wish to accompany them to the forest location where the ritual takes place. The rite instructs him in the last male secrets, and celebrates his procreative power as well as the emergence of a new parental couple.

In contrast to the male initiation of other Anga groups, among the Ankave women are not totally excluded from the rituals.[8] No woman enters the forest ritual space, but mothers and sisters have to be present in the village, and to respect a series of food taboos and behavioural restrictions in order for the ritual to go well. Throughout the period the initiates' septums are healing after having been pierced, their mothers are secluded in a large collective shelter built for the occasion; they are obliged to respect numerous daily behavioural constraints and food taboos, which, for the most part, are similar to those imposed on their sons in the bush. As I have shown elsewhere (Bonnemère 2008: 86; 2014), what is re-enacted here is the symbiotic relation between a mother and her child during pregnancy and the child's infancy. Reiterating this early relation is necessary for it to be transformed into another type of relation. This transformation takes place during the collective rituals, and is marked at their closure by a reciprocal exchange gesture: the boys give smoked small game (birds, rats) that they have hunted during their stay in the forest to their mothers, who reciprocate with cooked tubers. Now the relation between them is no longer symbiotic; it has become one in which exchange is possible between them.

The elder sisters of the boys (who ideally are not yet married) are not secluded as their mothers are, but they must respect two major food taboos: on eating red-pandanus juice and on chewing betel. They are the last ones to lift the taboos. The prohibition on red pandanus is automatically lifted the first time it is consumed again, while that on chewing betel is ritually cancelled. But while it is the newly initiated brother who gives his sister the areca nuts necessary for lifting the taboo, his mother had received them from the hands of the ritual expert. This difference may point to the fact that the ritual involvement of the boys' mothers has now come to an end, while that of their sisters will continue long after the collective stages of initiation are completed. Underlining their relationship through a ritual gesture made by the brothers to their sisters at the very moment the ceremonies are completed means that the sister's role does not stop here. She accompanies her brother while he undergoes the initiation ordeals; 'she helped him', as the

Ankave say, and she will accompany him again when his wife has his first child.[9] In short, to be married and become a father, a boy needs a sister to marry on account of the bridewealth given for her, and he needs a childless sister to act in the ritual of his first child.

As soon as the pregnancy is known, the parents of the father-to-be, together with his wife's parents, organize a big meal. This is the occasion for announcing to the young man that from this day on he will have to stop eating red-pandanus juice and game in general, as well as drinking water.[10] He is also no longer allowed to engage in the usual male activities such as making knots. The latter prohibition keeps him from building houses and fences, and from making bows, arrows and traps. One of his sisters also ceases to consume red-pandanus juice from this day on.

Their parents tell the young couple to make a special barkcloth called *ogidze*, which is dyed with red-pandanus juice, laid to dry in the sun and then folded and wrapped up for use some months later. Other barkcloths, ordinary ones this time, need to be made, and more quickly: two are for the father-to-be (one to wear over his head; the other, called *iZiare*, to be attached around his neck and let hang down to cover his buttocks); another is given to his unmarried elder sister and another to the mother-to-be. Lime must also be prepared for chewing betel after the birth, and to trade for vegetal salt with their Iqwaye neighbours.

When these ordinary capes are ready, the *tsewange'* ritual expert covers the head of the young man in a ritual performed in the forest. The pregnant woman and her husband's sister can put on their own capes themselves. For a man, wearing a bark cape in such a way, on the head, is so unusual that it is a sure sign that he is expecting his first child. He cannot take it off until his wife has given birth. His special appearance also indicates that he is in a taboo state, especially abstaining from red-pandanus juice. His wife can, and even must, consume it, in great quantities, since, as we have seen, their child feeds on it and its blood is made from it.

During the entire gestation of a man's first child, there are thus three persons who are united by the fact that each has received a new bark cape to wear in the same way and for the same period of time. They form a triad linked by special attitudes and taboos required from especially two of them, the father-to-be and his sister, that recall practices known as couvade (Bonnemère 2009: 221–22). Because the father-to-be is not the only one to be placed in a state of taboo, Ankave couvade practices could be appropriately termed a rite of co-parenthood, as Laura Rival, speaking of the Huaroni of Amazonia, calls it (Rival 1998: 631), rather than a paternity rite, as many anthropologists used to say. Moreover, the prohibitions that the expectant mother has to respect must be considered conjointly with those falling on the father-to-be and his sister: both abstain from eating foods that would become blood and cause the pregnant woman to haemorrhage, and they abstain from performing tasks which could prevent the foetus from coming out of her body. It is as though the father-to-be and his sister form a pair acting together in order to help the expectant mother deliver the child. The first-birth ritual is not only the third and last stage of male initiation, but also the moment when a new parental couple comes into being with the ritual support of the future father's sister.

The birth marks the beginning of a new period of ritual gestures and rules of conduct for the persons who were already involved during the pregnancy. First, a strict fast, including abstaining from water, red-pandanus juice and chewing betel, is imposed on both young parents for three days after the delivery. The only food the young mother can, and must, take is sugar-cane juice, since it makes her milk come in. In effect, the Ankave think that colostrum is a bad food for the newborn, and that it becomes good milk only after she has drunk this sweet juice. After the three days of fasting, the ritual expert gathers three special varieties of sugar cane, which he gives to the young father after having magically treated them. This will be his only 'meal' for two more days. Like the sugar cane given to the young mother, the three canes for the father have been collected by his sister from the married couple's garden.

Usually between four and eight days after the birth, a time during which the men have gone into the forest to catch marsupials, the *tsewange'* ritual takes place. Just before dawn on the chosen day, the grass shelter, where the young mother stayed, is destroyed by her mother in the presence of other kinswomen, and all then descend the path to the big river. The young mother washes in the running water, is rubbed with fragrant-smelling leaves by her sister, and finally puts on a new bark skirt. Once this has been done, all the women walk up to the village, not far from the place where the public phase of the ritual will be held. The young mother, her sister, her husband's sister and a woman whose husband has most recently gone through the *tsewange'* ritual hide in some high grasses and talk softly.[11] This will go on for a few hours, during which other women finish preparing a big meal of various species of tubers.

Once the male part of the ritual has taken place, the whole line of men leaves the forest and walks down to the hamlet, handsomely adorned, each having attached to his forehead a band of the *ogidze* bark piece that the father-to-be prepared during his wife's pregnancy.[12] The young father heads the line, carrying a long pole (*me'wa*) that a companion has cut for him. Tied to it are shell ornaments and braided necklaces for his wife. The new mother, together with the wife of the man accompanying her husband during the male ritual and her husband's sister, slowly crawl or walk bent over as they emerge from their hiding place.[13] Things are organized so that the men and women arrive at the same time and gather in the centre of the plaza where the public phase of the ritual will soon take place (Bonnemère and Lemonnier 2007: 170).

When the women are seated, the ritual expert takes the *me'wa* pole brought by the young father and gives the ornaments to the new mother. Her husband, or another man, chops the pole into long, thin pieces, which he plants in the ground in a circle within which he soon places even thinner pieces. The expert then sets fire to the base of this small structure with a bamboo torch. Afterwards, he offers areca nuts to the wife and to the husband's sister, who sits next to her. Both lift the taboo while chewing betel, spitting first into the fire. The marsupials that have been caught and gathered for this day are cooked in a bark wrapper or in an earth oven, after having been singed over the *me'wa* fire. One of the marsupials, a *tse' arma'* if available – because it grows fast – is prepared by the two sisters of the new parents, that is to say the mother's sister and the father's sister. The ashes from the fur mixed together with yellow-orange earth (*omoxe'*) and a bit of water are rubbed onto the newborn by its maternal grandmother. The baby is then quickly passed over the flames, while the old woman whispers a magical formula, 'to heat the bones', the Ankave say.

The *tse' arma'* is cut up by the two sisters, who cannot eat it because it goes entirely to the mother. The young father's sister distributes the other marsupials to all the other women and to their very young children, with the exception of herself and the newborn's paternal grandmother. For the father's sister or mother to eat some of the marsupials would be like eating their own brother or son, since all share the same blood. The day ends with everybody eating the taro and sweet potatoes that were cooked in great quantities during the morning.

To recapitulate: the transformation of the symbiotic relationship between a woman and her son during the collective phases of the initiation rituals is the first essential act of the process in which, eventually, he becomes a father. Crucially, his sister too has to intervene ritually, first when he is still a boy, but in a minor mode, and much more strongly when her brother is expecting his first child. At that time she has to respect the same taboos – on eating red-pandanus sauce and on chewing betel – as those imposed during the collective rituals, thus associating herself with the father-to-be, in order that they may act as a pair in protecting the pregnant woman from haemorrhage when giving birth.

The first-birth ritual celebrates a man's new status as a father and a new parental couple, but it is more than this, I suggest, for this ritual is also preparing a man to become a maternal uncle. This is why his sister has to be present, for she will be the one who, in having children, will permit her brother to attain this highly valued position. For the Ankave, to be a maternal uncle is to be endowed with a capacity to act for related people – a capacity that women have spontaneously, as it were. A man acquires this capacity through a long, gradual process, which transforms the relationships he has with the two most closely related women in his life: his mother and one of his adult but still-childless sisters. Becoming a maternal uncle and thus being able to act on and for, and sometimes against, the children of his sister is the culminating point of a man's life. But what exactly does it mean to be a maternal uncle?

Being a Maternal Uncle

As noted above, individuals have the same blood as their mother, her siblings, and their own siblings by her; it follows that they and their mother's brother share blood. For this reason, maternal kin in general, and the maternal uncle in particular as the main representative of this group, are considered responsible for the well-being of uterine kin, for their physical development and fertility. This protective behaviour manifests itself during initiations: a mother's brother is his nephew's 'partner of pain' (Herdt 2004: 25); he carries him on his back when he has to go through the rebirth corridor made of branches and is beaten by the men. When his niece's breasts begin to grow, he puts some earth on them to speed their maturation.

So, when all goes well, that is when the father of a child makes the gifts that are due to the maternal kin (see below), good health, growth, and fertility are guaranteed. But maternal relatives have to be looked after continuously: a sister's children will never, for instance, pronounce their mother's brother's name for fear that he will be offended and so make the child lose weight by cursing them. Similarly, one never speaks too loudly when he is present. Even though no embarrassment characterizes their relationship – one may ask a maternal uncle for areca nuts, food or land without him being able to refuse – one must conduct oneself properly in respect of him because his protection can easily turn into a power of destruction. If a maternal uncle feels he does not receive enough from the man who married his sister and from that man's group, and therefore thinks his benevolent acts are not sufficiently acknowledged, he can send curses towards his nephews and nieces.

Here follow some brief examples of relations with the maternal uncle as expressed in daily life. One day, under the shelter where we used to cook food, Kia'uni, her brother and her children were chatting without any restraint because, I was told, the children's father was absent. In another case, the eldest son of a widow chose to live with his maternal uncle when his mother decided to remarry and take her two youngest children with her. Or again, the only child of a woman who was recently widowed chose to live with his mother's brother, considered him as his father and called him

'Daddy'. The affection that one man felt for his maternal uncle moved him to ask people to call him 'Paul', the first name of his mother's brother.[14] Samuel prepared lime, a lengthy and demanding task, for his maternal uncle, who had asked him for some. More generally, the children of a man who in the past opened a garden on the land of his maternal uncle can also use it, which means that one of them can inherit some of the land. The brother of a woman may also give land to his sister's son, even if he has children himself.

The relation that everybody has with their maternal uncle is thus very close. The situation described at the beginning of the chapter, and the comment made by Michael, a maternal uncle, leads me to suggest that this bond is almost of a filial kind. Michael succeeded in getting his little niece to swallow her medicine because he is the one who, together with his sister, suffered when she was born. He adds that he was thus the beneficiary of *Simo'e* and *tuage'* gifts – prestations people owe to their maternal kin, especially during their infancy, and which continue until initiation for boys and until marriage for girls.

Some gifts are made for all children, the firstborn having a special status associated with more specific prestations.[15] When a child begins to crawl, their father brings a piece of pork or cooked game and offers it to the oldest of his brothers-in-law, who will share it with the child's other maternal kin; this is the *miaru'wa* gift. A second prestation of pork or game, called *noZe nangwen'*, is made by the father of a child, usually after their maternal uncle has indirectly requested it, in other words after he has remarked that his nephew or niece has grown well. In saying this, he is asserting his role in the child's development, and when such a sentence is pronounced, the gift is as much to prevent a negative action as it is to compensate a positive one on the part of the mother's brother. He and his group consider that having received the *miaru'wa* gift several years earlier is not enough to thank them for having aided the growth of a sister's children. Such disguised claims may be made several times in respect of a particular child.

Another mandatory prestation is called *Simo'e*. It is a male pig, which is given raw after a boy has gone through the collective phases of the initiations. It is cooked by the maternal uncle, who receives and shares it with all his brothers and sisters. Some Ankave comment on this gift by referring to the help of the maternal aunts and uncles in preparing the boy's adornments, while others speak about the blood that was spilled by the novice when he was beaten with cassowary quills during the rituals. As we know, this blood is the same as that which circulates in the bodies of the mother's brothers and sisters. Whatever the reason given, the *Simo'e* gift is the last of those prestations linked to a child's growth that are made to the maternal kin. It is the only one that is marked by a counter-gift, a mother-of-pearl shell called *memia'*, which the young initiate will wear as a necklace. When all these gifts have been made, a boy has reached an important stage of his life: he has grown up and is less at risk than during his infancy of becoming the victim of malevolent actions on the part of his maternal kin. Another period of his existence will start when he becomes a father himself, and has to make gifts to his brother-in-law to ensure the well-being of his own children.

In the case of a girl, the *Simo'e* gift is the first of the marriage prestations called *tuage'*; her parents always bring it to one of her mother's brothers, who will share it with his siblings and give his niece a female piglet in return. This is the *potije'* gift, which the girl may dispose of as she likes; in particular, she can keep the money obtained when the pig, once grown, is killed and its meat sold. This piglet is usually the first in a long series of pigs that every married woman raises. It is said that the *Simo'e* gift will help a woman to get along with her husband. Finally, if a uterine nephew or niece dies young, their maternal uncle receives either a small amount of money after the funeral or a piece of eel when the ritual marking the end of the mourning period is organized, a year or two after the death.

So, the maternal kin, wife-givers, are the main beneficiaries of the gifts that are made throughout a person's life. For a man to become a maternal uncle is a long and gradual process in which his sister plays a major role, not only because she will bear his nephews and nieces, but also because she must be present in person when he goes through the rituals during which, among other things, his relationships with his mother and with his sister are transformed. The sister is an essential figure for her brother because she is the one who makes him a maternal uncle, a most powerful status in the Ankave world, one that can confer fertility on people but which can also be used to cause death.

Notes

1. The *Simo'e* and *tuage'* gifts are, respectively, the entire pig that is given to the maternal uncle at the initiation of his uterine nephew, and the pork or game that is regularly given by a man and his group to the parents of his spouse over the course of their marriage. The brother of the mother of the bride always receives the first *tuage'* gift.

2. Karembola men of Madagascar similarly describe 'their sister's son as "born from their own belly", "as crying for their breast"' (Middleton 2000: 112).

3. Certain demographic phenomena nevertheless make it hard to respect exogamy in every clan. Notably, some members of the Idzadze clan, which accounts for 50 per cent of the total population, find it hard to avoid inter-marriage (Bonnemère 1996: 84).

4. I refer to 'his' first child since the ritual is performed even if his wife has already had a child from a previous marriage. Conversely, if a man with

children remarries a young childless woman, the ritual is not done when she becomes pregnant because he already went through it in the past.

5. The juice of the red pandanus is a prized food, obtained by cooking the big pandanus fruit and pressing its seeds. It is usually consumed as a sauce, which is poured over sweet potato and taro during collective meals.

6. Patrilineal transmission is not described using an idiom of 'blood'. The analysis of the myth relating how the sexes were pierced would seem to suggest that the source of children's spirits (denge') is their fathers' semen (Bonnemère 1996: 243); what are surely transferred in the agnatic line are rights to land. Cf. Poole's account of the transmission in semen of the clan finiik or agnatic spirit of the Bimin Kuskusmin (Poole 1981).

7. What I call 'affection names' are terms of address that differ according to gender and to the mother's clan affiliation; accordingly, all men whose mothers are from the same clan are called by the same 'affection name'. These names are used in contexts of food sharing or when people have not met each other for a long time. They express care and love. Husbands and wives never use these names to address each other (Bonnemère 1996: 146–47).

8. The Ankave belong to a set of groups called Anga, whose 80,000 or so members speak twelve related languages (Lemonnier 1981). Well-known Angans in the anthropological literature are the Sambia (Herdt 1981, 1987), the Baruya (Godelier 1986), the Iqwaye (Mimica 1988) and the Kamea (Bamford 1997).

9. See note 4.

10. He can drink water found in tree holes as well as sugar-cane juice.

11. The man who was most recently initiated will be the ritual sponsor of the young father during the tsewange' ritual held secretly in the forest.

12. For a brief description of what happens during the male part of the ritual, see Bonnemère (2009: 225–26).

13. Not much is known about this posture: for some women it evokes their position during their seclusion for the collective stages of initiation, when they cannot stand up and must spend their time sitting or crawling inside the collective house erected for the occasion.

14. All Ankave have local names (Bonnemère 2005), but more and more often they also have a biblical name, either after having been baptized or through their own choice.

15. The gifts made for a first child number four: the first, the dzilu'wa, is given when the pregnancy is announced, the other ones when the baby is born. The gift called xenej onanengo' ('to please the maternal aunt') is made to the sisters of the new mother, and consists of one of the marsupials caught after the birth. The gift nie'wa Su'wa ('to show the child') is given to the maternal grandmother of the baby for having rubbed some omoxe' earth on the newborn's body and transmitted this knowledge to her daughter.

References

Bamford, S. 1997. 'The Containment of Gender: Embodied Sociality among a South Angan People', Ph.D. diss. Charlottesville: University of Virginia.

Bénéï, V. 1997. 'De l'importance de la relation frère-sœur au Maharashtra (Inde)', *L'Homme* 141: 25–54.

Bonnemère, P. 1996. *Le pandanus rouge: corps, différence des sexes et parenté chez les Ankave-Anga, Papouasie-Nouvelle-Guinée*. Paris: Éditions du CNRS/ Éditions de la Maison des Sciences de l'Homme.

―――― 2005. 'Why Should Everyone Have a Different Name? Clan and Gender Identity among the Ankave-Anga of Papua New Guinea', in S. Tcherkézoff and F. Douaire-Marsaudon (eds), *The Changing South Pacific: Identities and Transformations*. Canberra: Pandanus Books.

―――― 2008. 'Du corps au lien: l'implication des mères dans les initiations masculines des Ankave-Anga', in I. Théry and P. Bonnemère (eds), *Ce que le genre fait aux personnes*. Paris: Éditions de l'EHESS.

―――― 2009. 'Making Parents: First-birth Ritual among the Ankave-Anga of Papua New Guinea', *Australian Religion Studies Review* 22(2): 214–36.

―――― 2014. 'A Relational Approach to a Papua New Guinea Male Ritual Cycle', *Journal of the Royal Anthropological Institute* 20(4).

Bonnemère, P., and P. Lemonnier. 2007. *Les tambours de l'oubli: la vie ordinaire et cérémonielle d'un peuple forestier de Papouasie/Drumming to Forget: Ordinary Life and Ceremonies among a Papua New Guinea Group of Forest-Dwellers*. Pirae/Paris: Au Vent des Îles/Musée du Quai Branly.

Burridge, K.O.L. 1958. 'Marriage in Tangu', *Oceania* 29(1): 44–61.

―――― 1959. 'Siblings in Tangu', *Oceania* 30(2): 128–54.

Godelier, M. 1986 [1982]. *The Making of Great Men: Male Domination and Power among the New Guinea Baruya*. Cambridge: Cambridge University Press.

Herdt, G.H. 1981. *Guardians of the Flutes: Idioms of Masculinity*. New York: Mcgraw-Hill.

―――― 1987. *The Sambia: Ritual and Gender In New Guinea*. New York: Holt, Rinehart and Winston.

―――― 2004. 'Sambia Women's Positionality and Men's Rituals', in P. Bonnemère (ed.), *Women as Unseen Characters: Male Ritual in Papua New Guinea*. Philadelphia: University of Pennsylvania Press.

Jamous, R. 2003 [1991]. *Kinship and Rituals among the Meo of Northern India: Locating Sibling Relationships*. Oxford: Oxford University Press.

Lemonnier, P. 1981. 'Le commerce inter-tribal des Anga de Nouvelle-Guinée', *Journal de la Société des Océanistes*, 37: 39–75.

Middleton, K. 2000. 'How Karembola Men Become Mothers', in J. Carsten (ed.), *Cultures of Relatedness: New Approaches to the Study of Kinship*. Cambridge: Cambridge University Press.

Mimica, J. 1988. *Intimations of Infinity: The Mythopoeia of the Iqwaye Counting System and Number*. Oxford: Berg.

Pauwels, S. 1990. 'La relation frère-sœur et la temporalité dans une société d'Indonésie de l'Est', *L'Homme* 116: 7–29.

Poole, F.J.P. 1981. 'Transforming "Natural" Woman: Female Ritual Leaders and Gender Ideology among Bimin-Kuskusmin', in S.B. Ortner and H. Whitehead (eds), *Sexual Meanings: The Cultural Construction of Gender and Sexuality*. New York: Cambridge University Press.

Rival, L. 1998. 'Androgynous Parents and Guest Children: The Huaorani Couvade', *Journal of the Royal Anthropological Institute* 4(4): 619–42.

7

The *Vasu* Position and the Sister's *Mana*

The Case of Lau, Fiji

◆●◆

Simonne Pauwels

> [I]n the days of the late chief, one lady could sit higher than Tui Nayau and speak
> loud in his presence because her mother was his elder sister.
> —A.M. Hocart, *Lau Islands, Fiji*

The position or office of *vasu*[1] in Fiji has been described and analysed many times (e.g. Wilkes 1845; Hocart 1915, 1923, 1926, 1929; Thompson 1940; Sahlins 1962, 1981; Williams 1982: 34–37; Hooper 2004).[2] It is founded in kinship in the sense that it refers to the relationship between a sister's child or children, who are said to be *vasu*, and their mother's brother(s). Where it is most meaningful, however, it does not involve just the brother and the sister's child, but all the people on the mother's brother's side and all those on the side of the father's sisters' children. 'All the people' is a more or less inclusive term, for its reference depends both on the status of the mother and her brothers and on that of the father, as well as on the importance of the event which brings them together and during which the *vasu* fulfil their function. The higher the protagonists' status, the more inclusive will be the group of reference, the largest being the chiefdom (*vanua*) of a high chief. When a person is spoken of as being *vasu*, the *vanua* ('place', 'land', 'people') to which they are *vasu* is always specified. They are said to be '*vasu* to Vuanirewa', where Vuanirewa is the name of the ruling clan of the Lau chiefdom, or 'to

Lakeba' or even 'to Tonga'. A *vasu* has the right to seize the property of his mother's people; the verb used is *vasuta*. This property excludes the mother's people's houses and wives, but it would seem that certain important *vasu* could sometimes even set their heart on a married woman.[3]

I begin by considering the kin relations in which the *vasu* is implicated in order to show how the efficacy of the *vasu* relation extends well beyond them. As will become clear, an examination of the sister's position, and particularly that of the eldest sister, illuminates the *vasu*'s supremacy over their maternal uncle, even if the latter is a paramount chief. A brief complementary analysis of certain rituals reveals the importance here of ideas about fertility. Finally, I show how in the chiefdom of the Lau islands the *vasu* position is the link which makes it possible to give meaning to the relationship between the high chief, *turaga levu*, the *Sau* or *Tui* title holder, who comes from the outside (Sahlins 1981), and the 'people of the land', *vanua*. We need to know that it is the 'mutual facing' (*veiqaravi*) of these two groups, which, in the Lau islands, is the foundation of society. As Steven Hooper writes: 'The idiom of mutuality (*vei-*) and facing (*qara*) pervades Lauan/Fijian language and social and ritual practice. The importance of complementary interactive partnerships and of mutual obligation is constantly emphasized' (Hooper 2004: 245).

My analysis here, which is based on the history of the founding of the present-day chiefdom in the Lau islands and in contemporary ethnography, explains how the *vasu* doubly represents the collectivity: as *vasu taukei* in relations inside the *vanua*, and as *vasu levu* in relations between one *vanua* and another. In both cases, sisters are of the first importance, to the *vasu taukei* as sisters of the 'people of the land' (*i taukei ni vanua*) and to the *vasu levu* as sisters of chiefs (*turaga*).

Here it is important to note, firstly, that what is valid in Lau may not be valid elsewhere in Fiji. Even in the Lau archipelago, differences can be noticed according to origin, rank, village or island. Some of these can also be explained by Tongan influence. The data discussed here were by and large collected on the chiefly island of Lakeba, which, at one point in its history (the early nineteenth century), had at least two Tongan villages with several hundred inhabitants. Secondly, not only men are *vasu*, women are too, even if Hocart writes that 'the term is never applied to a woman' (Hocart 1929: 40), a point of view shared by Williams (1982: 34). In Lau, the sister's children hold the *vasu* position as they do in many other places in Fiji (e.g. Toren 1990: 55–56, 85; 1994). As will become clear below, an analysis of all the relations linking two pairs of opposite-sex siblings connected by marriage illuminates the *vasu* phenomenon. I turn now to a description of these relations as they are evinced in daily interaction and in certain rituals.

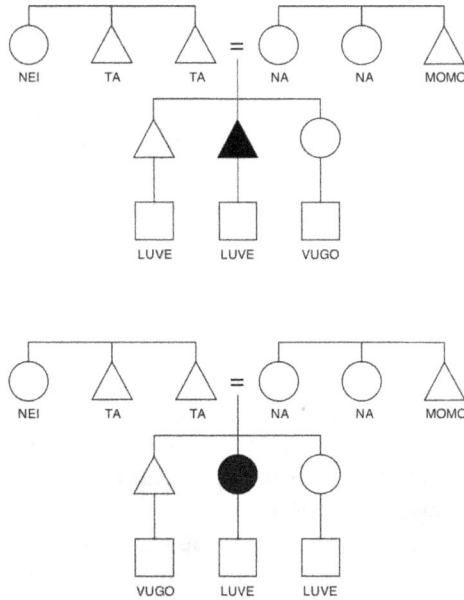

Figure 7.1: Dravidian aspects in the terminology

The kinship terminology is Dravidian (see Figure 7.1). The maternal uncle is distinguished from the father and the father's brother, the paternal aunt is distinguished from the mother and her sister, and the children of opposite-sex siblings are distinguished from the children of same-sex siblings. The early ethnography of the Lau islands described the preferred marriage as one between the children of a brother and sister. 'Marriage of a man with his cross cousin, that is the daughter of his mother's brother, or the daughter of his father's sister, is preferred, and he may joke and have sexual intercourse with his female relatives in this category' (Thompson 1940: 43). Since the mid twentieth century, however, this marriage has been considered as being 'too close because of the brother and sister', that is to say, because of the opposite-sex sibling relationship in the parents' generation.[4] Today, the most encouraged form of marriage is found two generations below, that is between the great-grandchildren of a brother and sister. Even so, an important mark of marriage between cross-cousins still exists: the father-in-law of a man and a woman is called by the same term as the mother's brother and the father's sister's husband (*momo*), and the mother-in-law is called by the same term as the father's sister and the mother's brother's wife (*nei*). But Dravidian terminology does not only divide people into kin one may marry and kin one may not marry; it also distinguishes between same-sex and opposite-sex relationships.

Sisters and Brothers and their Offspring

In Lau, a brother and sister each has two terms to use in reference to their opposite sex sibling – *ganequ* and *wekaqu*. There is a difference in the way the two are understood. *Gane* denotes only the relation between 'a real brother and a real sister', biological brothers and sisters and opposite-sex children of same-sex siblings. *Weka* may refer to the opposite-sex grand-children or great-grandchildren of same-sex siblings (see Figure 7.2). The word *weka* is generally said 'to carry the *tabu*', and, as an informant spec-ified: 'When somebody is said to be your *weka* you are reminded that it's your sister where you were likely to forget or had never been told. *Weka* is a warning word'.

Veitabui, 'tabu (forbidden) to each other', an expression that is used all over Fiji, seems to be used rarely in Lakeba. At a more inclusive level, all kin – that is to say, anyone to whom you can trace a bloodline – are *vei-wekani*, 'kin to one another, related'.

The term *vasu* is not used to denote the relation between a man and his sister's children; they are *veivugoni*, *vugo* being the term used to designate the child of an opposite-sex sibling. A man and his sister's children and a woman and her brother's children are *vugo* to one another (see Figure 7.3). The mother's brother is called *momo*, as is the father's sister's husband,

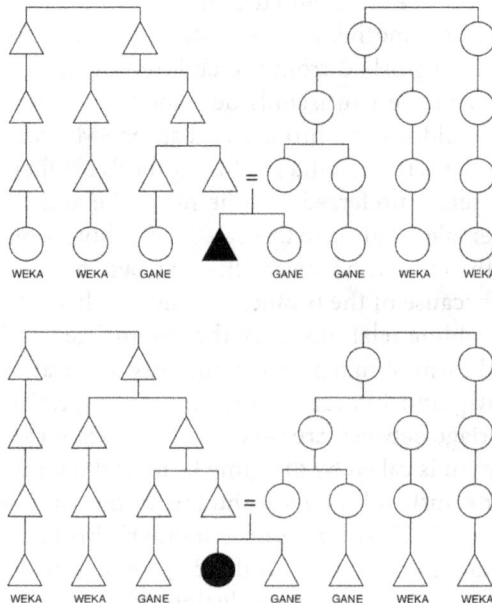

Figure 7.2: The *gane* and *weka* relationships

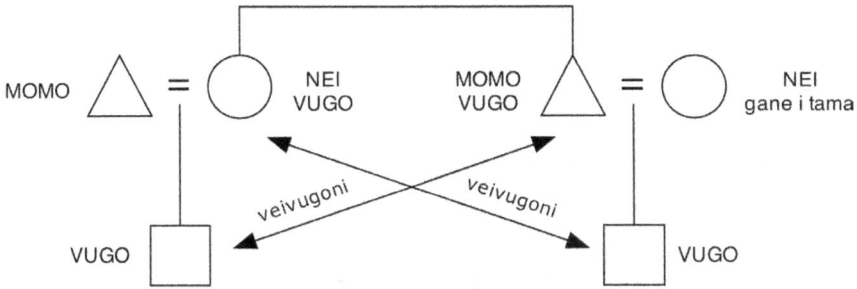

Figure 7.3: The *vugo* relationship

and the father's sister is called *nei*, as is the mother's brother's wife. But the mother's brother's wife can also be called *gane i tama* or literally 'sister of father', giving a hint that the term *nei* is predominant on the sister's side: the wife of my mother's brother is like my father's sister.

The relationship terms between the children of a brother and sister are best illustrated through an examination of two brother and sister pairs linked by marriage, as in Figure 7.4. There are two terms to differentiate same-sex cross-cousins, one for a man (*tavale*) and one for a woman (*dauve*), though some people no longer use *dauve*, having replaced it with *tavale*. There is only one term for opposite-sex cross-cousins, *davola*, but Ego can also, jokingly, call them *wati*, which means spouse. Cross-cousins are distinguished from same-sex siblings and parallel-cousins (which is not the case in Tongan or Samoan terminology). The mother's brother is not, however, differentiated from the father's sister's husband; neither

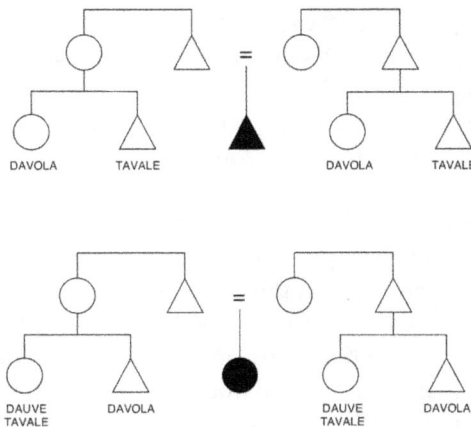

Figure 7.4: Cross-cousin terminology

are his children differentiated from the father's sister's children. Clearly kinship terminology alone cannot tell us a great deal about the *vasu* phenomenon.

Interaction between Opposite-Sex Siblings and the Mana of the Sister

Since Hocart's time, the relationship between brother and sister seems to have changed somewhat. Nowadays, at home, when they are adults but still single, biological brothers and sisters can stay in the same room together. Even though they are not supposed to, they can speak to each other, but jokingly. They cannot wear each other's clothes, and a sister cannot do her brother's laundry. In fact, boys contrive not to be in the house. Avoidance is much stronger between classificatory brothers and sisters. A bachelor will not come into the house when a classificatory sister, whom he calls *weka*, is present. Once married, biological brothers and sisters can no longer speak to each other. A brother will only come into his sister's house if his brother-in-law has invited him to drink *yaqona*.[5] If a sister visits her brother's house, she will speak to her sister-in-law to communicate with her brother. Her brother, if present, will not look at her but 'count the plaits of the mat'; he is embarrassed to be there. But for every ritual organized by his sister (marriages, the firstborn child's birthday, the eldest child's twenty-first birthday, funerals), the brother will come with taro, a pig and so on to cook at his sister's place. At Christmas, he will make a point of giving the children of the house fish and taro to take to his sister's. Such gifts are called *cokonaki*, 'food for a special day'. Sisters also receive the first fruit from their brothers' gardens. In the garden, there is a special mound for them, just as there is for the chief, the church and, sometimes, for the owner of the land and so forth. These gifts of first fruits are all called *i sevu*.

For a woman, her brother is somebody to lean on, someone who can help her when she has problems. Or, as an informant summarized it: 'He comes in with her food on every occasion. Her husband looks after her in the house, but when there is a function (*soqo*) it's her brother, not her husband. If the brother is not there, there will be a lot of gossip. The sister will be very quiet and pity herself'. A sister will also go to her brother's house if there is a ceremony, but she will go empty-handed, 'because it is her house'. If she has a good relationship with her brother, she will go to every ceremony in his house, but she will make him wait for her, knowing that nothing can start without her. 'She's the big boss here, not the brother's wife; she has to fade away'. It is quite usual to see the wife working in the kitchen while her sister-in-law sits in the house giving orders and welcoming the visitors with their gifts. Her husband and her children prepare taro and a pig for her brother, but they do it on the children's behalf, 'to show the mother's brother that they are good *vasu*'. I return to this later. An important difference between brother and sister appears here. When a man plants taro, he says, 'it's for my sister'; when a woman plaits a mat, she does not say, 'it's for my brother', she says, 'it's for the birth/marriage of my brother's child (*vugo*)'.

To have no sister or brother is to be *daku lala* ('with an empty back'), or without back-up so to speak. That is why parents without a daughter or a son take in somebody else's child, so that their children can learn how to be cross-sex siblings. After a few years, the child will return to its parents. A real sister is called *i coricori ni salusalu*, 'the stringer of the garland', the one who makes the garland for her brother. When the sister makes the garland for her brother, she attracts other people's esteem. Like the garland, she is his source of pride. One man told me that, since he has no sister, he has never worn a garland in his life, and that he felt pitiful or wretched (*vaka-loloma*, without *loloma*, 'love').

The eldest child, boy or girl, has a special position. To be the firstborn (*ulumatua*) means to be the only one of a kind and to remain so. That is why the eldest is the only subject of many rituals: the only one to have a first birthday party, a twenty-first birthday party, a big marriage feast and so on. As a friend said:

> Everything is done to the eldest, because he or she is the eldest. If you do it for the next one also, he can say to his elder sibling, 'we are the same'. And that is unthinkable! Everybody has to listen to the eldest. The other siblings, all the others, are basket carriers (*i colocolo ni kato*). The eldest must look after the siblings who follow and they must serve the eldest.

In Lau, not everybody would say, as in Tonga, that every sister is higher than her brothers, but even so one often hears remarks like, 'Every sister is not an elder sister, but . . .'. and there are households in which even the younger sister is looked upon as an elder sister. An examination of the situation of eldest sisters – that is to say, women who are the firstborn of a set of siblings – throws light on the position of *vasu*. The case of the sister who is *ulumatua* (eldest of a sibling set) is a special one. Elder sisters in general are distinguished, as is shown by the following example from Hocart: 'in the days of the late chief, one Lady could sit higher than Tui Nayau and speak loud in his presence because her mother was his elder sister' (Hocart 1929: 52). The reader is asked to keep this example in mind because it mentions two women – the chief's *vasu* and the chief's elder sister, both apparently superior to him.

One of the marriage rituals, called *vakamamaca* ('making dry' or 'putting on dry clothes after getting wet'), is also called 'drying of the tears'. It is performed by the bridegroom's sisters, especially the eldest, in order to tell the bride not to worry, not to cry. She is presented with a mat, cloth, *masi*[6] and oil and acknowledged in the following words: 'You came in swimming, your feet are not yet dry, you cry because you've left your parents, but don't worry, you're welcome'. The mat is for the bride to stand on while she rubs the foreign soil from her feet so that it falls onto the mat. The *masi* and the cloth are for drying the foreign water, the oil to make her smell like Lakeba. As an informant told me, 'This carries a lot of meaning'. Its implication is that an eldest sister can very easily let her sister-in-law be cast off if she does not agree with the marriage. Even after this ritual has been performed, the couple will be under the watchful eye of the eldest sister. She can try to break up the marriage if she thinks her sister-in-law does not take proper care of her brother. She can put a curse on her and say to her face, 'don't expect children'. An eldest sister has the right to say such things and to bring about ill effects because 'the *mana*, good or bad, is with the firstborn'.[7] When a young couple is childless after a few years of marriage, they will send somebody to ask the sister if she has cursed them. If so, forgiveness will be asked with the gift of a whale's tooth in the ceremony called *ibulubulu*.[8] In the case of continuing conflict, it is usually the unmarried eldest sister who stays in the house and her brother and his wife who leave.

When the brother has offspring, this is regarded as evidence of a good relationship between him and his eldest sister. As father's sister to the newborn baby, she will bring a special mat for the child; she will also fish for the mother in order to feed the child. It is she who is said to give her brother's children the most respectful love and care; she is sometimes compared to the grandmother. When her brother's children come to her house, she will do everything to make them feel comfortable. She gives them all the love and attention she cannot show her brother. If a father is very angry with one of his children, the only safe place for the child is its father's sister's house, even if she is a younger sister, for the brother cannot go to her place, cannot be angry in front of her; if a child is sitting beside its father's sister, the father is 'out of order'. In such a case, the child becomes almost like the sister, and the sister always has the last word; at one point in a conflict, she will say to her brother's child, 'You can go home now and I don't want to hear any more about this'.

All this is a matter of *mana*. A father's sister, and even more so a father's eldest sister, has *vosa mana*, 'words that are *mana*', or 'effective speech': what she says will happen. It is even worse when she does not utter the words, but only thinks them. Some translate *vosa mana* as 'prophecy'. Chiefs have *vosa mana*, as do parents and grandparents, but among kin, the father's eldest sister has the highest, the strongest *vosa mana*. Even the gift of a whale's tooth cannot always appease her. Indeed, the underlying idea is that it is not she the whale's tooth has to coax but the ancestors and the gods who make her words *mana*.[9]

The eldest sister's *mana* is described as giving the power of life and death, a power that confers high status on her children as *vasu* to their mother's brother, their mother's people, their mother's village of origin or even, if their mother is the sister of a high chief, the whole chiefdom. As one informant put it: '*Vasu* is a one-sided thing, only because of your mother. It's the sister who produces the *vasu*'. And it is the sister's *mana*, which comes from the ancestors and the gods, that gives sister's children a high status.[10]

Proper recognition by the mother's brother and his people of the sister's children as *vasu* requires that they themselves be acknowledged in ritual by the sister's husband and his people. If the ritual of *vakalutulutu* is not performed, the mother's brother can act as if he does not to know his sister's children, and they will not be allowed to come to his home or his village. *Vakalutulutu* means 'to fall from a height', and was described to me as 'dropping your child like a parachute with everything you bring'; the other name of the ceremony is *kau mata ni gone*, 'bringing the face of the children' to the mother's brother or mother's people. Usually it is performed only for the eldest child of an eldest sister. That day, the father and his people bring the child swathed in barkcloth and a lot of valuables to the mother's brother's house or village. The person carrying the child on his shoulders puts it down on a mat in front of the mother's brother. This gesture tells the people present that the child is of higher status, as does the amount of valuables. The father and his people have to give as much as possible because, 'the more you lose, the higher you are; my child is higher than you, that's why I bring a lot'. The mother's brother and his people also make gifts, as provisions for the guests' journey home, but there will be fewer of them for 'it should not be an exchange, otherwise we become equal again'. What is important to notice here is that if the sister is the highest, her children will be high too, but not without the assistance of their father's side. But, even though it is the father and his people who present the child and the valuables, it is said in the end that it is the mother who presents her child. Once this is done, the child is *vasu i taukei*, native *vasu*, to his or her mother's brother's house, village or *yavusa*, the largest origin group, and from now on can come freely and exercise *vasu* rights, taking what he or she wants without asking in the uncle's house or garden.[11]

Taking without Stealing

Hocart called this taking without asking 'seizing' or even 'stealing' (Hocart 1915, 1923, 1926), but the latter is clearly too strong. Take the example of the *fono*, which as far as I know is of Tongan origin (Hocart 1915: 640; Rogers 1977: 168–69; Biersack 1982: 200–1). The *fono* is the first part cut from the biggest pig of the *burua*, the last funeral meal consisting of the food cooked in all the ovens (*lovo*) by close kin, or brought uncooked by those who are less closely related and who have presented themselves to those drinking the funeral *yaqona* so as to be known again and to 'strengthen the blood ties'. The *fono* is the pig's belly – the part most cooked as it was touching the stones in the earth oven. This portion is then laid in front of the drinker of the first cup in the kava circle. This person is always the highest-ranking member of the group, the highest in the chiefly line. Once the *fono* is in front of him, as his status is too high for him to do it himself, his spokesman will shout '*Fono!*' This word offers the *fono* 'to whoever is ready to take it'. Many people in the gathering will look at each other trying to ascertain who among them is the first drinker's highest *vasu*. Sometimes two or three people will rush for the *fono* at the same time. Those who were absent will ask 'who ate the *fono*?' or 'who *vasuta*?' And there will always be continuing discussion and gossip about the legitimacy of the *vasu* who took it. In fact, the point of these discussions is to find out who was the highest *vasu* present. This can be the eldest child of the first drinker's eldest sister, but it can also be the eldest child of his father's, or even great-grandfather's and so on, eldest sister if this person is of higher rank – that is to say, if this person has a very high status not only because they are the descendant of an eldest sister, but also because this eldest sister was of chiefly status, for example, the descendants of the eldest sister of a high chief of Lau who married the high chief of Bau, the highest ranking chiefdom in Fiji. In such a case, the *vasu* will not run to get the *fono*, but will walk to it and just touch it to claim it, and some other *vasu* will bring it to him or her. It is only after the *fono* has been touched that the portion of the pig to be given to the high chief (*yaco*) is carved and brought to his house and the 'leftovers' shared out. A lot of ink has been spilled over the question of whether the *fono* is the ancestors' or the gods' portion or not. As they are Christians, nobody in Lakeba today would say this sponta-neously, but I believe I have gathered enough evidence to be able to say so. The ancestors and gods are with the sister and her children; they are the seat of their *mana* and the recipients of their share of the gifts or sacrifices. One informant told me: 'It doesn't look good when the first cup-drinker sits for a while with the *fono* in front of him, with no *vasu* to take it, because it looks as if he has no *weka*'. The reader will recall that the first meaning of *weka* is, for a man, 'sister'; only secondly does it refer to all his kin. My informant's remark suggests that when a man has to sit for a while with the *fono* in front of him, untaken, it implies that such a man's words are not *mana*.

As the ritual is performed today, it does not accord with Hocart's use of the word 'stealing'. The *fono* is offered by the highest-ranking person present to his highest *vasu* as a personification of the gods and ancestors and of their *mana*, although it may look like stealing when two or more *vasu* run to get it. To strengthen his argument, Hocart also mentions the fact that the *vasu*, having stolen the offering, is beaten by his uncle's sons (*tavale*), but he adds, 'at the same time [there is] good humour with which the cousins insult and rough-handle one another for there is no hostility on either side' (Hocart 1923: 11–12; see also 1915: 642). In other words, the beating is mutual. The picture is not of someone stealing and getting a beating for it, but of someone taking something and then entering into a mock fight with someone else. Mock fighting, teasing and joking are characteristic of day-to-day behaviour between those who call each other *veitavaleni*, cross-cousin.[12] During rituals, the joking relationship between *veitavaleni* is very often enacted at the end of the ritual day, as part of it and as the moment of return to profane time. Even if in Lakeba today nobody seems to remember the 'beating' of the *vasu* or the mock fight (and Hocart does not mention it for Lau), it seems to me that if it did happen it was a way of separating the sacred from the profane, especially when we learn from Hocart that, 'his [the *vasu*'s] cousins in some places, if not all, abuse and beat him but cannot recover the stuff' (Hocart 1915: 642).

The relationship between an eldest sister's children and the mother's brothers is extremely respectful on both sides and, most of the time, they use a go-between to speak to each other.[13] Otherwise, the eldest sister's child will in general use the word *momo* to address his uncle, but in addressing his sister's child, the uncle will use a cardinal pronoun, *kemudrau* (second person dual, 'you and somebody else') or *kemuni* (second person plural, 'you as one of a group') or even *ko ira* (third person plural, 'they') to address his nephew or niece, especially when they are of high status. These polite pronouns are normally used to address chiefs or other high-status persons. The last, *ko ira*, was explained to me in the following way: 'even the *vasu* person is not included but referred to with this word'. I suggest that the mother's brother is really speaking to the ancestors and gods whom his sister's child represents, shelters or lives with. Because of Christianity, people in Lakeba do not like to talk about these entities, but in conversations today they are called, with an undeniable complicity, the 'unseen beings'. Unseen, yet full of efficacy or *mana*.

How Sisters and Daughters Helped Establish the Lauan Chiefdom

My analysis shows that the *mana* of the sister's children and their superiority over their maternal uncle stems from the sister's superiority over the brother; in this section I look at the impact of these facts on the founding of the present chiefdom in the Lau islands.[14] As there is not sufficient space here to go into all the historical details, I mention only those that reveal the recurring structure of marriages. Unlike other more warlike regions of Fiji, the territory of the Lau islands, up until the missionaries' arrival, was mainly built on repetitive marriage strategies established in order to exploit politically the prerogatives of the *vasu* position. Lakeba's oral tradition, sometimes confirmed in Tongan texts, enables us to go back with certainty as far as the sixteenth century. It recounts several migrations from the north-west, the south and the west. Each time, the first action mentioned on the arrival of a new group is that of the leader of those already living in Lakeba giving a wife to the leader of the new arrivals. Around the beginning of the seventeenth century, a group large enough to be a marriage-alliance partner with the highest Tongan authorities was living in a fortified settlement built on high ground.[15] The oral account recorded in the 'Itukutuku Raraba' tells that when a new group, accompanied by its priests and deities, arrived, the two leaders of this group 'took away' two of the daughters of the leader of the group already occupying the island'.[16] One of these leaders turned out to be a cannibal and was killed while the other received the title *Sau*, 'high chief' and half the land.[17] From then on, according to the account, each group fulfilled a ritual function; apparently a period of peace was established under the aegis of a real chief, and marriages contracted with islands to the north and south of Lakeba allowed them to be brought into Lakeba's zone of influence. I return below to this connection between marriage and political influence.

Around 1760, things changed and the Lau islands became part of the history of those to the west. At this point in time, the Bau chiefdom, still the most important, took possession of the little island of Korolevu inhabited by, among others, the Levuka, a people renowned as navigators, most of whom emigrated to Lakeba. In 2012, one of their descendants, the spokesman, related their history as follows:

> Levuka people come from Bau, they were there before the Viti Levu people.[18] They lived peacefully together and they became fishermen to the chief of the mainland. This was in the sixteenth or seventeenth century. At that time in Lakeba, the *Sau*, Ginigini, had a daughter, Asinate Lagi. She was a princess. One day her mother went down to the reef to fish. She said to her daughter: 'You stay inside in order to preserve your complexion. I have taken the mats and the *masi* outside. If it rains you must bring everything inside'. The rain came and the flood washed everything away to the sea. When the mother saw this, she became very angry and banished her daughter. Asinate went to the beach, made a raft with coconuts and drifted away. She arrived near Bau. Two fishermen from Bau, Levuka people, came fishing there and found her. She was very beautiful. They wrapped her up in the sail of the canoe and then hid her in the

rafters of their house. They fed her. One day the fishermen caught a fish, a *saqa*, which is taboo to anyone but the chief.[19] They fed it to the young girl. The little children used the bones for their toy spears and fish hooks. Someone from the chief's house discovered this and they were driven off the island because they had not given the *saqa* to the chief. They took Asinate with them. They asked her where she came from: 'From towards the sunrise'. So they travelled in the direction of Lakeba where Ginigini was very happy to see his daughter alive and he offered her to the Levuka people in marriage. But they answered: 'We cannot, we regard her as a sister or a daughter after living together such a long time'. 'Then, let us divide the land', said Ginigini. 'We don't need that much land, just a place to dry our sails in the sun'.[20] Since then, the Levuka people have lived in the village of Levuka, nowadays more and more interlocked with that of Tubou.

At the time of the Levuka people's arrival, the inhabitants of Lakeba, of different origins, were in conflict with each other. They went to war for the title of *Sau*. When Asinate's brother, Fuakilau, was killed, she asked the people of Levuka to help her avenge her brother. In exchange, her father promised to hand over to them his title of *Sau*. In their turn, the Levuka people asked the Bau warriors for help and won the battle.[21] As promised, Codro, chief of the Levuka people, became *Sau*, but he was a *Saurara*, 'a hot chief, an oppressor'; he consumed the island's population, taking everything he wanted. He said: 'This taro place is sprinkled with salt water, so it's mine', a reference to Levuka people being sea people (*kai wai*). He did the same with the pigs, the girls, the men. So the survivors decided to go to Nayau island to get a new, strong chief.

Here I have to draw attention to two points. What the oral tradition presents as a tale about a shipwrecked princess is in fact probably the story of the forced migration of people who were the high chief of Bau's fishermen and navigators, not only because their island was confiscated but also because Bau was trying to extend its zone of influence eastward.[22] This explains why an army of Ra warriors (under the influence of Bau) rallied to help the people of Levuka take power.[23] Secondly, contrary to the usual pattern, the new arrivals from Levuka refused the gift of a wife and land the *Sau* offered them.[24] There was therefore no marriage on which to found this chiefdom. This absence of a marriage and of a gift of land is a metaphor for a chiefdom that eats itself. According to my informants, 'Codro', which is a nickname, refers to 'entangled, irregular waves – when you can see the water boiling'. His name means chaos and is closely related to the sea. Codro represents sterility; not only is he 'hot', but he does not cultivate his own gardens and sprinkles salt water over other people's. He also illustrates the fact that a fisherman-navigator cannot change office, cannot become *Sau*.[25]

Women of the Land in Ritual

In the 'drying of the tears', described above, the sister welcomes her brother's wife as if she has been shipwrecked, and transforms her through the ritual into a person from Lakeba, erasing the marks of her origins and voyage. In the ritual of 'bringing the face of the child', it is the mother who is said to present her child to her group of origin and to make them a *vasu taukei*, native *vasu*. There is, moreover, another ritual called *rova*, which is performed, for example, when a high chief from another chiefdom comes to visit the village of Tubou, that of the paramount chief of the Lau islands. In this case, the women who are natives of the village wait on the shore with pieces of barkcloth and a *tabua* (whale's tooth) worn by a woman from the chief's clan.[26] When the men on the boat, apart from the chief and his close bodyguards, see them, they swim ashore and, attracted by the women, are lured by them into the centre of the village. There the village men are waiting for them. An informant told me:

> It's a way of saying to the guests that they are welcome, that they are not shipwrecked people we are going to eat. Women have to accept you first. It's not easy to be *vulagi*, a 'stranger', the women have to take away your foreign smell, to clean up the salty water and the soil before you are taken into the *veiqaravi* circle, the circle where you face each other. The women run right to the place where the *veiqaravi* is to take place. The weakness of the men in this 'fight' is that they had to travel and to swim. It's the women who shout that you are a *vulagi*. *Rova* is a lifesaving act by the women, nothing to be afraid of.

My informant added: 'Any time the women can say, "You are still wet, you swam to this land, you never came by boat"'. The ritual represents men who have been shipwrecked but who are 'saved' (from being eaten) by the native women. It is only after this that these men's chief can be welcomed as a guest. He will be received with different gifts inviting him to drop anchor, to lower his flag, to be dried and so on. But in the end it will be said, 'The stranger is a guest, even if he's a chief, he is still a *vulagi taukei*'.

This conclusion is confirmed by the fact that the paramount chief of the Lau islands too, when he returns after a long absence from his island, is welcomed in this manner by the women of the *vanua*, with the same proposals of services and so forth. This clearly shows that not only is the foreignness of the Lau chiefdom still present in people's minds, but also that it is fundamental. When the remains of Ratu Mara, the last high chief of Lau, were brought back from Suva to Lakeba, the military honours were performed on the jetty but, when the coffin crossed the boundary of the sacred village square, he was welcomed by the *tama* of the *vanua* women who, sitting facing each other separated by a long line of *masi*, guided him towards his house.[27] This same path is followed when the newly installed Tui Nayau arrives from Nayau island to be installed as the *Sau ni Vanua ko Lau*, 'Paramount chief of the Vanua of Lau', in Lakeba, or when the chief's children are presented during the *kau mata ni gone* ritual to their mother's chiefdom. This *masi* path links the exterior and the interior, as if they were coming together to constitute a fertile chiefdom, a chiefdom that is *sautu*, 'creating peace and prosperity'.

The first man to take this path was Rasolo, who held the title of Tui Nayau on Nayau island in Codro's time.[28] The inhabitants of Lakeba appealed to him and his brothers to free them from the latter's yoke. His youngest brother, whose mother was from Lakeba and who was therefore *vasu taukei* to Lakeba, put them to flight with the help of his warriors, and Rasolo was installed as the first *Sau* of the Vuanirewa dynasty, who still hold the title today.[29] The reader is asked to note, firstly, that Rasolo was a foreign chief with a father from Nayau and a mother from Totoya island.[30] He married several women of different origins. Oral tradition has remembered four of them: the first from Tonga, the second from Nasaqalau (a village on Lakeba), the third from Totoya and the fourth again from Tonga. Secondly, under the reign of Codro's son, Rasolo brought the Levuka people back to Lakeba. This was probably for two reasons. On the one hand, the Levuka people were, and still are, important intermediaries between the high chiefdom of Bau and the chiefdom of Lau. On the other, the Levuka people are navigators: the ensemble of offices essential to the constitution of a chiefdom is never complete without them. Traditionally the tie between a chiefdom and its navigators is sealed by a marriage between one of the *Sau*'s daughters and the navigators' leader. In this case, Rasolo gave one of his daughters (from his fourth union) in marriage to Codro's son, the Daulakeba, the chief of the Levuka people. Such a marriage is the opposite of one that binds a high chief from outside the *vanua* to a woman of the *vanua*. Rasolo himself had married a woman from Nasaqalau who was the eldest daughter of the leader who was *Sau* before Codro.

The Son of the Woman of the Land

The case of Soroaqali, the son of this marriage, is a good illustration of my argument so far. First, he is the only one of Rasolo's sons to have a *vanua* mother. He is therefore the only one to be *vasu taukei* to Lakeba and the islands under its influence. If he had taken on the position and title of *Sau*, he would have held simultaneously the two highest functions possible, which *a priori* would have been desirable since he had *mana* from the interior, from the *vanua*, through his mother, and strength and valuables from the exterior through his father. But this does not take into account Soroaqali's own political analysis of the situation.

Today when the inhabitants of Lakeba talk about Soroaqali, they always mention the same facts, which they summarize as follows: Soroaqali didn't want to become Sau, he said to his brothers Malani (the elder) and Taliai Tupou (the younger), 'I'm already a chief, I have a *taukei* mother, I'm *vasu*, you be chief and I'll help you'. A hundred years ago, one of Hocart's informants attributed similar words to Soroaqali when speaking to Taliai, his younger brother: 'Be you chief that I may look after you', and Hocart added a remark: 'He himself had quite enough power without the chieftainship' (Hocart 1929: 41). The underlying idea is that Soroaqali should have become chief. One informant said:

> Malani's mother is from Tonga, he's not *vasu* to Lakeba. That's why they were always fighting [they were not stable as they would have been as *vasu* to the place]. So they [Malani and Taliai Tupou] had to get warriors from Tonga, where they were *vasu*, to fight their wars [Taliai Tupou's mother from Totoya was also of Tongan descent]. They had no strength in Lau.

Another informant explained: 'The *vasu* place is higher than the chiefly status. He has access to the land, he is *vasu taukei*'. What he calls 'access to the land' means access to the wealth of the *vanua*, that is to say, the chiefdom as far as it reaches.

Indeed, Soroaqali seems to have kept his promises and to have served his brothers as *vasu taukei*; he appears to have been a great traveller, collecting the valuables intended for his brothers who succeeded one another as high chief. In 1825, William Cary's account shows Soroaqali was at Vatoa island (the far south of the Lau archipelago) with his own boat (Cary 1998: 26–27).[31] There he found Cary, the only survivor of the shipwrecked whaler *Oeno* from Nantucket, and took him under his protection. Cary relates that Soroaqali was sailing to the island of Ono to receive the first fruits (*isevu*) for the high chief, his elder brother Malani: 'The natives were expecting us, it being the time for their annual visit to collect tribute, and had large quantities of provisions cooked and all things prepared for the annual feast . . . [T]hey brought us the provisions they had prepared and presented them with a great deal of ceremony' (ibid.: 22). Evidently Soroaqali travelled round the chiefdom for his elder brother Malani with the authority of a *vasu taukei*, the person who cannot be refused whatever he asks for or takes.

In May 1827, Dumont d'Urville dropped anchor at Lakeba. He wrote: 'At about half past three, a little canoe arrived transporting four or five Kaï-Bitis and TonMaK informed me that one of them, called Toureng-Toki, the king's brother, was asking for permission to come aboard; this was immediately granted him' (Dumont d'Urville 1830: 408). Toureng-Toki was Soroaqali. He was to spend a week on Dumont d'Urville's ship, the *Astrolabe*, because contrary winds made it impossible to put the visitors ashore, and they were taken on a long voyage, which ended on the island of Moala. By questioning Toki and Tomboua-Nakoro, Dumont d'Urville obtained the names of a hundred and nine islands or islets in the Fijian archipelago (ibid.: 413).[32] His travelling companion Tubou na koro described Soroaqali to Gaimard, the naturalist aboard the *Astrolabe*: 'Toki is the brother of the king of Laguemba [Lakeba], the richest of all the Viti [Fijian] islands: he is a very commendable, very rich chief, who possesses more than fifty wives and I would be sorry to see him far from his country' (ibid.: 699).[33] Today Soroaqali is above all renowned for his animosity towards the Tongans, and the fact that until the day he died he refused to convert to Christianity.[34] As the Tongans were involved in the success of Christianity, these two facts are connected. It should be noted that even Hocart, in a comprehensive genealogy of the Vuanirewa chiefdom, mentions neither the name of Soroaqali's wife nor his offspring. The memory of the phrase addressed to his brothers concerning his *vasu* position is all the more remarkable, and reflects the full weight of the *vasu taukei*.

Even though all my informants confirmed the statement '*Vasu taukei* outranks *vasu levu*', the latter's position is important. A 'great *vasu*' is the child of a high chief's eldest sister married to a high chief of another chiefdom. It will then be said, for example *koya bika vanua ki Bau*, 'she presses down on (*bika*) the *vanua*', 'she sits on the land of Bau', 'she holds the land (*vanua*), it becomes an ally in war'. The 'pressing down' is compared to a stone put on a mat so that it is not blown away. It is explained that: 'Bau will not fight Lau, the sister's son will not fight Lau, rather he will help in war against some other enemy. Otherwise Bau is a *vasu ca*, a bad *vasu*'. The last part of this sentence leads one to believe that the possibility exists. Indeed, Lau's most famous *vasu levu* illustrates this point perfectly. His name was Kamisese Mara Kapawai.[35] He was of very high rank in Bau at the time of the first missionaries on Lakeba (1835). He was *vasu levu* to Lakeba, to the Moala group and to the island of Ono, through his mother and both his grandmothers.

The missionary Thomas Williams, staying in Lakeba on 27 August 1841, wrote in his journal:

> Much stir on the beach caused by the arrival of a canoe from Bau. Not knowing whether the intention of those on board was peaceful or otherwise (war being expected from that quarter) multitudes of Feejeeans and Tonguese assembled on the sand armed with muskets, clubs, lances . . . Several of our people struck the water in defiance of the supposed foe. A small piece was fired by those on board and answered by several from shore. The latter waited anxiously until a messenger sent by them

should return and state who were the visitors, and what their intention. When the name of Campsis was announced, the *oa* of respect was given and things went on as usual. (Williams 1931: 35)[36]

Clearly, at the time tension between Bau and Lau was high. What usually happened when a *vasu levu* visited the chiefdom was very similar to what Cary had related for the visit of a *vasu taukei* to one of the islands of the chiefdom (cited above), and was described by Williams as follows: 'The *Vasu* then walked up to the King, having two whales' teeth in his hand, which – after a short speech, referring to his coming and its object – he presented, receiving in return an expression of the King's wishes for prosperity and peace' (Williams 1982: 36). In exchange for tribute, the first fruit offerings, the *vasu* was a source of prosperity and plenty, which follows from the *mana* vested in the sister and her children and the *vasu* being the representative of the ancestors and gods. One of my informants summarized the train of thought as follows: 'Tribute is given to the *vasu* who gives it to the chief. We cannot refuse through the *vasu*', and he added a historical example to support his argument. He said, 'Vuetasau, Malani's son, who was *vasu taukei* because of his Tubou mother, was "acting", while Taliai, the High Chief and his father's younger brother, was "sitting"'. This means that Taliai was living in Tubou while Vuetasau was travelling around to collect the first fruits and, later, to wage the so-called Christian war.[37] My informant emphasized that Vuetasau acted as *vasu taukei* and not as Taliai's potential successor. Sahlins, in the introduction of his analysis of the war between the Bau and Rewa chiefdoms, stresses the influence and action of the high chiefs' sister's children in each other's chiefdom (Sahlins 2004: 11), but he considers the high chief's younger brothers and heirs as the chieftainship's active side (Sahlins 1981: 122). Indeed, this is often the case in Bau, but it seems that, in the Lau and Cakaudrove chiefdoms, tasks were more divided between the chief and the *vasu taukei* of the *vanua* (Sahlins 2004: 231).[38] With this conclusion, Soroaqali's statement to his brother makes complete sense.

Conclusion

The different descriptions of the *vasu* position can now be summarized. Everyone is a *vasu taukei* to their mother's people, village, island or chiefdom, depending on her rank.[39] Not everyone is a *vasu levu*, this status being accorded only to the children of eldest sisters.[40] A high chief's younger sisters will preferably be given in marriage to minor chiefs within the chiefdom; their children will be *vasu taukei* to the chiefdom and be allowed to take what they want, but they and their mother's chiefdom will have to assist the high chief in collecting artefacts for an even higher chief or, perhaps, in waging war against him.[41] The elder sisters of a high chief are given in marriage to the high chiefs (or their brothers, who may become high chief on the death of their brother) of other chiefdoms.[42] Their children will be *vasu levu* to Lau. They can take whatever they want, but they are also collectors of tribute or first fruits, bestowing prosperity and peace (*sautu*) in return. As *vasu levu*, they bestow on their mother's chiefdom what the chief himself bestows on his own chiefdom. That is to say, a chiefdom is blessed with the *mana* of its high chief, acquired from the *vanua* through the installation ritual, but also with that of its *vasu levu*, through the elder sisters given in marriage to other high chiefs. The *vasu levu* often live in their mother's village or chiefdom so that their own chief (who may be their father) has easy access to the valuables such as *tanoa*, 'wooden bowl in which *yaqona* is prepared', mats, *masi*, boats and *magimagi*, 'sinnet', and he, in turn, will reciprocate with prosperity and peace. I leave the last word to Thomas Williams:

> However high a Chief may rank, however powerful a King may be, if he has a nephew, he has a master . . . But it is not in his private capacity, but as acting under the direction of the King, that the *Vasu*'s agency tends greatly to modify the political machinery of Fiji, inasmuch as the Sovereign employs the *Vasu*'s influence, and shares much of the property acquired. Great *Vasu* are also *vasu* to great places, and, when they visit these at their superior's command, have a numerous retinue and increased authority. A public reception and great feasts are given them by the inhabitants of the place which they visit; and they return home laden with property, most of which, as tribute, is handed over to the King. (Williams 1982: 35)

Thomas Williams had observed what Soroaqali promised his brothers he would do.

Notes

1. See also Douaire-Marsaudon and Cayrol, this volume.
2. Hocart writes: 'A nephew is spoken of as *vasu*, which appears to be a title, not a real kinship term' (Hocart 1929: 40). Williams writes: 'The word means a nephew or niece, but becomes a title of office in the case of the male' (Williams 1982: 34).
3. In his journal entry for 1 January 1842, the missionary Thomas Williams wrote: 'Appealed to by Jonah Lolou from Waciwaci [a village on Lakemba island] to assist him with the property to present in the place of his wife whom Campsis had determined to take to Bau. Campsis was appeased' (Williams 1932: 52). Campsis is the way Williams wrote the name of the most famous *vasu* to Lakeba, Kamisese Mara.

4. As far as I know there is actually no such case in Tubou or Levuka village.
5. *Yaqona*, or more commonly kava, is a drink made from the root of the same name (*Piper methysticum*).
6. *Masi* is barkcloth made from the paper mulberry (*Broussonetia papyfera*).
7. With these words one of my friends summarized a long talk on *mana*.
8. *Bulubulu* is a ceremony of forgiveness, 'burying' resentments (*bulu*, to bury, *ibulubulu*, burial place, grave).
9. As they do with the chiefs too.
10. When speaking about *mana* and kinship, I never heard Lauans argue that they experienced a decline of *mana*, as it seems to be the case in Lau and elsewhere when it comes to religious discourse (Tomlinson 2007). Kinship seems to be a realm where *mana* is not threatened because the relationship with the ancestors on a *mataqali* or family level are still very much alive.
11. A *i taukei* is one who belongs to a place, also a landowner, one who is *vasu i taukei* is the child of a woman of the land. The *yavusa* is the largest kin group, sometimes spread over more than one village, and made up of people with the same origin story.
12. Same-sex cross-cousins, who could or should be brothers-in-law, behave like this because of the marriage possibility; opposite-sex cross-cousins also have a joking relationship alluding to the possibility that they could have married.
13. Things are different when the mother of the sister's child is younger than her brother.
14. My sources are numerous: Dumont d'Urville (1830), Hocart (1929), Reid (1979, 1990), Young (1982, 1993), Cary (1998) and the 'Itukutuku Raraba ni Yavusa ko Lakeba' (unpublished manuscript, c.1930, 14pp). The original is kept at the NLTB (Native Land Trust Board) in Suva, but some villagers have a copy at home. The document is a general report on Yavusa Lakeba, containing oral statements made to the Native Lands Commission in support of territorial claims. Nearly every *yavusa*, 'tribe, largest kin-group making up a *vanua*', has a written version of these statements. The Lakeba report is supposed to have been completed in the 1930s. I also make use of accounts by people who today live on the island of Lakeba, the seat of Vuanirewa high chiefdom whose territory today covers the whole of Lau province.
15. One of these was the *Fale Fisi*, the 'House of Fiji', which traditionally gave husbands to the Tu'i Tonga's sisters, who were forbidden to marry a Tongan and whose descendants were the Tamahà, the most sacred people in the Tongan hierarchy (see Douaire-Marsaudon, this volume).
16. 'Itukutuku Raraba Ni Yavusa Ko Lakeba', (p.1). 'Take away' (*kauta*) here has the meaning of 'to steal, to elope with'.
17. This is the first time the title appears in the Lau chiefdom's origin tale. In the 'Itukutuku Raraba', the moment is described thus: 'This was also the occasion

on which their custom (*vakavanua*) of giving a function, a duty (*tavi*) to a chief was seen for the first time' (p.2). See also Sahlins (1981).

18. Bau was the name given to Korolevu by its new occupiers; Vitu Levu is the name of Fiji's main island.

19. The giant trevally (*Caranx ignobilis*).

20. Later, this place became the landing place of the first missionaries in Fiji, and then the burial place of some of Fiji's most important personalities: Ma'afu, Ratu Sukuna, Ratu Kamisese Mara. This part of the story also helps to explain why Levuka people, who are navigators, have hardly any land on Lakeba.

21. Tradition has it that the inhabitants of the Ra region, in the north-east of the main island, Vitu Levu, were the warriors of the Bau chiefdom.

22. The *Gonedau* or fishermen-navigators were also the 'fishers' of turtles and 'fishers' of enemies for cannibal sacrifices.

23. Sahlins writes: 'Sometime in the latter half of the eighteenth century, one such army, complemented by warriors from northeast Viti Levu (Nakoro-tuba), had successfully stormed the inland fortress of Kedekede at Lakeba, Lau' (Sahlins 2000: 319).

24. We must remember that the first person to hold the title of *sau* and his brother had 'taken away' the leader's two daughters. It is only after the cannibal brother's murder that the title of *sau* and the land were given.

25. On the other hand, all important chiefs are accompanied by *Gonedau* who perform at least two functions for him, that of fisherman (*dau qoli*), and not only of fish but also of turtles, even of enemies for sacrifices to the gods of cannibal chiefs, and those of their warriors and that of navigator (*dau soko*).

26. These then are women born in the village and not wives who have come from elsewhere. They can be called 'sisters of the village men'. In theory, they are only the *vanua* women, but today at least one woman from the chiefly clan is present.

27. The *tama* is a shout of reverence to a chief specific to each village and, in some cases, to each sex and/or rank. *Masi* is also the symbol, with *yaqona*, of the *vanua*. *Masi* strips are tied on to the future chief's right and left upper arm by two *vanua* representatives during the installation ritual. All the *vanua* chiefs are also called the *masi* of the *vanua*.

28. He is sometimes called the first Tui Nuyau, but the title may have existed in Nayau before him. What is certain is that he is the first Tui Nuyau to be installed as *Sau ni Vanua ko Lau* in Lakeba.

29. 'Which made him strong in Lakeba' my informants always specify, for he could count on the help of those to whom he was *vasu*. Rasolo, however, whose mother was from the island of Totoya and of Tongan origin, could not.

30. It should be noted that today Totoya is part of the chiefdom of Lakeba, but at the time the Moala group of which Totoya is part was under the influence of the Bau chiefdom.

31. He is mentioned by the name of 'Toka, the brother of the head chief of Lahcameber' (Cary 1998: 26).
32. We learn later that Tomboua-Nakoro is the representative of Naulivou, the paramount chief of Bau, in Lakeba, and also his nephew (Dumont d'Urville 1830: 700), the son of Tanoa. His mother was from Bau, but unfortunately we do not know if his grandmother came from Lakeba and therefore whether he was a *vasu taukei*.
33. Extract from Gaimard's journal in Dumont d'Urville (1830).
34. At the time, they represented about a third of Tubou's population, and his brother's wives had increased the number by arriving accompanied by a large court.
35. Ratu Sir Kamisese Kapawai Mara, Fiji's first prime minister and late president, was his namesake.
36. Campsis is Kamises Mara Kapawai. Later, Williams spells it Kamsisi. The *oa* is the *tama* already mentioned above.
37. He disappeared, presumed drowned, in 1857.
38. Even if, from the Lauan point of view at least, Kamisese Mara Kapawai is clearly regarded as a *vasu* and as the high chief of Bau's potential heir. Research on the origin of the mothers and grandmothers of the Bauan high chiefs' brothers and heirs would probably reveal that, like Mara, they were primarily 'active' in their mother's place of origin.
39. Vuanirewa informants will say in private that the children of a Vuanirewa woman with a *vanua* man are not *vasu* but *kete*, 'belly, stomach'.
40. Some say children of elder sisters are.
41. Historically, Bau or Cakaudrove were 'higher' than the Lauan chiefdom. As one informant put it, 'Taking is their right, helping is their obligation'.
42. Ratu Sir Kamisese Mara's two eldest daughters married prominent chiefs of Cakaudrove and Bau.

References

Biersack, A. 1982. 'Tongan Exchange Structures: Beyond Descent and Alliance', *Journal of the Polynesian Society* 91(2): 181–212.
Cary, W.S. 1998 [1828]. *Wrecked on the Feejees*. Fairfield, WA: Ye Galleon Press.
Dumont d'Urville, J.S.C. 1830. *Voyage de la corvette l'Astrolabe exécuté par ordre du Roi pendant les années 1826-1827-1828 et 1829 sous le commandement de M. J. Dumont d'Urville, capitaine de vaisseau*, Vol.4, Pt.2. Paris: J. Tastu.
Hocart, A.M. 1915. 'Chieftainship and the Sister's Son in the Pacific', *American Anthropologist* 17(4): 631–46.
——— 1923. 'The Uterine Nephew', *Man* 23: 11–13.
——— 1926. 'Limitations of the Sister's Son's Right in Fiji', *Man* 26: 205–6.
——— 1929. *Lau Islands, Fiji*. Honolulu: Bernice P. Bishop Museum.

Hooper, S. 1982. 'A Study of Valuables in the Chiefdom of Lau, Fiji', Ph.D. diss. Cambridge: University of Cambridge.

———— 2004. 'Who Are the Chiefs ? Chiefship in Lau, Eastern Fiji', in R. Feinberg and K.A. Watson-Gegeo (eds), *Leadership and Change in the Western Pacific*. London: Athlone Press.

Itukutuku Raraba Ni Yavusa Ko Lakeba, n.d., c.1930. Manuscript.

Reid, A.C. 1979. 'The View from the Vatuwaqa: The Role of Lakeba's Leading Lineage in the Introduction and Establishment of Christianity', *Journal of Pacific History* 14(3): 154–67.

———— 1990. *Tovata I & II*, Suva: Fiji Museum.

Rogers, G. 1977. '"The Father's Sister Is Black"': A Consideration of Female Rank and Powers in Tonga', *The Journal of the Polynesian Society* 86(2): 157–82.

Sahlins, M. 1962. *Moala Culture and Nature on a Fijian island*. University of Michigan Press.

———— 1981. 'The Stranger-king, or Dumézil among the Fijians', *Journal of Pacific History* 16(3): 107–32: 11–13.

———— 2000. *Culture in Practice: Selected Essays*. New York: Zone Books.

———— 2004. *Apologies to Thucydides: Understanding History as Culture and Vice Versa*. Chicago: University of Chicago Press.

Tomlinson, M., 2007. 'Mana in Christian Fiji: The Interconversion of Intelligibility and Palpability', *Journal of the American Academy of Religion* 75(3): 524–53.

Thompson, L. 1940. *Fijian Frontier*. New York: American Council Institute of Pacific Relations.

Toren, C. 1990. *Making Sense of Hierarchy: Cognition as Social Process in Fiji*. London: Athlone Press.

———— 1994. '"All Things Go In Pairs or the Sharks Will Bite". The Antithetical Nature of Fijian Chiefship', *Oceania* 64: 197–216.

Wilkes, C., 1985 [(1845].), *United States Exploring Expedition: Tongataboo, Feejee Group Honolulu*, Vol. 3. Suva: Fiji Museum.

Williams, T. 1931 [1815]. *The Journal of Thomas Williams, Missionary in Fiji, 1840–53*, ed. G.C. Henderson. Sydney: Angus and Robertson.

———— 1982 [1858]. *Fiji and the Fijians*, Vol. 1: *The Islands and Their Inhabitants*, ed. G.S. Rowe. Suva: Fiji Museum.

Young, J. 1982. 'The Response of Lau to Foreign Contact: An Interdisciplinary Reconstruction', *Journal of Pacific History* 17(1): 29–50.

———— 1993. 'Lau: A Windward Perspective', *Journal of Pacific History* 28(2): 159–80.

8

'Sister or Wife, You've Got to Choose'

A Solution to the Puzzle of Village Exogamy in Samoa

◆●◆

Serge Tcherkézoff

In Samoa, the principle of village exogamy goes back as far as family accounts stretch, to the late nineteenth century. This poses a puzzle, because the families (*aiga*) that make up a village (*nuu*) are generally far from related (*aiga*), and even so Samoans are unanimous in condemning marriage within a village. Why should this be so? Village organization could provide an answer: at a certain encompassing level of representations, all villagers are brother or sister to each other. This village organization is perhaps the most striking example of the high salience of the brother–sister relationship (*feagaiga*) in Samoa.

The overarching brother–sister link becomes evident if we analyse the composition of the village (*nuu*) not just as a group of families (*aiga*) but as made up of three ceremonial groupings that include everyone, and that are also called *nuu*: first, the family (*aiga*) representatives (*sui*), also called family heads (*ulu*), in everyday usage *matai*, usually translated as titleholders or chiefs; second, their sons; third, their daughters. The deep meaning of the word *nuu* is 'community'. A village is a set of families, but as a community it is a circle of chiefs made as one, and these chiefs have sons and daughters who thus stand to one another in a brother–sister relationship. The marital links within the village are put at the back of the scene, nearly invisible, except when a marriage occurs inside the village.

Available literature is virtually silent concerning the condemnation of intra-village marriage, which has thus escaped discussion and analysis.[1] The reason, I believe, is two-fold. First, the issue is expressed in specific cases, rather than as an absolute rule, such as would apply to incest. Secondly, an understanding of marriage demands analysis at village level, and not only, as the literature to date reflects, at the level of the family (*aiga*). This is evident, for example, in the following conversation, in which a young woman spoke wistfully of her cousin.

> 'She isn't happy with her husband'
> 'Why not?'
> 'Because she was in love with someone else'.
> 'Why didn't she marry him then?'
> 'Because the parents didn't want them to'. [A pause] 'Didn't you know?' [Another pause, and then, in hushed tones:] 'They're from the same village'.

The problem caused by a couple's common origins does not surface in conversations about defining ideas of family or village, but always in personal stories like this. Much later, one discovers that a couple one knows is 'from the same village', but nobody talks about it, because what they have done is 'unseemly'. One then notices that such couples, who are rather uncommon, are never at the forefront of village life. It becomes apparent that there is a glaring contradiction between village endogamy and the status system. Moreover, it is easier to understand why the prohibition on village endogamy is not expressed as it is for incest: 'It is absolutely forbidden (*sa*) to marry your relative (*aiga*), it would be committing incest (*matafaile*)'. Apart from family and village custom, *sa* is used for all prohibitions decreed by religion and government. When asked why families do not wish their children to marry within the village, however, Samoans invariably answer that it is because it is unseemly, shameful or bad (*mataga, ma, leaga*), implying that the problem arises once the act has been committed, and thus has to do with the consequences of such a union.

FaaSamoa: A Village Country

The broadest idea of social organization is 'Samoan custom' or *aganuu faaSamoa*, shortened to *faaSamoa*: rules of respect that require everyone to know more or less how to assess their own status with regard to others. Respect is assessed once village and family names are known. All persons are defined by these two reference points and, within the village, hierarchy is clear. Every time the family heads (*matai*, chiefs) gather, they must know where to sit, when to speak and when to take kava, the ceremonial drink (only one person drinks at a time).

The family (*aiga*) is defined by at least one founding title (*suafa matai*), which is passed on by ritual bestowal and kept by each generation. The duty of bearing this title is called *matai*. All families have a *matai*, or chief, who represents the ancestor, and all family members are said to be the *matai*'s 'children' and he their 'father'. When the person invested with the founding name – the *matai* – dies, another is chosen. The founding ancestor is usually a man. Anyone who can state and convince others of any genealogical link with a founding ancestor, or someone subsequently chosen to bear the ancestral title, is 'related' (*aiga*) to this title, and hence to the family. All Samoans are thereby linked to many families through an extensive cognatic and genealogical memory stretching back four to ten – and in some cases over twenty – generations. In order to maintain an effective link, however, a Samoan must take active part in work required for ceremonial exchanges with other families.

The 'chief' is the head of a family, and there are as many chiefs as there are families. A chief is chosen by all family members, and no primogeniture or lineage preference rule necessarily applies; individual aptitude is much more important, and they can very well lose his right to bear the founding title for inappropriate conduct. The invested person is the receptacle of the ancestor's persona and, as such, becomes the 'family's *matai*'. One of the ceremonial expressions used for the office of *matai* is 'the entity-from-above here below' (*o le atua o lalonei*). The name-founding ancestors were superhuman entities – 'gods' as the word *atua* has been translated by missionaries or, often, demigods from a union between a god and a mortal. The other founding ancestors were born to these first ancestors, and received a name and land from them as a reward for their support during a war. Thus all founding ancestors have some antique, divine authority and a family's *matai* is its living receptacle.

At first sight, it would appear that the village exogamy rule refers to the *aiga* (family), because nobody may marry one who claims to belong to the same *aiga* (whether or not they live in the same village). This is incest, *mataifale*, lit. 'facing inwards in the house' (*mata-i-fale*). It is necessary, however, to find out more about the village, or *nuu*, which is the basis for defining the concept of 'country' (*atu-nuu*, lit. 'a chain of villages') and 'custom' (*aga-nuu*, lit. 'the essence of village life'). These ideas are evinced in two key forms: the hierarchy of titles, and rights to land.

Names are titles whose value varies according to their antiquity, and, because a genealogy's length only makes sense when compared with others, a name's rank has to be visible and acquire substance by interacting with other names.[2] Since the early twentieth century, the country and district are both too large for day-to-day interaction, so it is in village meetings that the hierarchy of titles becomes visible. A village consists of a number of families (from ten to forty or more), whose representatives (the 'chiefs', *matai*) meet to deal with issues affecting the community.

A family name can be handed down as a title only if it is attached to land; its status derives from its rank within the 'sacred circle' of titles that define the village's history, and in whose terms the ages of the various genealogies are compared. The *nuu* is thus a 'sacred circle' of *aiga* families, although there are other terms that refer merely to its geographical location. This circle is part of the definition of an *aiga*, which cannot exist unless it belongs to a village and the land attached to it.[3] I turn now to an examination of the groups referred to as *nuu*, which together form the village, also known as *nuu*.

The Village of Chiefs and the Village of Servants

The *fono* is the council of *matai*, the family heads or chiefs, who regularly meet and make decisions affecting village life. As in all meetings in Samoa, they meet in a house, seating themselves in a circle, literally a 'circle of chiefs'. If there is a family which, according to the genealogy of its name, far outranks the others, the meeting takes place in the great house of this 'great' family, but more often than not the various great houses of various prominent families host the meetings in turn. The building is often round, but if it is oval or rectangular, as is sometimes the case, the seating order is the same. The family chiefs sit with their backs against the posts located along the house perimeter. The houses have no walls and are made up of a base on which posts that support the edge of the roof are arranged in a circle, oval or rectangle. A clear hierarchy is attributed to the posts. Without going into details, there are four sides, already ranked, and within each side order starts from the middle post and goes down on both sides, until reaching the next 'side'.

At each meeting, then, the circle of chiefs reveals a hierarchy among family chiefs, and therefore a hierarchy among family names ('titles'). All meetings are held in an open traditional house, with the whole village able to see and listen to the proceedings from outside. The hierarchy is therefore regularly displayed. It determines the order operating in other groups taking part in communal village life, which is discussed below.

Samoans have different ways of referring to the circle of chiefs in their conversation or ceremonial rhetoric. It can be just 'the *fono*', more explicitly 'the *fono* of *matai*', or 'sacred circle' (*o le alofi sa*). As previously stated, the chiefs (the family heads invested with the title of the family) can be ceremonially referred to as *o atua o lalonei* ('the god here below'), and this hallowed title is used for the village's chiefs collectively. They are 'the village *matai*' (*o matai o le nuu*), which is the expected expression, but which is also said in reverse as 'the *nuu* of the *matai*' (*o le nuu o matai*), 'the village of chiefs'. Thus, just like the village, the group of chiefs on its own can be designated as *nuu*. Chiefs can be men or women, but there is always a majority of men.

One is bound to be struck by the importance of the chiefs' circle (constantly referred to by everyone, even if it only meets once a week or once a month), and then to notice that, when the chiefs' circle makes a decision, those who carry it out are men living in the village who are not chiefs. They cultivate a common garden, repair buildings or, when there is a crisis, act as police (for example, to force a recalcitrant family to comply with a decision).[4] They also cook and serve food to the chiefs' circle. They are known as *taulelea* (singular *taulealea*). Some younger Samoans are not aware of the term's origin, but it fairly certainly means, 'those who look after [preparing] the kava (*lea*) [for the chiefs]'.

Such duties are known as 'doing service' (*tautua*), and the men as the 'servants' circle'. Service is highly thought of, and it is an honour to do *tautua*. Everyone, whether chief or not, explains the service ethic by the saying that, 'service is the way to power [i.e. being a chief]' (*e ala i le pule le tautua*). Servant status is seen as a prerequisite for becoming a *matai*. All accounts indicate that, in the past, all young men became members of the servants' group at puberty after undergoing the tattooing initiation rite. Those who later became chiefs had to have been through this stage. The concept persists today but, for some, there is a major difference. A person is regarded as a child until leaving school. Those who continue to the end of junior secondary school, and those who win a scholarship to study overseas, can become *taulealea* only if, and when, they finish their studies and come home. Sometimes, the kudos that comes with a qualification, particularly if it leads to a well-paid job, prompts the family to make the young adult a *matai* without first doing communal service.

When *taulealea* meet to plan and allocate the tasks assigned to them, they sit in a circle in one of the houses, just like the chiefs, and the seating arrangement mirrors theirs. The meeting is known as the *fono* of the *taulelea*. As individual persons, they are '*taulelea* of the village' and, significantly, the expression is reversed, as with the family heads, to ceremonially designate the group as a whole – that is, 'the village of the servants', the '*nuu* of the *taulelea*' (*o le nuu o taulelea*). Just like the whole village, and the chiefs' group, the servants' group on its own can be called a *nuu*. Its members are only men.

Affinity, Residence and Gender

Taken together, the *matai* and the *taulelea* account for the village's entire male population (excluding the *tamaiti*, lit. 'children little', a term that includes both pre-pubescent children and school children up to final-year university students). Samoans do not, however, think of *matai* as representing a single-sex or even gender-exclusive whole. Neither of the two words meaning 'men' (*tane* or *tamaloa*) is used to refer to these two groups together. *Taulealea* are always men, but the same is not true of chiefs (*matai*). There is a small but well-documented percentage of women *matai* and, more to the point, Samoans do not use any sex- or gender-related terms to refer to *matai* leadership.

Among those sitting in the circle of chiefs, there is, occasionally, the husband of a daughter of the family who came to live in his wife's family and has been chosen by them to bear one of the family's secondary founding titles. In such cases, the man always comes from another village, and often from a family that does not have a 'great' title (or that does, but the man has no hope of bearing it, as the current incumbent is young). He hopes that his wife's family will improve his prospects, even if it means living with his wife in her family's village and on its land. His wife's family may prefer him over local candidates to bear the name if he has many good qualities, whether traditional (he is a hard-working gardener, good at public speaking) and/or modern (he is a senior public servant or has a similarly good job). The family may grant him a secondary title that it holds so that he can sit in the village chiefs' circle and lend extra weight to the family's interests. A fairly large family would have several founding ancestor names from secondary lineages. In addition, a family chief can create a new, secondary chief's title, and grant it with the whole family's consent.

Such a member of the circle of the chiefs (in his wife's village) is not distinguished in any formal way, even if, privately, people may explain to outsiders that this man is *faiava*, lit. 'he who has made a wife' (*fai*, make; *ava*, wife – a term without status connotations). *Faiava* designates men who came to live in their wife's village, but this identification is somewhat silenced when the man has become a chief (*matai*) in his wife's family. When this man goes back to his own village and family, he is usually not considered there as a chief (*matai*). He joins the group of the servants (*taulelea*) to which he belonged before he married, went to live in his wife's village and there obtained a title that made him a chief.

Within this category, sitting in the circle of chiefs as an in-marrying husband from elsewhere, there can be another type: he has a high title in his own family, he did not receive a title from his wife's family. He is thus not a chief in his wife's village, but is nevertheless at home there, and the host village allows him to sit on the chiefs' council, particularly if his name is relatively 'great'. When decisions have to be made on village matters, his opinion counts as advice (*fautuaga*), not authority (*pule*). I have, however, seen one such man who, because of his public speaking ability and knowledge of the country's major genealogies, had become a central figure in his host village. Everybody sought his advice and it carried great authority.

Men who fall into the category of in-marrying non-chief can chose to live on their wives' land for various reasons. Some hope to acquire a title there. Increasingly, men from villages located very far away from the capital, who marry a girl from a village close to town, choose to live with their wives. There is, however, a heavy price to pay in terms of authority in the couple and sharing household chores. Parents-in-law wield their authority over such a man who, from his first day, does all the chores performed by the young men of the household: cooking, gardening, repairs and serving his wife's parents. Such a husband is not treated any differently to his wife's brothers of the same age or younger. He fully shares the tasks that punctuate the family's home life, in which brothers 'do service' (*tautua*) to their sisters. In addition, the wife's parents give him orders in the same terms as their sons: 'Hey! Boy (*sole*)! Go and do the . . . !' When speaking about his mother-in-law, he designates her as 'my mother', and in the same way his father-in-law is his 'father'. In short, he has become a quasi junior son of the family, and somehow, at least in public, a quasi young brother of his wife.

The chiefs' and servants' circles together, excepting the children *tamaiti*, account for the entire male population of a village. While this fact may seem insignificant at first glance, it has a major consequence: a male in-law from another village who settles in his wife's village will be integrated into the two existing ceremonial circles discussed. Both groups are called *nuu*, 'village', but bear in mind that *nuu* can mean the 'village as a community', the 'village of chiefs' (*nuu o matai*) and the 'village of servants' (*nuu o taulelea*). In other words, male in-laws are integrated in the host village, and their affinal status is partly cancelled out. People know that these men are 'part of our *faiava*' ('wife-makers'), but this will not be said openly of those in-marrying men who are chiefs. In community terms – that is, in terms of *nuu* – these men, whether chiefs or servants, do not belong to a separate category.

The few women who sit in the circle of chiefs, the 'village of the chiefs', are always local village women. Where a family chooses a woman to bear the title, she is a *matai*, and all terms used when addressing a male chief are used with her. There are also women who are chiefs in their own villages, but who settle in their husbands' villages. In the (rare) cases I heard about, the husband himself was a high-ranking chief and, in all the cases, the stay was temporary. If the circle of chiefs accepts her, the woman-chief can sit in the circle where her husband is already, but more on a temporary visiting basis.

I have not come across (nor did I ever hear about) a case where a woman who settled in her husband's village was chosen by his family to receive a title.

In sum, there are permanent male in-law members in the chiefs' circle, but no permanent chiefly women members through marriage. It could happen that a woman, chief in her own village, marries a non-chief from another village, but the idea that she might follow her husband to his village struck my informants as preposterous. The other possible scenario – the husband living in his wife's village – met with the comment, 'Well, if he's long-suffering enough to live in his wife's village, he will of course be in the *taulealea* circle'. The 'long-suffering' remark relates to the fact that the husband would be in the group that serves the village: the chiefs' circle of which his wife is a member. It is not an issue for a sister to have a higher status than her brother, for she belongs to the 'side' that 'communicates with God', while her brother 'makes power' by bearing the headship title or, if he is a servant, 'uses strength' to 'do service' for the family and village. It is, however, clearly a problem for a wife to have a much higher status than her husband.[5]

The Village of the Ladies

All women in all villages conduct a number of activities together in the *komiti* (women's committee). The term itself immediately indicates that it is a borrowing. Even though the committee system has been integrated into Samoan villages, it is not so assimilated as to have a Samoan name. The issue falls outside the purview of this study, but a brief discussion is warranted. First, the Protestant missionaries came as couples and imported gender-segregated teaching and division of labour. Missionaries' wives would gather all the village women – a category that made sense to a Western wife's mind, and thus included both the daughters of the village and the wives who had come from other villages – and would teach them together.[6] Then, in the 1920s, the New Zealand administration set up health committees that were managed by women. Grouping village women together confirmed the system introduced by the missionaries. Shortly before independence, some local elite groups used this structure as a basis for a true women's movement (see e.g. Grattan 1948; Schoeffel 1977, 1978a, 1978b, 1979; Schoeffel-Meleisea 1982; Aiono 1992, 1994, n.d.). The outcome of this was complex in its finer details, but, in essence, family chiefs' wives, non-chiefs' wives and village daughters spent more time doing things together for the village community than separately.

This trend still prevails today, and gives the appearance of a 'village women's circle'. Disputes arise, however, between those wives who claim to have authority over the whole women's group based only on age, and the village-born ladies who counter that, by definition, the former group are 'not from here' and therefore have no say. Also, at some ceremonial events in certain villages, only the village women ('village daughters') gather; they exclude the in-married wives. However we look at it, it does not help us understand village exogamy, for men and women. We must now ask if any group of women can be a ceremonial *nuu* group.

The two groups making up the *nuu* village – the chiefs and the servants – are themselves *nuu*. Are there any other village components that have a *nuu* status? When this question is posed, informants unanimously reply that there is just one other group that constitutes a *nuu*: the *tamaitai*, interpreted as the 'ladies of the village'. Particular ceremonial practices reinforce this conclusion. For example, in some villages, the village holds a Sunday banquet or *toonai*, and the villagers sometimes gather in *nuu* groups rather than simply having a family meal. Three *toonai* can be observed – the chiefs' meal (*matai toonai*), the servants' meal (*taulealea toonai*) and the ladies' meal or (*tamaitai toonai*).[7]

The *tamaitai* ladies' group includes women born in the village and living there either permanently or temporarily. This, therefore, includes young (post-pubescent and, nowadays, school graduate) girls and young unmarried women, and also women who have married a man from another village and who brought him in, or who, although usually living (or have been living) in their husbands' villages, have temporarily (or permanently after separation or their husband's death) returned to their village. The etymology of *tamaitai* is not certain, and I have translated it as 'ladies' (as most Samoans do in order to discriminate from the word *fafine*, which refers to a woman only as wife or sexual partner of a man). I might have said 'single women', for these women, even if married, belong to, take the initiative in and have rank in the *tamaitai* group independently of any husband. Everything depends on the family name to which they belong in their own village.

Tamaitai women who bear titles with which they were invested by their families, such as headship titles from female founding ancestors, are known as *saotamaitai*.[8] Ideally, a *saotamaitai* should remain single and entirely devoted to perpetuating the 'sister' title. Such a title is known as the *feagaiga* of a male founder. *Feagaiga* is the ceremonial term for any brother–sister relationship, as well as the sister herself within this relationship. It is said that, in families which have this type of title –only some of the older families in each village do, and sometimes only one of them – a young girl, even a pre-teen, would be invested with the name and known as an *augafaapae* (etymologically, the trans-generational line of the foundations of the title's stem house) or, more commonly, *taupou*.[9] When she eventually marries, another *augafaapae* is chosen. The married woman keeps the female ancestor's name, the *feagaiga* title.

When English-speaking Samoans explain the cultural identity of a *tamaitai* to a foreigner, they make a significant distinction by saying that the *tamaitai* is 'not a woman, but a lady'. Samoans say that, to them, the English word 'woman' corresponds to *fafine*. The Samoan *fafine* can be used for a female animal (preceded by the name of the animal species) or for a woman, but only when her only social definition is as a wife (especially a de facto wife) or an untitled *taulealea*'s wife (even legally married); the category *fafine* is ineligible for special ceremonial names that are used for chiefs' wives (see below).

What role do *tamaitai* play in a village? Nowadays, the *tamaitai*'s role is restricted to dances and gift giving at great feasts between villages, various ceremonies, weddings, chief investitures and church dedications and so forth, insofar as such dances and presentations, along with fine mat weaving, are often (or always in the case of the other functions such as health surveillance networks) carried out by the whole women's group, which includes both the daughters of the village and married women from outside. What was probably the most important *tamaitai* role, that of chaperoning those who were ceremonial virgins (*augafaapae*), has disappeared, as the last ceremonial virgins were instated in the 1920s.

There is, however, an ideologically important distinction between the village daughter and the woman from outside who came as a wife. Whenever there is some ambiguity or dispute, Samoans can soon be heard to mention the distinction: 'Who do you think you are, talking like that? You're not a village *tamaitai*'. Although ceremonial virgins are no longer instated, expressions are still used today that indicate that the concept is still ideologically relevant, and that all village single women have a responsibility towards the village. If an unmarried single woman commits the error of allowing herself to be seduced before marriage (and cannot keep it a secret because the boy brags about it or she falls pregnant), she will be accused of bringing shame not only on the family but the whole village.

This *tamaitai* ladies' group is a *nuu*. Individually, each woman is a village 'lady', and collectively they are all the *nuu* of the *tamaitai* (*o le nuu o tamaitai*). When the ladies meet, they sit in a circle that follows the hierarchy of the circle of chiefs, each lady being a 'daughter' or 'sister' of a chief.

'Our Daughters, Our Sisters'

The ladies' *nuu* completes the *nuu* group that makes up the village *nuu* as a whole: the *nuu* of the chiefs, of the men-servants and of the ladies. Like the circle of the servants, the ladies' *nuu* is a single-sex group. There is an essential difference with the men-servants' group, however, as the ladies' circle is not defined by a function, such as service to the village, but first and foremost by belonging.

This belonging is referred to by two terms: 'daughters' and 'sisters'. When referring to the ladies' circle, Samoans say, 'The *tamaitai* are our village daughters (*teine o le nuu*)'. *Teine* generally means a young unmarried woman. If she remains single, she will no longer be *teine* but, after some time, *tamaitai*. For older women, the word *teine* becomes either an affectionate or slightly mocking term. In a nutshell, if the person speaking is the woman's relative or fellow villager, they would say *teine* for 'young girl'. When she is a woman, but in a sense that overrides her status as a wife to the point where the word does not indicate whether or not she is married, the term used is *tamaitai*. *Teine* assumes virginity, as does *tamaitai* if she is not married; if she is married, *tamaitai* implies that her marital relationship is left 'outside' the area in which she is referred to as *tamaitai* – that is, her village. In order to specify that such a woman is a virgin, a speaker will say *teine muli* if she is young, or *taupou* if she is older. If a person wishes to state unambiguously that a woman of any age has lost her virginity, whether legitimately or not, they will use the term *fafine*. Calling a woman *fafine*, when she is known as a *tamaitai* in the area, is a very grievous insult.

Another statement relevant to this investigation is, 'The *tamaitai* are the *feagaiga*'. The word *feagaiga* means both the 'brother–sister relationship' and 'sisters' themselves. The term is specifically applied to the relationship between names that have become titles, and which belonged to a male ancestor and his sister respectively. In honorific language, it is used for all the family's daughters. The chief will say to them, 'You are *feagaiga* and should behave accordingly'. This opens up a vast area for observing women's ceremonial role in the family, insofar as it is linked with perpetuating founding names and with brother/sister avoidance behaviour that is regularly referred to in the literature, as well as the value attached to premarital virginity (e.g. Mead 1930; Schoeffel 1979; Shore 1982; Aiono 1986). There is also the distinction between, for example, *tamatane* descendants (of both sexes) of the brother or son of a reference ancestor, and *tamafafine* descendants (of both sexes) of a sister or daughter of this ancestor. (Taken together, those who are *tamafafine* can be referred to as *feagaiga*.) This intra-family concept extends to the village level. If a chief speaks about the village ladies, they can even say, 'They are our *feagaiga*, they are the village's *feagaiga*'. In other words, the ladies' circle includes the 'sisters' of all the 'brother–sister relationships' that define each family within the village.

Stories about decisions regarding succession in a great family of the chief title in the 1930s indicate that the 'brother-side' members (*tamatane*) are responsible for presenting candidates; the duties of those on the 'sister-side' (*tamafafine* or *feagaiga*, among whom women bearing *saotamaitai* titles hold most authority) are to ease tensions caused by rivalry between the various brother-side branches. The sister-side should also hint at the best choice, as it is understood to have mystical communication with the founding ancestors and to know what is best.

Premarital virginity for a family's daughters is considered by Samoans a condition for perpetuating the family name; indeed, contemporary observation suggests that, as pointed out above, when an unmarried daughter is seduced and the matter discovered, the shame taints not only the whole family, but the entire village. Given this, it is easy to see links between *feagaiga* sister status in the family and *feagaiga* sister group status in the village. Although some of the expressions mentioned above are unknown today to young Samoans, the accompanying ideology still clearly holds sway in village life. *Tamaitai* ladies are the village sisters. They are, thus, sisters to all the men in the village, and it follows that marrying within the village is the height of unseemliness. This is a first answer to the puzzle posed by the condemnation of village endogamy. But what about in-marrying wives?

Wives: Status, Residence and Asymmetry with Husbands

Another fundamental difference between the ladies' circle and the men-servants' circle is that no woman who comes to live in the village as a wife can ever be taken into the ladies' circle; but, as we now know, male in-laws who are not chiefs are admitted to the men-servants' circle, and male in-laws who are chiefs to the chiefs' circle. Where do the wives who come from outside fit in, seeing that they are not in the ladies' circle?

Within the broad category of in-marrying wives, the group of chiefs' wives stands out because of its combination of similarities with and differences from the other groups. These women gather in a circle as do other groups, faithfully reproducing the hierarchy of the chiefs' circle, but even so the differences outweigh the similarities. First, the group is restricted to chiefs' wives. Second, the names used for this group exclude the term *nuu*. Female in-laws are not treated like male in-laws; far from being integrated like the men, these women form a separate group.

They are known as *faletua ma tausi*. The name itself lacks unity, as the group is made up of two types of member: *faletua* commonly means the wife of a chief whose title is in the *alii* order, while *tausi* means the wife of a chief in the *tulafale* order; *ma* simply means 'and'. All Samoan *matai* chiefs are classified in a national as well as local hierarchy that is based on age and genealogy (the national hierarchy is not very visible, while the local one is fairly visible at district level and very obvious at village level). Cutting across everything, however, is a massive dualistic distinction that sometimes has a ternary extension. The chiefs known as *alii* have various duties attaching to their status, such as not saying much, remaining seated at meetings, eating lightly and drinking tea in small cups, all of which are signs, not of weakness, but of greater sacredness. Few words and gestures are needed, as the authority represented by these chiefs is great. Other chiefs, known as *tulafale* (or *failauga*, lit. 'orators'), speak more, make their speeches standing, eat more at meetings and feasts, and claim genealogies generally springing from those of *alii* chiefs. Overall, orator chiefs are vested with less sacredness than *alii* chiefs but, in a given locality, an orator chief's title may have a greater rank than all the *alii* present (see Shore 1982). Finally, some very great *alii* are entitled to specific honorific formulae, and their wives are ceremonially known by a third term, *masiofo*. The wives' group known as *faletua ma tausi* bear a name that entirely derives from their husbands' status rather than village status. Note that the group does not represent all village wives, as it excludes the wives of men classified as servants. There is no group that takes in all those women who marry in, no 'circle of wives' that could function as such.

What about women who marry in to the village as wives of non-chiefs – that is, as wives of 'servants'? They do not form a group and can only be referred to by their in-law status as 'the non-chiefs' wives' or *o ava a taulealea* – *ava* being the ordinary term for 'wife' (without any status marking), one that would be offensive in reference to a chief's wife. They do not have any ceremonial or other name denoting group status. With regard to their tasks, in addition to the work they do in their husbands' families, they occasionally accompany their husbands when they meet in the servants' circle, such as when the circle is required to cook communally.

Setting aside the difference between chiefs' wives who make up a group and non-chiefs' wives who do not, the common feature shared by all wives is evident in their designation as 'our *nofotane*' (from *nofo*, stay, live, and *tane*, man, husband). They are women who 'stay/live with their man'. They are their 'husbands' wives', and this relation of possession is clearly marked in the system of possessive markers. Most kinship terms require the-*o*-class possessive marker, indicating that the possessor is not the cause of the possession: 'my mother' is *lou tina* and *lou* ('my') applies also to 'my land', the real possessors of which are my ancestors; but 'my wife' is *lau ava* (*lou/lau* differentiation).

In-marrying husbands, on the other hand, are referred to by a term indicating that they sought to 'make a wife' (*fai-ava*), and therefore came to live with their wives; *faiava* is always used to specify the residence issue. The asymmetry evident in the terms *faiava* ('wife-maker') and *nofotane* ('she who is by her husband') is reinforced by the words that precede the terms, whether implicitly or explicitly. In the expression 'the *faiava* men of our village', the word *tamaloa* will be used for men; *tamaloa* applies only to male humans, not to animals. When distinguishing the gender of 'the *nofotane* women of our village', however, only the word *fafine* can be used (never the word for 'ladies', *tamaitai*), and *fafine* is used of female animals, not just for female humans. This distinction arises from social organization. Thus in Samoa the word *fafine* (which occurs in all Polynesian languages to indicate female) necessarily includes the idea of non-virginity. This is why all Samoans, whether men or women, agree that the term is 'impolite'. It designates not only 'wife' (which is generally *ava* or *nofotane* when residence is specified), but connotes that 'she is not-a-lady', a non-*tamaitai*. In contrast, the word *tamaloa*, for a man, does not imply anything about status (chief or servant) or about residence (in his village or as in-law in his wife's village).

The vocabulary denoting kinship-by-marriage-and-residence conveys the same bias. The term for men in their circles (chiefs' or servants') has nothing to do with their wives' statuses, whereas the term for married women precisely depends on the status of their husbands. Moreover, the terms remind the hearer that the man who came to his wife's village 'made' something (a wife), whereas the woman who came to the man's village is simply 'she who stays in her husband's home' (*nofotane*).[10]

This instance of asymmetry is offset by the fact, indicated by all older informants, that a certain trend in custom was for the woman to move to her husband's village, with the opposite being rather rare.[11] It would seem that today, and for the last two generations, it is more a matter of convenience – and a cause of instability of residence. The choice is made in terms of the husband's hopes of receiving a title, the distance from town, and the status difference in the two families' founding titles. There is a third option that is available to very few people – that of buying land in the 4 per cent of the country's surface area that is freehold, thus being independent from both families. I have encountered only a few couples who have been able to opt for this for financial reasons (one was a central-bank department manager and his wife was a teller at the same bank) or as a result of upbringing (one was a pastor's son, and therefore less caught up in the *matai* title system).

The most telling asymmetry is that between in-law statuses. A village is a *nuu* and is made up of three *nuu* groups plus the wives, but not the male in-laws. The husbands partially disappear from the scene, but the wives stand out clearly. The husbands are assimilated, but not the wives. The husbands blend into a system that refers to titles (either as a *matai* chief or as one of a group of servants that is said to be 'the way to become a chief'). Wives are identified only in terms of their husbands.

The Village: Three *Nuu*, Two *Nuu*, One *Nuu*

There are three *nuu* in the village which is itself a *nuu*: the *nuu* of the chiefs who are the embodiment of the deceased ancestors and the founders of the land names; the *nuu* that includes all the male non-chiefs and male in-laws; and the *nuu* of the village daughters (but only those born to the village's founding families, excluding the wives). It is instructive to look here at what Samoans say when asked to explain what constitutes a village (*nuu*). The most common reply was to list all sorts of groups. Usually *matai* chiefs were placed first, then the women's committee or, if the informant was elderly or a village woman, the ladies' circle, followed by the chiefs' wives (if it was a conversation with a married woman, the latter order was reversed), the 'servants' circle' and, finally, the various religious or sports groupings (congregations, new churches, the village choir, sport teams).

The view offered by Aiono (Aiono 1984: 24, 1985, 1986: 104, 1994) is restricted to non-religious and non-sporting groups, and she mentions five groups – the chiefs (mentioned first or sometimes last) and then (always in the same order) the ladies, servants, chiefs' wives and village children. Aiono offers a diagram, emphasizing the fact that the five-component unit is in fact one plus four. There are five circles with the chiefs' circle in the middle of the diagram. The line joining this circle to each of the four others is explained as a *faiatoto* or *faiafaasuli* link – that is, a 'blood link' or the 'position of being an heir to the family's founding name'.[12] Each of the four circles connected to the chiefs' circle is defined by a relationship with them: the *tamaitai* are the chiefs' daughters, the *taulealea* are the chiefs' sons, the *faletua ma tausi* are the chiefs' wives and the *tamaiti* are the chiefs' children. This is significant both in terms of the order followed and the intention of presenting the village as a single family. In fact, Aiono expressly states in one of these five-circle presentations that 'this is the *Aigapotopoto* writ large in the *nuu*' (Aiono n.d.: 2). The first word means the *aiga* family when all members meet formally for an important decision (*potopoto* means to gather individuals or assemble).

The 'one plus four' pattern can be reduced to three. In the past there were only three formal groups: the chiefs, ladies and servants (Aiono 1994: 3). It can then be further reduced to two, emphasizing that 'the *Tamaitai* [single women's group] . . . is the unit in the ideal social organization that repeats the authoritative level of the *matai* group itself; the Samoans refer to the *nuu* as having a *Nuu o Tamaitai* [single women's village] and a *Nuu o Matai* [chiefs' village]' (Aiono n.d.: 2). Aiono has previously stated that 'the *Tamaitai* of the village occupy a place in the social system equal to that of the village *matai*' (Aiono 1985: 2). If taken further, the analysis returns to the starting point, with the chiefs' circle being the whole system's central circle, the model being repeated by the others for their internal organization. In a sense, says Aiono, 'the word *Nuu* also refers to the social organization of the *Faamatai* or specifically to the *Matai* Group' (Aiono n.d.: 5). In any case, whether village organization is seen as a single group or five or more, it would clearly appear to be expressible in terms of the following: the chiefs, chiefs and ladies, the three kinds of *nuu* (chiefs, ladies, servants), these three *nuu* groups plus the wives and children.

An expression often used by Samoans is, *nuu o tamaitai ma nuu o matai*, 'the ladies' village and the chiefs' village', or, in reverse order, *nuu o tamaitai ma nuu o alii*, where *alii* has replaced *matai*, giving rise to ambiguity. The word *alii* or 'chiefs' is (or became in the nineteenth century) also a polite way of referring to men in general in a speech or ceremonial address, like the English 'gentlemen'. Similarly, the word *tamaitai* is used as the English 'ladies' when women are referred to in public; *fafine* is considered impolite and quite inappropriate for speeches because of its 'non-virgin woman' connotation. This alone has led various observers to see in this expression the notion of a 'village of gentlemen and a village of ladies', thus a male/female division, opening the door to the Western bias of trying to view any society as primarily a grouping of 'men and women'.

The summary picture that emerges here, however, is not at all a 'male/female/division'. It is a ternary configuration, based on the family model, with the ancestors made present in the chiefs and their sons and daughters. It is essentially one of a world of consanguinity, where an agnatic ideology – in the limited sense that any chief, whether man or woman, is 'father' to the members of the family whose name they represent – totally ignores kinship by marriage. Only the fathers and their sons and daughters are included. Bringing the fathers together in a single circle suggests that all these sons and daughters are each others' brothers and sisters. Significantly, when Aiono emphasized the importance of the relationship between the chiefs and single women within a village and was asked about the servants' circle, she replied spontaneously that 'the *aumaga* are the brothers of the *tamaitai*' (*aumaga* is one of the names that can be applied to the servants' *taulealea* group).[13]

This brother–sister relationship is also at work between the chiefs and the ladies' circle, as it is essentially the chiefs' circle that symbolizes the village, and the chiefs say that 'the ladies are the village's *feagaigai* sisters'. *Matai* chiefs are mostly men and, whether men or women, are said to be their family's fathers. All other men, younger or older, are their juniors in status terms. They do service for their chief and, through them, for the community. The relationship between the chiefs' and servants' circles is a father–son or older-brother–younger-brother relationship that supersedes age (an older man will say to a younger *matai*, 'You are my older brother').

The ladies' circle, however, includes both the daughters and sisters (aunts and so on). A man owes respect to a woman in his family and age group and, all the more so, to an older woman, as she is his *feagaiga*, or classificatory sister. As far as a man is concerned, a younger brother cannot do any more than he can. All he can do is help him (*fesoasoani*). A female blood relative, however, is supposed to have a special relationship with the origin (gods, founding ancestors), which used to be ritually condensed in the ceremonial virgin figures, but is more or less deemed to be the purview of all female kin (Schoeffel 1979). In a way, the chief owes respect to his *feagaiga* sisters.

Something of this relationship is clearly at work in the collective relationship between the village chiefs and the village ladies (even if ancient tales of war about the virgin ladies' sacrifice in offering themselves to the enemy, if the village is about to be invaded, are no longer part of the collective consciousness), and the reduction of the village to the two first groups, the chiefs and the ladies, emphasizes this. For example, if a servant commits an offence, he is fined but it is his family, and therefore his chief, who pays the fine to the chiefs' circle. If a virgin 'falls', however, according to the *matai* chiefs, the entire village is put to shame.

'Sister or Wife, You've Got to Choose'

The findings on village exogamy thus far can be summarized as follows. A man who is an in-law in his wife's village and a chief in his own family, or who has acquired this title in his wife's family, is admitted to the village chiefs' circle in his wife's village. If he is not a chief, he is assigned to the men-servants' circle in his wife's village with the same status as her brothers, both in terms of duties and forms of address. If the man stays in his own village, his wife becomes one of his village's in-laws. She is a *nofotane* who is going to stay with her husband. If she marries a chief, she joins the chiefs' wives' group, but this group does not belong to the village and is not a *nuu*. If she marries a non-chief, she has no group to join, and is simply a servant's wife.

What happens if both spouses are from the same village? For the man, nothing happens in terms of the status he enjoys because of who he is. If he is a chief in his own village, he remains so, even if some shame is bound to pursue him wherever he goes. This shame is cast upon him from elsewhere – that is, from what has happened to his wife's status as a result of the endogamous marriage. Likewise, if he is a servant in his own village, he remains so. In either case, the man will continue to belong to his own village circle, whether it is that of the chiefs or the men-servants.

For the woman, however, the situation is different. Whether she marries a chief or a servant from her own village, she is excluded from the ladies' circle. If she marries a chief, she will be faced with joining the chiefs' wives' group. If she marries a servant, she will not belong to any formal group. In either case, she has now to associate with the *nofotane* women who have come from outside 'to live with their men'. And in either case, she is no longer 'at home' in her own village; she loses this fundamental identity of 'being from such-and-such village' and an 'heir to this land'. In each and every case I know of, this logical set of options meant that, in all marriages made within a village, the wife was compelled by the community to take on the status of a wife and, in so doing, lose the status of village lady.

There was a case involving a woman who was one of the country's last surviving ceremonial virgins within one of Samoa's great families. Through circumstances unknown to me, she married a chief in her own village and, despite her fame and previous status, was not admitted to the village's ladies' circle. She was reduced to staying at home for many years, and then to spending much of her time away from home. When she divorced, for unrelated reasons, she rejoined her initial circle, though without the same honour as before. Forty years later, she explained to me that, as she was the first *tamaitai* lady and the first among them to bear a title (*saotamaitai*), she could never associate on a daily basis with women who were defined solely in terms of being *nofotane*, 'she who stays with a man'. She had to seclude herself in her house, or to leave the village. 'You see', she said, '*tamaitai* or *nofotane*, you've got to choose and make sure you get it right'.

Notes

1. I have found only four references to the phenomenon: Gilson (1963, 1970: 22), Schoeffel (1979) and Aiono (1986: 104).
2. Variation of value with age brings other important considerations into play: the longer the genealogical record (which is kept active by interaction), the more the network of 'related' people expands and the greater the investment can become in exchanges with another family.
3. See e.g. Tcherkézoff (1998) on the issue of a village's right to exile the occupants of family land.
4. In Samoa, the state police force in practice operates only in the capital. It only intervenes in a village if requested to do so by a member of the public or the council of chiefs. Such a request is always seen as shameful for a village because, as visitors are told, 'The real police in Samoa are the *matai* and the whole *faamatai*' (the whole respect system generated by the hierarchy of family titles borne by the *matai*).
5. I will not dwell on the complex issue of the different types of superiority here. Suffice it to say that brother/sister inequality is totally

unrelated to husband/wife inequality. The former is the whole/part and sacred/temporal type, a hierarchy in the holistic Dumontian sense, whilst the latter is the more ordinary type, unequal measures of the same attribute – in this case strong/less strong or *malosi/vaivai*; on the distinction between hierarchy and inequality, see Tcherkézoff (2008b).

6. For more details and quotations from missionary accounts, see Tcherkézoff (2008a).

7. For further examples, see Schoeffel (1979).

8. Often male founding ancestors' sisters.

9. The word *auga* conveys the notion of a flow or steady stream (Milner 1966: 29), as in 'the years drifting by' or 'the succession of *matai* bearing this name' (*o le auga a matai* or the word *auganofo* explained above); *pae* means the house foundations; the (abutting stone) foundation height is a direct and regulated sign of a family title's rank in the village circle.

10. Another instance of this asymmetry occurs in the language of the sexual act, known from the male point of view as 'doing' (the 'thing'), while the female partner 'is touched, wounded, knocked', and all kinds of similar metaphors (Tcherkézoff 2003: 277–412).

11. According to accounts made to me regarding the 1930s.

12. *Faia* is a passage between two points, such as a log thrown across a stream to cross it (a term still used to indicate a relationship by blood or marriage); *toto* means blood; *faa* is a causative prefix; and *suli* means heir.

13. This comment came during questions in response to Aiono (1994).

In memory of Aiono Dr. Fanaafi and Koke Aiono.
As I was just about to send Aiono Dr. Fanaafi the final version of this chapter which owes so much to her wisdom, sad news came of her passing away, in August 2014, after a long life dedicated to keeping the FaaSamoa ('Samoan language' and 'Samoan custom') alive and rich, through her researches and the educational programmes she had implemented in the country. The whole field of Samoan Studies, and indeed the whole of Samoa, have lost their Feagaiga.

References

Aiono, F.L.T. 1984. 'The Confessions of a Bat', *Savali* (Apia, Samoa), July, pp. 22–29.

⸻ 1985. 'The Woman in Samoan Society', unpublished lecture delivered at the Unesco conference 'Decade of the Woman', Dubrovnik.

⸻ 1986. 'Western Samoa: The Sacred Covenant', in C. Bolabola, D. Kenneth and H. Silas, M. Moengangongo, F. Aiono and M. James, *Land Rights of Pacific Women*. Suva: Institute of Pacific Studies, University of the South Pacific.

_____ 1992. 'The Samoan Culture and Government', in R. Crocombe, U. Neemia, A. Ravuvu and W. von Buch (eds), *Culture and Democracy in the South Pacific*, Suva: Institute of Pacific Studies, University of the South Pacific.

_____ 1994. 'The Brother–Sister Relationship', unpublished lecture delivered at the Ecole des Hautes Etudes en Sciences Sociales, Pôle de Marseille, May.

_____ n.d. 'The Samoan Culture and Government', unpublished paper (expanded version of Aiono 1992).

Gilson, R.P. 1963. 'Samoan Descent Groups: A Structural Outline', *Journal of the Polynesian Society* 72(4): 372–77.

_____ 1970. *Samoa, 1830–1900: The Politics of a Multicultural Community*. Melbourne: Oxford University Press.

Grattan, F.J.H. 1948. *An Introduction to Samoan Custom*. Apia: Samoa Printing Co.

Mead, M. 1930. *Social Organization of Manuʻa*. Honolulu: Bishop Museum Press.

Milner, G.B. 1966. *Samoan Dictionary*. London: Oxford University Press.

Schoeffel, P. 1977. 'The Origin and Development of Contemporary Women's Associations in Western Samoa', *Journal of Pacific Studies* 3: 1–22.

_____ 1978a. 'Gender, Status and Power in Samoa', *Canberra Anthropology* 1(2): 69–81.

_____ 1978b. 'The Ladies' Row of Thatch: Women and Rural Development in Western Samoa', *Pacific Perspectives* 8(2): 1–11.

_____ 1979. 'Daughters of Sina: A Study of Gender, Status and Power in Western Samoa', Ph.D. diss. Canberra: Australian National University.

Schoeffel-Meleisea, P. 1982. 'Women's Associations and Rural Development', *Pacific Perspectives* 11(2): 56–61.

Shore, B. 1982. *Salaiʼilua: A Samoan Mystery*. New York: Columbia University Press.

Tcherkézoff, S. 1998. 'Is Aristocracy Good for Democracy? A Contemporary Debate in Western Samoa', in J. Wassmann (ed.), *Pacific Answers to Western Hegemony: Cultural Practices of Identity Construction*. Oxford: Berg.

_____ 2003. *Faasamoa, une identité polynésienne (économie, politique, sexualité): L'anthropologie comme dialogue culturel*. Paris: L'Harmattan.

_____ 2008a. 'Culture, Nation, Society: Secondary Change and Fundamental Transformations in Western Samoa. Towards a Model for the Study of Cultural Dynamics', in S. Tcherkézoff and F. Douaire-Marsaudon (eds), *The Changing Pacific: Identities and Transformations*. Canberra: Pandanus Press.

_____ 2008b. 'Hierarchy Is Not Inequality, in Polynesia for Instance', in K. Rio and O.H. Smedal (eds), *Persistence and Transformation in Social Formations*. Oxford: Berghahn.

9

The Sister's Return

The Brother–Sister Relationship, the Tongan *Fahu* and the Unfolding of Kinship in Polynesia

——————— ◆●◆ ———————

Françoise Douaire-Marsaudon

At the beginning of the twentieth century, the relationship between a brother and a sister and their respective offspring in Oceania attracted the attention of anthropologists. Hocart (1915) described how, in Tonga, during the kava ritual performed for a high chief, a person outside the kava circle – generally the chief's sister's son or his grandchild – might come and seize the ceremonial food (*fono*) set aside for the chief. Hocart was thus one of the first anthropologists to pay attention to the ceremonial prerogatives of the sister's child, called *vasu* in Fiji and *fahu* in Tonga. He brilliantly demonstrated that these prerogatives throw light on the conception of chiefship in the Pacific region (ibid.: 640–45). Later, Radcliffe-Brown (1924) compared the relationship which links uterine nephews to their maternal uncle, first among the Bathonga of South Africa and, second, among the inhabitants of the Friendly Islands, as Tonga was once known.[1] Hocart and Radcliffe-Brown were both particularly curious about the ceremonial aspects of the relationship between a man and his sister's son and the position of the latter as *vasu* in Fiji or *fahu* in Tonga, and both identified the sister's son's behaviour during the rituals as 'predatory'. '[T]he sister's son is permitted to take many liberties with his mother's brother, and to take any of his uncle's possessions that he may desire. And there also we find the custom that, when the uncle makes a sacrifice, the sister's son takes away the sacred portion offered to the gods, and may eat it' (Radcliffe-Brown 1924: 542–43). For Hocart and Radcliffe-Brown, the *vasu/fahu* is able to steal the offerings made to chiefs or gods and to eat them because, as the chief's sister's son or the chief's grandchild, he is superior to him in status. It follows that the *vasu/fahu* should not receive any supernatural punishment for stealing the chief's or the god's food.

Rivers had also taken an interest in the brother–sister relationship in Oceania, but from another point of view, having been surprised by the very close relationship he found between a person and their father's sister in Tonga:

> In Tonga a man honours his father's sister more than any other relative, more even than his father or his father's elder brother. In the old time, it was believed that, if he offended her, disobeyed her, or committed any mistake in the regulation of his conduct towards her, he would die. The father's sister or *mehekitanga* usually arranged the marriage of her *fakafotu* or brother's son and she could veto one [marriage] arranged by his parents or by the man himself . . . There is some degree of community of goods between nephew and aunt; the father's sister can take anything belonging to her nephew and the latter will not say a word. (Rivers 1910: 42–43)[2]

Rivers did not mention the *fahu*; rather, he observed an important detail in the relationship between a father's sister and her brother's children: 'a father's sister can take anything belonging to her nephew and the latter will not say a word'. In other words, Rivers showed that because she outranks her brother, the father's sister has, over her brother's child, the same 'predatory right' that the *fahu/vasu* or uterine nephew/niece has over their mother's brother. Rivers was thus the first anthropologist to point out that the relationship between the father's sister and her brother's child was the exact symmetrical opposite of that between the mother's brother and his sister's son (Rivers 1968, I: 367).

After 1930, the theme of the relationship between brothers, sisters and their respective offspring in Oceania disappeared almost completely from anthropological and historical works, and it was not until the 1970s that the theme again came to the fore – usually in reference to a more inclusive issue: rank (Kaeppler 1971; Bott 1981), economic privileges (Lévi-Strauss: 1984: 216–18), ceremonial exchange (Kaeppler 1978) and descent groups (Biersack 1982). Additionally, Rogers (1977), who had done extensive fieldwork in Niuatoputapu, Tonga, analysed the bonds linking a woman and her brother's children, focusing, like Rivers, on the father's sister's role. He argued that, in this patrilineal society, there existed a matrilineal principle which gave a symbolic power to female lines, which explains the special prestige accorded to women. Wood-Ellem (1981) threw new light on the brother–sister relationship by showing how the emblematic figure of the brother/sister pair could be used as a symbolic basis for the management of political power, while I have myself looked at Tongan history and examined the role of opposite-sex siblingship in the political strategies of marriage, right to the very top of Tongan society (Douaire-Marsaudon 1998). As will be evident in what follows, the work of Biersack (1982) is particularly relevant for my argument here.

The present chapter sets out to reconsider the phenomenon of the Tongan *fahu* and the implications of opposite-sex siblingship. I argue that the brother–sister relationship acquires its full meaning when the brother and sister have produced their respective offspring: each of them is, in their own way, the true 'parent' of the other's child. This appropriation of descendants through opposite-sex siblingship is evinced in the *fahu* who is thus the core of the unfolding of kinship relations over generations. As such, the *fahu* mediates between the domestic and the political spheres.

Tongan Kinship Rules: The Sister as Absolute Senior

Tonga is considered one of the most stratified societies of Polynesia (Sahlins 1958), but what is much more important is that the hierarchical principles that rank persons and groups are rooted in the kinship sphere.[3] As Gifford observed: the 'ranking of individuals within the Tongan family . . . is the key to the organization of Tongan society in every stratum. From bottom to top and from top to bottom of the social ladder, one general scheme of family organization prevails' (Gifford 1929: 19). The principles of rank hierarchy are expressed by the dichotomy *'eiki/tu'a* or chief/commoner. As James rightly puts it, 'They do not denote a simple notion of dominance of one over the other but rather an order of precedence in which *'eiki* is the superior' (James 1990: 2).

These principles are relatively simple, even if their combination is intricate, depending on circumstances. The elder is *'eiki* (chief) or superior to the younger (who is *tu'a* or a commoner), and within the extended family group, called the *kāinga*, the elder line is superior to the younger line, whatever the age of the person concerned.[4] Sisters (and female cousins in this classificatory system) are superior to brothers (and male cousins) whatever their respective age, which means that the youngest sister is superior to all her brothers, even to the eldest one. The principle of (female) sex transcends the principle of seniority. The father's side is superior to the mother's side. These rules work only between two consecutive generations (thus not between grandparents and grandchildren) within the patrilineal group called the *kāinga*.

According to these rules, there are two main principles which structure kinship, seniority and sex. But what is more singular is that, among siblings/cousins of the same generation, the sister appears as a kind of absolute senior because of her sex. During the period between the seventeenth and nineteenth centuries, the paramount chief, the Tuʻi Tonga, supposed to have been engendered by a powerful god, was of very exalted rank, but his sister, the Tuʻi Tonga Fefine, had the supreme rank. I return to this point below, following my discussion of Tongan kinship terminology. Beginning with Ego's generation: what does the terminology tells about the brother–sister relationship?

A Terminology Structured by the Principle of Opposite-Sex Siblings

In terms of Murdock's (1949) classification, Tongan kinship terminology belongs to the Hawaiian type, which means that it does not distinguish between siblings and cousins, or between cross and parallel cousins (Figure 9.1).[5] Throughout Polynesia, two main principles of sibling differentiation are analytically relevant: those of sex and seniority.[6] Another principle of prime significance is the specification of the sex of siblings in relative terms: same sex as the speaker or different sex. So, a sister refers to her sister by the same term as a brother refers to his brother; in Tonga it is the term *tokoua* which is thus reciprocal. But sister and brother use other terms to refer to one another. In Tonga, a brother refers to his sister by a female-significant term, *tuofefine*, and a sister refers to her brother by a male-significant term, *tuangaʻane*.[7] Thus, the principle of relative sex is present in Tongan terminology at level G0 with the reciprocal term *tokoua*. But there is also, and simultaneously, the specification of absolute sex with the two terms *tuofefine* and *tuangaʻane*: both of these are used by siblings of opposite sex, and both indicate simultaneously the sex of alter and the sex of the speaker. Not only are brother and sister in an opposite sex relationship, but their actual sex matters too. One might also observe that brother and sister are differentiated by sex, but to be a sister of a brother is not quite the same as to be a brother of a sister. In other words, the terminology accords with the hierarchical principle that ranks sisters above brothers.

It is illuminating to compare these terms with those used by spouses: husband and wife use the same term *hoa* to refer to the other. Thus *hoa* is not a term of relative sex specification; *hoa* means companion and could be used for two persons of the same sex, for a pair of friends, for example. Despite the sexual nature of the relation between spouses, the sex specification is not relevant in the terminology used by married couples. By contrast, the sex distinction is not only present but emphasized for a brother/sister

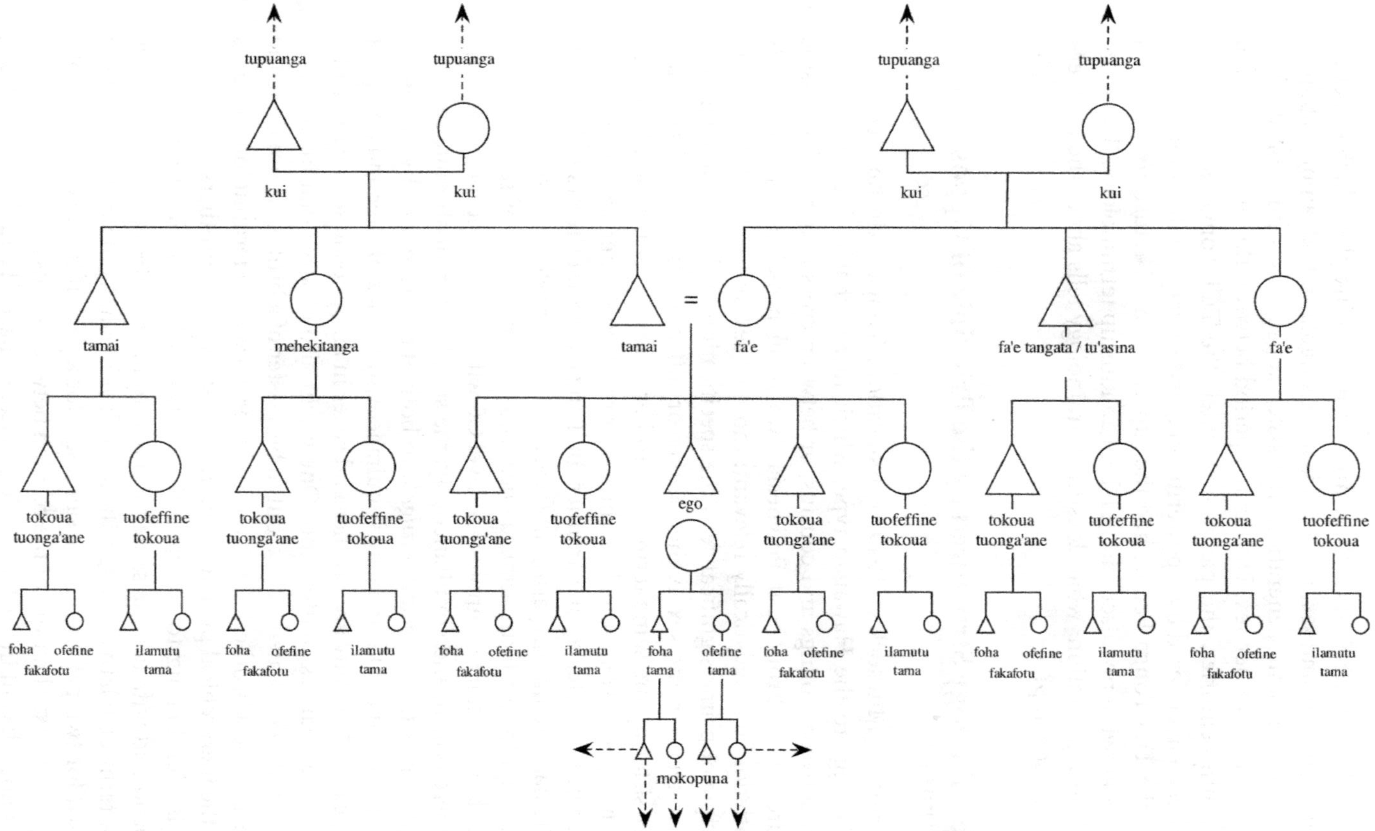

Figure 9.1: Tongan kinship terminology

pair. This makes sense, for sexuality may be ignored where it is fitting and, by the same token, marked out and emphasized by a strong taboo where it is not, as in the brother–sister relationship.

If we look now at Ego's parents' generation (G+1), it is easy to see that the opposite-sex principle also structures this level. *Fa'ē* is the term for the mother and all her siblings of the same sex; *tamai* is the term for the father and all his siblings of the same sex. Specific terms appear for siblings of opposite sex to the father and mother: *mehekitanga* for the father's sister and *fa'ē tangata* (literally 'male mother') for mother's brother.[8] Thus, on level G+1, two aspects of the terminology attract attention: first, among a group of fathers and mothers, two brother/sister pairs emerge, the father and his sister on the one hand, the mother and her brother on the other; second, on the mother's side, among a group of mothers, *fa'ē*, the terminology operates a distinction between female mothers, *fa'ē*, and male mothers, *fa'ē tangata*. The opposite-sex principle also structures the level of Ego's children (G–1). A man refers to his brother's children with the same terms he uses for his own children, a woman refers to her sister's children with the same terms she uses for her own children.[9] But specific terms appear for the father's sister to designate her brother's children, *fakafotu*, and for the mother's brother to designate his sister's children, *'ilamutu*.

It is noteworthy that, on the three levels which form the core of Tongan kinship terminology – G0, G+1 and G–1 – the opposite-sex principle (which requires non reciprocal, special terms) does not deal with the relation between alter and Ego, nor that between Ego and the linking relative, but with the relation between alter and the members of the same generation. In other words, what is at stake here is the opposite-sex principle between or among siblings and cousins. Thus Biersack (1982) rightly observed that consanguineous kin are divided into two classes: parallel-siblings and their children, and cross-siblings and their children. Following Lévi-Strauss, she called these two 'matrixes' – the cross-matrix and the parallel matrix – 'the two structures of exchange' (ibid.: 181).

According to Biersack, cross-cousin marriage or marriage with the MBD, which was in vogue among Tongan chiefs, was part of this system of relationships:

> In the post-contact period, there was a marriage referred to as *mali fatongia*, 'marriage duty', a duty, Gifford tell us, that is incumbent upon BC [brother's children] ... The purely indigenous expression is *takai fala*, 'rolling up the mats', for it is said of the woman that she goes to roll up the mats of her father's sister's son'. That Tongan MBD marriage is intelligible as a relationship among relationships, as a constituent of the system of exchange exemplified in the cross-matrix, is, of course, consistent with the fact that it is the FZ who chooses her BC's spouses. (ibid.: 6)

This kind of cross-cousin marriage was called *kitetama*, and was the only form of matrimonial union which was named.[10] Today, the *kitetama* is no longer practised (probably because it was condemned by the Church), except among those who are of chiefly birth. This cross-cousin marriage (*kitetama*) was systematically practised between the three royal lines, at least from the end of the sixteenth until the nineteenth century (see below). If, however, we examine Tongan terminology, it becomes apparent that there is nothing special about *kitetama* or MBD marriage: the maternal uncle and the father-in-law (man speaking) are not referred to by the same term, as is the case in Fiji, where cross-cousin marriage is the prescribed matrimonial union.[11]

Respect, Avoidance and Exchange between Brother and Sister

As in all hierarchical relationships, respect (*faka'apa'apa*) and avoidance are mandatory in the relation between brothers and sisters, but the taboo on their relationship (as well as between cousins in this classificatory system) seems particularly significant with regard to sexuality: any allusion, by gesture or words, to things or ideas related to sexuality or para-sexuality (like pregnancy or childbirth) is prohibited between brothers and sisters. Brothers and sisters are not supposed to share any cloth or to finish the other's food. A brother should not enter a house where his sister is alone, he should not appear before his sister in slovenly dress (without a shirt), he should not speak badly in her presence. All boys of the same generation in a given family sleep in a *fale uo* (bachelors' house) from the first signs of puberty until they marry, whereas girls stay at home with their parents. Moreover, the prohibition concerning allusions to sexuality must also be observed by other people present: if there is a meeting at which opposite-sex siblings are present, all the participants have to respect the same prohibition.

The brother–sister relationship is also positively marked by exchanges of goods and services. The direction of the flow of goods and services clearly shows who is superior and who is inferior: the sister is the chief (*'eiki*), whereas the brother is the commoner (*tu'a*). The brother honours and helps his sister by giving food (generally raw, *tokonaki*) at certain important moments of the year, but also whenever she asks for it. The sister is also supposed to make a gift to her brother of some *koloa* (mats, barkcloth or coconut oil) in return but, for her, it is not compulsory. The brother must also give his sisters the *polopolo* or the first fruits of his harvest and fishing (just as any commoner has to give their first fruits to their chief): yams, breadfruit, pigs and so forth. When asked about help, care and gifts given to their sisters, my male informants said that this is their *fatongia* for their sisters, that 'it's an honour to do that for them'. The word *fatongia* means 'duty'. The same term is used by Tongan villagers to speak about the link with their chief. This behaviour between brothers and sisters must be observed by the parties concerned from the first signs of puberty until death.

According to Biersack, because of the incest taboo operating in the cross-sibling relationship, 'exchange between cross-siblings is effectively suppressed' (Biersack 1982: 4). My own observations do not correspond with this. To my mind, the incest taboo between brother and sister is the tip of the iceberg constituted by their rich and ambiguous relationship. The main part of this relationship, but much less visible than the taboo itself, is composed of an important series of exchanges based on what Tongans call '*ofa*, 'good love': tenderness without sexuality, help and care. These exchanges of goods, services and feelings between brothers and sisters are lifelong, but their relationship acquires its full dimension when both of them have engendered their respective offspring.

The Mother and the Mother's Brother

The term *fa'ē* is applied to the mother and to all her real and classificatory sisters. A child should behave respectfully towards their mother, even if a lot of freedom is permitted between them. Some anthropologists have seen a principle of hierarchy between a mother and her child (Rogers 1977: 160). It is true that the mother is considered the pedestal for her child, particularly in the aristocratic milieu, blood and rank being, in traditional ideology, transmitted through the mother. It is also true that the mother's side (*kāinga 'i fa'ē*) is, according to kinship rules, the inferior side (*tu'a*) of the child's *kainga* kin group, the paternal side being the superior one ('*eiki*). Moreover, a Tongan mother knows that, even if her children must respect her, she has no control over their lives: this power is held by the father, and even more so by the father's sister. In any case, it seems to me that the mother–child relationship is too free to be considered as typically hierarchical. After the birth rites, even if a child is considered a member of the paternal clan and subject to its authority, the bond that ties a child to their maternal group (*kāinga 'i fa'ē*, mother's side) is and remains strong by virtue of their relation to their mother's brother.

As noted above, the relationship between the mother's brother and his uterine nephew or niece in Tonga is 'oriented': the latter is *fahu* to their mother's brother, and thus in a superior position. The nephew or niece can, in principle, take what they want from the maternal uncle. Futa Helu told me the following story: one day, his sister's children, three boys between six and eight years old, came to him and asked for money to buy sweets;

when he refused, because he had no money on him, they said, angrily, 'You know, Futa, if we wanted to, we could sell you!'[12] Of course, they could not 'sell' him, and a mother's brother is never obliged to give what he does not possess. What these young boys were expressing was their felt sense of rank as *fahu*: because they take precedence over their mother's brother, he has to submit to their desires. Thus today, the best way for a youth to get to Nuku'alofa, the Tongan capital, is to look for a maternal uncle going there. In fact, the mother's brother is supposed to help and support his sister's children as much as possible and throughout his whole life.

There is one difficulty, however, in considering the relationship between the mother's brother and their uterine nephew/niece as simply hierarchical: in Tonga, as we have seen, hierarchical relationships are usually marked by avoidance and taboos, but this is not the case between the mother's brother and his nephew/niece. On the contrary, their relationship is said to be *fa'iteliha*, free of constraint (see also Rogers 1975: 270), and could even be classified as a 'joking relationship'. This single characteristic is sufficient to make the relationship between any man and his sister's child a special one.

During the life-cycle ceremonies of his sister's child, the *fa'ē tangata* (mother's brother) observes a specific form of behaviour that recalls his low status: he spends his time in the kitchen, cooking for family and guests. At births in particular, he fulfils an important duty: besides cooking for guests, he keeps young coconuts warm for his sister. This supportive action (*ta'ota'o veifua*) 'follows the belief that the warm juice of a *veifua* (young coconuts) will hasten and increase the mother's own milk' (ibid.: 267). Here, the *fa'ē tangata* indeed appears as 'male mother'; interestingly, Rogers was told that the maternal uncle was doing it 'for the benefit' of his own children.

When his sister's child (*'ilamutu*) marries, the maternal uncle walks behind, anointing their shoulders and arms with coconut oil. During the ceremony, the *'ilamutu* sits on the lap of the maternal uncle, who presents his uterine nephew or niece to the spouse's kin as a valuable person he has to protect.

In the past, it was the mother's brother who circumcised his sister's son.[13] He could perform this operation because both of them, uncle and nephew, were supposed to share the same blood. In Tonga, according to traditional ideas, blood was transmitted only by women; in other words, a mother transmitted her blood to her children – male and female – but only her daughter will transmit this blood to her children. Consequently, brothers, their sisters and their sisters' children are truly 'consanguineous' (excluding, for the brothers, their own children and their brothers' children).

The Father and the Father's Sister

The term *tamai* refers to the father and all his brothers, real or classificatory. *Tamai* are 'eiki, considered to be 'chiefs' within the *kāinga*. Because of his rank within the family group, the *tamai* is surrounded by many taboos, the strongest being the prohibition on touching his head (the seat of ancestry). He is the *ulu o'e famili*, the head of the family, and as such he has the power (*pule*) to command and control family affairs. If he is a titled chief, he transmits the title, the land and authority over the land. While all the children must obey the father, there is a slight difference in the behaviour of a father towards his son and his daughter: with the latter, a father has an easier, less constrained relationship than with the former.[14]

All the father's sisters are referred to by the term *mehekitanga*, but the most revered is the senior sister of the real father, or the eldest of his real sisters.[15] Within the *kainga* group, the father's sister, in accordance with the rules of hierarchy, occupies the highest rank. She is surrounded by the strongest taboos. She has the power to make her brother's wife sick when she is pregnant or to make the birth difficult, thus provoking the sickness or death of the baby (Gifford 1929: 331; Rogers 1977: 164). If a miscarriage, sickness or death befalls someone – a baby, a child or even an adult – people first check that everything is all right between this person and their paternal aunt. Indeed, the father's sister can intentionally put curses on people, and this is one of the reasons for behaving very respectfully towards her, but the curse may also happen independently of her will:

> Near the capital Nuku'alofa in Tongatapu, a woman miscarried repeatedly for years. She believed that her barrenness was due to her father's sister, who had been insulted by her mother, who died without making up the quarrel. She took a gift to her father's sister, and weeping, begged her on her knees to lift the curse she had undoubtedly placed (*talatuki'i*) on her. The aunt said she had done nothing, but agreed that a curse may have fallen even without her conscious agency because of the mother's ill-tempered behaviour towards her. (James 1990: 30)

It has been said that the *mehekitanga*, by virtue of her power to curse, possesses 'black power' (Rogers, 1977: 157–158). This 'black power' has been discussed by Lévi-Strauss and Valeri. The latter opposed the negative sacrality of the *mehekitanga* to the positive sacrality of the paramount chief, the Tu'i Tonga (Valeri 1989: 245, n.28). Lévi-Strauss was also interested in the father's sister's role in western Polynesia:

> in the two groups of islands [Tonga and Samoa], the father's eldest sister had supreme authority over her nephews and nieces. She could even curse them or make them

sterile, thus depriving them of descendants and compensating – one is tempted to say by analogy with the Fijian *vasu* – for her incapacity to succeed to her brother's titles in the agnatic group or, once married and living with her husband, to interfere in the affairs of the family in which she was born. (Lévi-Strauss 1984: 218–19)

Thus, according to Lévi-Strauss, the father's sister's powers are compensation for her double incapacity: as a female, because she cannot inherit; and as a sister, because, once married, she can no longer interfere in her family's affairs. Even so, though a chief's sister/daughter does not generally inherit his title, in the chiefly group the father's sister has her say about the inheritance both of the title and the land. Besides, concerning the 'incapacity of a sister, once married, to interfere in her family's affairs', Lévi-Straus was not well-informed. It is precisely after her marriage, when she has left the paternal *kāinga* where she was born for the marital *kāinga* where she lives, that the sister is required to return to her previous home and to play there, during the life-crisis rites of her brothers' progeny, her prominent role of *mehekitanga*.

At all life-cycle rites for her *fakafotu* (brother's children), the *mehekitanga* sits in the place of honour, generally beside the gifts of mats and barkcloth brought to the ceremonies by the participants. For a birth, the baby's *mehekitanga* comes with two important gifts: a name for the baby and a *pa'epa'e*, a little 'bed' consisting of a fine mat and a piece of tapa. These are presented to the baby's parents as a sign that the father's sister accepts the baby into the paternal *kāinga*. At the end of the ceremony, she lifts the taboos and receives the largest tapa piece and the most beautiful mat.

The *mehekitanga* does not exactly choose her brother's child's spouse, but it is true that her consent is required for the wedding.[16] If a father does not agree with his child's choice of a spouse, the best way to make him change their mind is to obtain the father's sister's support: if she asks the father – her brother – to accept his child's choice, he cannot refuse. During her brother's children's weddings, the paternal aunt sits in the place of honour; she receives the top layer of the wedding cake and the most beautiful mat and piece of *gnatu* (tapa). She may also, if she likes, distribute the *koloa* (mats, barkcloth and coconut-oil). She may even take all the *koloa* brought for the ceremony. One of my informants told me that, in this case, people whisper that she is a *mehekitanga kovi* (mischievous father's sister) but nobody protests.

For funerals, the *mehekitanga* sits close to the head of the deceased. During my first period of fieldwork, intrigued by the immobility of the paternal aunt sitting near the dead body, I asked naively: 'What does she do there the whole day? Does she pray for the deceased?' An informant replied:

'No, it's the priest who is here to pray, not the *mehekitanga*. She has nothing to do, just sleep'. Later, when I pressed the point, I got this answer: 'Shh, she is in contact with the dead, our ancestors'. At the end of the rite, the father's sister of the deceased person, the *mehekitanga* (or somebody who represented her, generally a grandchild or great-grandchild) lifts the taboos and the relatives of the dead must prepare a roll consisting of a mat and a piece of tapa for her.

In summary, for all these rites, the paternal aunt occupies the place of honour, takes or receives the best part of the *koloa* (gifts of mats, tapa and coconut oil) and lifts the taboos at the end of the ceremony. This is because she is *fahu* which, in this context, means 'above the taboos' or 'above the law' (see also Kaeppler 1978: 178). Her place is the opposite of the position of the *fa'e tangata* ('male mother'): she is in the place of honour, he in the place of lowest status.

The power to curse – a 'supernatural' force which operates with or without the father's sister's will – corresponds to the well-known Polynesian concept of *mana*. The *mehekitanga*, as the most sacred person in the family, possesses *mana*. But the source of her *mana* comes from elsewhere: from the ancestors she is responsible for representing among the living members of the *kāinga* during the life-cycle rites concerning her *fakafotu* (brother's children). Thus the paternal aunt mediates between living members of the paternal *kāinga* and their dead ancestors at any life-cycle event concerning them.

If we consider the *mehekitanga*'s power to curse in this perspective, it appears not as a negative one – as Valeri (1989: 245, n2) suggests – but as a power of sanction; it is what could happen if the 'right' things were not done. If feelings and duties are respected between a brother and a sister, if good behaviour is observed by the brother in relations with his sister, everything will be all right: the brother will have offspring and the sister's children will live and prosper.

The reader will have noted above the appearance of the term *fahu*. I turn now to an account of what it means to be *fahu* in Tonga.

The Tongan *Fahu*

In order to be able to sum up the Tongan *fahu*, I look first at its different meanings, beginning with some (historical) definitions. The oldest definition is given in a list of vocabulary by William Mariner, a young British sailor who spent four years in Tonga, at the beginning of the nineteenth century: '*Faoo*: to take away by main force, or by virtue of superior rank or authority; also to load, to burthen, to stock with' (Martin 1981: 426). There is no mention here of any kinship position; only the predatory 'right' of the *fahu* and their superior rank are alluded to. At the end of the nineteenth century, the Marist priests' dictionary proposed the following definition: 'Sister's children, he or she who is the sister's descendant, nephew. Formerly, he/she had the right to grab everything they wanted from their maternal uncle and his descendants' (Missions Maristes 1890: 44, my translation). This definition is more complete than many others: it specifies that the *fahu* position does not concern solely the sister's son, but all the sister's children, male and female, and, moreover, the sister's descendants; it also points out that the *fahu*'s 'predatory right' is exercised not only over the maternal uncle's goods but also over his descendants' belongings.

In Churchward's Tongan–English dictionary, the definition of *fahu* is as follows: '(man's) sister's son or grandson. In Tongan custom, one's *fahu* may take great liberties with one's belongings' (Churchward 1959: 19). This last definition also takes into consideration two points: first, the *fahu*'s position as sister's son or grandson; second, the *fahu*'s 'right' to take liberties with his uncle's belongings.

The most complete study of the *fahu* institution for this period was made by Gifford:

> The sister's children are *fahu* (Fijian *vasu*) to their mother's brother. They have the privilege of taking their uncle's goods, also the goods of his children, either during his life or after his death. Even one of the uncle's wives might be appropriated. At the wedding of a man's child, his sister's children may help themselves to the presents. The brother's children must show respect (*faka'apa'apa*) to the sister's children. The institution of *fahu* is a one-sided, non-reciprocal affair. The victims never have a chance to retaliate, but they exercise similar privilege toward their own mother's brother and his offspring. Towards one's *fahu* only respect and acquiescence must be shown. (Gifford 1929: 23)

Gifford's summary includes details already alluded to, but he specifies certain points: The term *fahu* denotes the sister's child for the mother's brother. The mother's brother and his offspring must show respect to the sister's children. The superior rank of the sister's child endows the *fahu* with the privilege of taking the mother's brother's belongings – a privilege which also obtains in respect of the maternal uncle's children, who are matrilateral cross-cousins to the *fahu* and, like their father, of inferior rank to the *fahu* and his own children. Towards one's *fahu*, one must show respect and obedience, just as one should towards a superior (for example, a commoner vis-à-vis a chief).

There is one point in the above description of the *fahu*'s privileges where my own observations do not corroborate those of Gifford: I do not know of any example of an uncle's wife being appropriated by a uterine nephew.

However, as we have seen above, there exists, in Tonga, a form of marriage called *kitetama* (see above) where a man appropriates his mother's brother's daughter.[17]

Today, *fahu* still denotes the sister's child vis-à-vis their maternal uncle, but the term is most often used to designate a ritual function during life-cycle rites: births, marriages and funerals. This ritual function consists in 'clearing the taboos' at the end of the ritual.[18] I was told that the person in the *fahu* position is able to lift the taboos because of their superior position in the kinship sphere: they are 'above the law', an expression used by Gifford at the beginning of the last century (ibid.: 18).

In Tonga, in accordance with kinship rules, the person who, in principle, holds the highest rank within the *kāinga* is the father's sister, the *meheki-tanga*. At the ceremonies for a birth or a wedding, she is given the place of honour; for someone's funeral, however, it could happen that the women in the position of father's sister are already dead; in this case, the place and the role of *fahu* will be incumbent on a descendant of the father's sisters or a descendant of a grandfather's sister (or great-grandfather's sister and so on), preferably of the female sex.[19]

In sum, as a function of their ritual superiority, the Tongan *fahu* is distinguished by economic and ritual prerogatives: the 'right to seize' the chief's or god's food, and the maternal uncle's belongings.

Economic and Ritual Prerogatives

Historical sources reveal some of the past exactions of *'ilamutu* or the children of powerful chiefs' sisters. Captain Cook witnessed such an act and reported it with surprise: 'He [the sister's son or *fahu* of the Tu'i Tonga] made no scruple of taking anything from the people even if it belonged to the king' (Beaglehole 1967: 954). The right to seize something from someone was abolished by the constitutional laws of 1875. Even so, the prerogatives of the *fahu* are still exercised today, having been reactivated at the end of the twentieth century, in the context of emigration and a drastic land shortage. Paul van der Grijp's case study of a Tongan village showed that *fahu* privileges were exercised by a woman who had asked and obtained access to her brother's land for her son, despite the fact that the law prohibited any *fahu* exercising their privileges (van der Grijp 1993: 193; 2004: 41; see also Rogers 1975: 270; Douaire-Marsaudon 1998: 162). During the last twenty years, this typical case has been repeated many times: access to a mother's brother's plantation has been granted to many a man without land. Nowadays, the right of access to the uncle's belongings is extended to his monetary income. Some informants told me that, if their maternal uncle has enough money, they can ask him for a ticket to go overseas.

It is worth considering these facts in context. In Tonga, residence is patrivirilocal: it is principally men and their children who stay on the land of the *kāinga*; the women of the patrilineal clan – daughters and sisters – and their children generally live elsewhere. Thus the *fahu*'s position gives sisters/daughters' children priority of access to the land of their maternal *kainga* – that is, their mother's paternal *kāinga*. It is as if the localization of the kinship groups (*kāinga*) on a patrilineal basis should not obliterate the rights of the female lines (Douaire-Marsaudon 1998: 169–79).

The *fahu* institution also operates at the top of the socio-political ladder, as already stressed by Gifford. The Tuʻi Tonga, the paramount chief of the whole of Tonga, as a descendant of a god, was of very exalted rank; but the rank of his sister, the Tuʻi Tonga Fefine, was even superior to his. Her children, called *tamaha* ('sacred child'), were the great *fahu* of the Tuʻi Tonga.[20] As Gifford noted: 'The Tamaha was the great *fahu* of the Tuʻi Tonga. To her, he made obeisance, as did inferiors to him. Cook, in 1777, tells of the Tuʻi Tonga *Pau* and the Tamaha Moungalakepa, to whom Pau paid the same homage that he received from his own subjects, embracing her feet with his hands' (Gifford 1929: 81).

Historically, the *fahu* institution played an important role in the political sphere, between chiefs and between local groups headed by chiefs:

> To the demand of the *fahu*, of a great chief, that chief and his dependants were obliged to accede. Thus all descendants of the Tuʻi Kanokupolu Tukuaho are *fahu* to the Haʻa Ngata Motua chiefs and to the commoners of this lineage. In other words the whole of the district of Hihifo, Tongatapu, is obliged to yield its best to the great *fahu* of the chiefs of the district, who here is the Prince consort Tungi. (ibid: 115)[21]

What Gifford is explaining here is that, because of matrilateral cross-cousin marriage (*kitetama*) practised among high chiefs, a large number of aristo-cratic clans, particularly in the royal family, found themselves, with regard to each other, in a mother's brother/sister's son relationship – in other words in a *fahu* position. In this case – and it is precisely that of the Tuʻi Kanokupolu royal lineage from Tukuhao with regard to the Haʻa Ngata Motua clan – the clan in the mother's brother position has to provide help and care to the clan in the sister's child position – or, to be more precise, in the *fahu* position. And here, 'help and care' mean not only food but also men, women, warriors, canoes, weapons and so on – in other words, a military and political alliance.

It is therefore the totality of the hierarchical kinship positions created by the *fahu* system that governs the exchange circuits among local *kāinga* groups. The asymmetry between the brothers' lineages on the one hand and the sisters' on the other, combined with patrivirilocal residence, leads to a generalized exchange of support – economic, political and, in the past, military – between local *kāinga* groups. We can thus see here that the institution of *fahu* does not only apply within the *kāinga* kinship group, as a bond of solidarity between a brother and sister and their respective lineage, but it also constitutes the main link in political alliances between local groups. The *fahu* system makes possible exchanges between the microcosm of domestic intimacy and the macrocosm of political action.

I noted above that, according to Hocart and Radcliffe-Brown, during the chiefly kava rituals, the *fahu* is the only person able to steal the chiefs' or gods' offerings and to eat them because of their ritual superiority to the chief, being his sister's child or his grandchild.[22] This act places a specific kinship relationship at the heart of a sacred rite: either that linking a maternal uncle and his nephew/niece, or that linking a grandfather and a grandchild. But this relationship involves a third person who makes these relationships possible, that is to say the sister or daughter. And sisters and daughters are women born of the paternal clan. When, in the course of the kava rite, the *fahu* seizes his grandfather's or his uncle's *fono* (portion of food) – hence his ancestor's *fono* (according to the chiefly ideology, they 'are' their ancestors during the *kava* ritual) – he can do so without endangering his life because he is descended from them through a privileged link, that involving sisters or daughters, in other words the female members of the clan[23].

In Tonga, as in Fiji[24], the term *fahu* is not a kinship term, though it has tended to be considered as such. It marks a position of hierarchical precedence activated during life-cycle and chiefly kava (*taumafa*) rituals. This hierarchical position is attributed according to three parameters: the relationship with the people present (the living); the relationship with the recipient of the ritual (new-born, married, deceased or chiefly); the relationship with the ancestors (the dead). In Tonga, this position generally falls to the father's sister (*mehekitanga*) or to a descendant of the grandfather's (or great-grandfather's and so on) sister, in other words to a descendant of the ancestors on the female side.

It can be seen that the *fahu*'s position of ritual superiority, whether during a rite pertaining to the chiefdom or a life-crisis rite, is associated with the idea of the privileged link which, in this patrilineal society, continues to connect the clan's sisters and daughters, as well as their descendants, to the clan's ancestors.

Conclusion

The *fahu* complex constitutes a condensed form of the obligations binding a brother and sister as evinced in ritual, economic exchange and socio-political strategy. These obligations are the other face, as it were, of the taboo marking the relationship. The taboo separates brother and sister while the *fahu* institution emphasizes their solidarity. Thus, it is when brother and sister have produced their respective offspring that their relationship takes on its full meaning: each is, in their own way, responsible for the other's progeny.

For the fathers and brothers of a *kāinga* kinship group, the *fefine* category, the 'female side', is not their wives (*hoa*) – with whom they have sexual relations – but their sisters (*tuofefine*) and their daughters (*ofefine*) with whom these relations are forbidden. The *fefine* category is fundamental for them, for the survival of the *kāinga* group depends on the goodwill of these sisters (*tuofefine*) and daughters (*ofefine*) – the sisters of the next generation. Thus each *kāinga* group, composed locally around a nucleus of men, entrusts its social reproduction to the goodwill of its women – sisters and daughters – who leave to reproduce elsewhere. Generation after generation, the men of the same group play the role of 'male mother' for their sister's children, born on the group's land but brought up elsewhere, being responsible throughout their life for providing them with food, help and protection.[25]

Thus the brother–sister relationship does not work exclusively before the sisters' marriage, as Lévi-Strauss' (1984: 218–219) claimed, but comes into full effect afterwards. One might say of Tonga, as Raymond Jamous said of the Meo of North India, that the double movement of marriage and begetting separates the sister from her brother and then provokes her return to the brother's group in order to ensure the continuation of generations (Jamous 1991: 223). In Tonga, however, the sister does not merely return to her native *kainga*. In oral tradition as in royal rites, the sister sometimes appears in the guise of the 'putative mother', and the mother's brother is always the one who helps and protects. The ambivalence of the roles allotted to the brother/sister pair can be found in myth. In the Tongan origin myth, the great gods and humanity originated (over several generations) from a series of incestuous couplings between opposite-sex twins. The populating accounts of the oral tradition often begin with a case of brother–sister incest. Nor are the royal rites at a loss. According to the French navigator Dumont d'Urville, during the investiture ceremony of a new paramount chief, the Tuʻi Tonga, the Tuʻi Tonga Fefine, or the late Tuʻi Tonga's sister, went to purify herself in a sacred fountain – a ritual that suggests that the Tuʻi Tonga Fefine has given birth to a child who can only be the new Tuʻi Tonga himself. At the same time, the ritual ablution also refers to incest between the late Tuʻi Tonga and his sister (see Douaire-Marsaudon 2002: 519–28).

Considering together these ritual representations and the everyday practices between a sister and brother, it becomes clear that the brother–sister relationship and the *fahu* system organize the unfolding of kinship (inside and outside *kainga* groups) and, at the same time, tend to appropriate descendants. Today, though the bonds of solidarity, in Tonga as elsewhere, are tending to loosen with globalization, the practices associated with the *fahu* complex are still very much alive, and seem even to be gaining in importance. This is unsurprising, given that, as I have shown above, these same practices have, generation after generation and beyond the necessary distinction between the sexes, inscribed in daily life the founding law of the *kainga* group – that is, the solidarity between male and female lines.

Notes

1. Note that Bathonga and Tonga are totally different societies – the homonym is pure chance.
2. Rivers (1910) showed that the father's sister's role in Tonga is the same on Pentecost Island and in the Banks Islands, both in the New Hebrides (now Vanuatu).
3. This rooting of social stratification in the kinship sphere is relatively common for societies termed chiefdoms like Tonga. In Tonga, the rank system is based on genealogical proximity with the paramount chief, the Tuʻi Tonga, begot by a god.
4. The *kainga* is a cognatic group with a strong patrilineal bias: residence is patrivirilocal, title and land are inherited in the male line. In its broadest sense, the *kainga* refers to the whole of Tonga and, in its strictest sense, to a brother/sister pair.
5. As Raymond Firth remarked, since the sibling relationship is a basic feature of Polynesian life, even a limited treatment of a few of the significant variables at the level of Ego's generation may help in the study of the whole terminology (Firth 1970: 272).
6. In English or in French, a brother is a male person of equivalent kinship grade, a sister a corresponding female person, the sex of the other sibling referred to not being considered.
7. This principle of relative-sex specification has two variants: in one variant, both sisters and brothers use an identical term for referring to each other, as in Futuna (*teina* for same sex, *tuagaane* for a sibling of opposite sex) and in Tikopia (*kave*). It is a way of saying: what is important or relevant is that our relationship is one of the opposite sex, not the actual sex of either of us (Firth 1970: 272).
8. Tongans sometimes use the term *tuʻasina* for the mother's brother, but it seems more and more in disuse. According to Tongans – though there is no real agreement on the subject – *faʻē tangata* refers to the elder mother's brother, and *tuʻasina* to a younger mother's brother.

9. Brothers and sisters do not use the same term for their children: a man refers to his children with two terms, one for his son (*foha*) and one for his daughter (*ofefine*); a woman uses only one term, for her son as well as for her daughter (*tama*).

10. We must remember that, in ancient Tonga (sixteenth to the nineteenth century), chiefs were polygamous and usually made the two types of marriage: exogamous with chiefs' daughters (from other *kainga*), endogamous with their MBD. Cross-cousin marriage (*kitetama*) was not allowed among commoners.

11. In Fiji, the mother's brother is called by the same term used for the father's sister's husband *momo* (Pauwels this volume) or *gadina*, (Cayrol this volume) and the father's sister is called by the same term as the mother's brother's wife (*nei*), which is consistent with cross-cousin marriage.

12. Futa Helu (head of the Tongan Atenisi University), personal communication (e.g. 5 November 1988).

13. Today, circumcision is performed in hospital.

14. For most of the commentators, this constrained relationship could be explained by the fact that there always existed rivalry between fathers and sons based on the patrilineal transmission of titles and land.

15. The term *mehekitanga* has equivalents in other societies of western Polynesia: *mahaki* on Wallis (Uvea) and *masaki* on Futuna. It is probably formed from the root *mahaki*, which means 'sickness'.

16. Cf. Biersack (1982), and see the passages from Rivers (1910: 42–43), referred to above.

17. This cross-cousin marriage was, in principle, restricted to the chiefs who, being polygamous, usually married both outside and within the clan.

18. Nowadays, the ritual of *kai fono*, which awakened the curiosity of Hocart and Radcliffe-Brown, is very rarely performed, probably because it offends Christian sensibilities, as it is related to the idea of chiefs' ancestors being considered as gods.

19. During funerals, a grandchild is preferred to a child because a child of a paternal aunt is, vis-à-vis the dead person, in a brother–sister relationship, and it is not considered proper for anyone to be too close to the dead body of a brother (for a female Ego) or a sister (for a male Ego).

20. All the Tu'i Tonga Fefine's children were called *tamaha* and were *fahu* to the Tu'i Tonga, but the oldest of these *tamaha* received ritually the title of 'Tamaha' and was the great *fahu*. Historical accounts show that she was considered a goddess.

21. Tu'i Kanokupolu is the title of one of the three royal lines. The Ha'a Ngata Motua is a very powerful clan of chiefs. Tukuaho, who bore the title of Tu'i Kanokupolu, was in the position of sister's child for all the clan of Ha'a Ngata Motua, and as such was *fahu* for all its members, chiefs and commoners. In

Gifford's time, the person who was in the position of *fahu* for this clan was Prince Tungi, Queen Salote's husband. Needless to say, the support of the powerful Ha'a Ngata Motua represented an appreciable winning card in the political game.

22. Today, the ritual of *kai fono* (eating the remains) is seldom practised, and only during royal kava rituals.

23. See also Pauwels, this volume.

24. See also Cayrol and Pauwels, this volume.

25 In the past, Tongan women, when pregnant, used to return to their paternal *kainga* to give birth, and still do so today.

References

Beaglehole, J.C. (ed.) 1967. *The Journals of Captain James Cook on his Voyages of Discovery*, Vol. 3: *The Voyages of the 'Resolution' and 'Discovery', 1776–1780*. Cambridge: Cambridge University Press.

Biersack, A. 1982. 'Tongan Exchange Structure: Beyond Descent and Alliance', *Journal of the Polynesian Society* 91: 181–212.

Bott, E. 1981. 'Power and Rank in the Kingdom of Tonga', *Journal of the Polynesian Society* 90: 7–81.

Churchward, C.M. 1959. *Tongan Dictionary: Tongan–English and English–Tongan*. London: Oxford University Press.

Douaire-Marsaudon, F. 1998. *Les premiers fruits: Parenté, identité sexuelle et pouvoirs en Polynésie occidentale (Tonga, Wallis et Futuna)*. Paris: Editions du Centre National de la Recherche Scientifique (CNRS)/Editions de la Maison des Sciences de l'Homme (MSH).

———— 2002. 'Le bain mystérieux de la Tu'i Tonga Fefine: Germanité, inceste et mariage sacré en Polynésie', *Anthropos* 97: 147–62, 519–28.

Firth, R. 1970. 'Sibling Terms in Polynesia', *Journal of the Polynesian Society* 79(3): 272–87.

Gifford, E. 1929. *Tongan Society*. Honolulu: Bernice P. Bishop Museum.

Hocart, A.M. 1915. 'Chieftainship and the Sister's Son in the Pacific', *American Anthropologist* 17(4): 631–46.

James, K. 1990. *'Rank Overrules Everything': Religious Hierarchy, Social Stratification and Gender in the Ancient Tongan Polity*. Christchurch: MacMillan Brown Center for Pacific Studies, University of Canterbury, New Zealand.

Jamous, R. 1991. *La relation frère–soeur: Parenté et rites chez les Meo de l'Inde du Nord*. Paris: Editions de l'Ecole des Hautes Etudes en Sciences Sociales.

Kaeppler, A. 1971. 'Rank in Tonga', *Ethnology* 10(2): 174–93.

———— 1978. 'Me'a Faka "Eiki": Tongan Funerals in a Changing Society', in N. Gunson (ed.), *Essays in Honor of Harry Maude*. Canberra: Australian National University Press.

Lévi-Strauss, C. 1984. *Paroles données*. Paris: Plon.

Martin, J. 1981 [1918]. *An Account of the Natives of the Tongan Islands*. Neiafu, Tonga: Vava'u Press.

Missions Maristes. 1890. *Dictionnaire tonga–français–anglais*. Paris: Chadenat.

Murdock, G.P. 1949. *Social Structure*. New York: Macmillan.

Radcliffe-Brown, A.R. 1924. 'The Mother's Brother in South Africa', *South Africa Journal of Science* 21: 542–55.

Rivers, W.H.R. 1910. 'The Father's Sister in Oceania', *Folklore* 21: 43–59.

———— 1968 [1914]. *The History of Melanesian Society*, 2 vols. Oosterhout: Anthropological Publications.

Rogers, G. 1975. 'Kai and Kava in Niuatoputapu: Social Relations, Ideologies and Contexts in a Rural Tongan Community', Ph.D. diss. Auckland: University of Auckland.

———— 1977 '"The Father's Sister is Black": A Consideration of Female Rank and Power in Tonga', *Journal of the Polynesian Society* 86: 157–82.

Sahlins, M. 1958. *Social Stratification in Polynesia*. Seattle, WA: American Ethnological Society.

Valeri, V. 1989. 'Death in Heaven: Myths and Rites of Kinship in Tongan Kingship', *History and Anthropology* 4: 209–47.

van der Grijp, P. 1993. *Islanders of the South: Production, Kinship and Ideology in the Polynesian Kingdom of Tonga*. Leiden: KITLV Press.

———— 2004. *Identity and Development: Tongan Culture, Agriculture and the Perenniality of the Gift*. Leiden: KITLV Press.

Wood-Ellem, E. 1981. *Queen Salote of Tonga: The Story of an Era 1900–1965*. Auckland: Auckland University Press.

10

How Would We Have Got Here if Our Paternal Grandmother Had Not Existed?

Relations of Locality, Blood, Life and Name in Nasau, Fiji

◆●◆

Françoise Cayrol

The first European observers were quick to notice that the societies of central Viti Levu – the main island of the Fijian archipelago – present a number of specific features. Following Fergus Clunie (1986), Alfred Gell suggested calling the ensemble they formed 'Viti', in order to clearly distinguish them from those in the east of the Fijian archipelago strongly marked by contact with Tonga (Gell 1993: 40). Some of these features concern kinship terminologies and, in certain cases, particularly the relationship linking a brother and sister. Thus, in Matailobau, situated in central eastern Viti Levu, brothers and sisters (*taci*) are distinguished with regard to seniority by the term *tuka*, to which an inalienable possessive (*-qu*) is suffixed: the only other slight difference being that, when addressing or designating his eldest sister, a brother will add an honorific particle (*ra*) as a prefix to this term: *ra tuka-qu* (Turner 1991a). A bit further north, in Nasau, it is the same: brothers and sisters (*'aci*) recognize the eldest (*'uka*), among whom elder sisters (*ra'uka*) are further distinguished.[1]

These terminologies are therefore part of the rare examples in the world of a sister's high status being clearly marked. In an article which brings to light the fundamental role of the brother-sister relationship in Matailobau,

James W. Turner noted that this distinction did not, however, affect eldest brothers' precedence in terms of eligibility for traditional responsibilities (ibid.: 185, 187). But until the turn of the century in Nasau, the title Tui Nasau, from *'ui* ('chief'), was held by an eldest sister who had returned to her native village after her divorce.[2] Similarly, in Nasau, unlike what seems to occur in Matailobau, in the absence of an eldest son, the eldest sister sometimes drinks the bowl of *yaqona* (kava) intended for her group of origin at a ceremony.

The presence of this honorific particle in Nasau terminology, and the fact that the status of 'eldest sibling' seems, under certain conditions, to supplant the gender distinction, raises questions regarding women's place, for women's inferiority has often been invoked in Fiji. As Toren (1990) shows, however, this is because women as wives are formally inferior to their husbands, while women as sisters may retain their status in their natal households. Thus in everyday ritual in the house and village hall, the wife must keep 'below', near the common entrance to a house, while the place called 'above', where men sit, is hierarchically superior (Toren 1988: 701–2; 1994a). The domestic character of women's activities and the fact they must show respect and deference to their husbands is crucial here, though the relationship between spouses undergoes a shift towards equality over time (Toren 1994a). Moreover, as I show in what follows, a woman may occupy several positions over the course of her life, and is caught up in diverse relationships in which her status varies. Parallel to this, men and the aspects of social organization with which they are associated have often been taken as the key to Fijian social organization (see e.g. Nayacakalou 1955: 47). Certainly group membership effectively depends in the great majority of cases on the father, but is it indeed the case that descent among the peoples of Viti – as opposed to those in eastern Fiji – may everywhere be properly characterized as patrilineal?

Two sets of several elements give us cause to doubt this. First, in Nasau, babies are welcomed at birth with these different expressions: 'Here is the *bure!*' for boys, using a term which refers to the old communal men's and bachelors' houses; 'Here is the *vale!*' for girls, *vale* being the word for family dwellings. The importance of the house throughout Oceania has already been demonstrated. In Nasau, *bure* is, as I show below, an idea of central importance. *Vale*, qualified by *levu* ('big'), designates the house of the eldest member of a lineage or a group, that of the chief and, beyond this, all the people who together make up 'the big house of Nasau'. Therefore, from the moment of birth onwards, social organization is decisively gendered.

Further, the most respectful forms of address for this type of elder place the latter at the centre of three kinds of differentiated relations, two of which pass through women. The first of these, which appears to be the most

complex, is focused on a person's paternal group and the '*ako* or *lavo* generational category. This distinction, characteristic of what Gell (1993) calls
Vitian peoples, means that if a father is *lavo*, his son will always be '*ako* like
his paternal grandfather, and so on. Each of these categories, '*ako* or *lavo*,
is usually combined with one of the constituent elements of the different
emblems of the group to which the person belongs: an animal, a plant, a
phenomenon, a star and so forth (*icavuʻi*).[3] These combinations, when used
to form an expression to address somebody, are most often worded as:
« ''ako child of' plus the name of the corresponding element or ''lavo child
of' plus the name of the corresponding element ». The two elements accompanying respectively '*ako* and *lavo*, are often contrasting with each other
as, for intance, ''*ako* child of sleep' or '*lavo* child of the sun', here referring
to some of the group's members' ritual powers, using the sun as a reference. Very much like titles, these expressions are highly valorized. Called
masumasu, from *masu*, which now means Christian prayer, they were used
to oblige or implore somebody. Till now persons so addressed say to be
touched to their 'inner depths' (*loma*), and consequently can refuse their
interlocutor nothing. But these expressions only acquire their full value
when completed by two others that position the person with respect to their
mother's group, through the famous *vasu* position – well-known to specialists of the region – and to their paternal grandmother's, through what is
called a *bula* relation, the term *bula* referring to 'life' and 'good health'. The
wording of these expressions is different: *vasu ki* ('towards') plus the name
of the mother's group, *bula ki* plus the name of the paternal grandmother's
group.[4] The latter relation can thus be glossed as: 'our paternal grandmother
is at the origin of life, how would we be here if she hadn't existed?'

This chapter attempts to shed light on the differentiated places of men
and women and what is expected of them, and to give an account of the
nature of the relations that pass through women.[5] I begin by describing
Nasau social organization to show how *bure* is linked to baby boys and *vale*
to baby girls, and, in particular how gendered affinal relations inform the
process of constructing houses and the big house, *vale levu*. Thereafter, I
return to the distinction between '*ako* and *lavo*, and the full value given by
the *vasu* and *bula* positions – the relationship to the mother's and paternal
grandmother's groups respectively. This will enable us to understand how
the number three could be a expression of the value in this society.

From One Mound, under One Name, in One Big House

Situated on the southern border of Ra province, Nasau is part of the Nalawa
tikina (district), one of the province's four districts. Placed under the
authority of the Tui Nalawa, the Nasau people, predominantly Methodists,

are above all connected to their own *'ui*, who resides in Nasau, one of the eight villages composing the *tikina* of the same name.[6] In these villages dwell the members of different exogamous groups, whose members are assumed to be siblings (*'aci*). The local origin of each of these groups is said to be linked to at least two brothers, the very first human ancestors present in the region. The mound (*'obu*), said to have been used as the foundation for the elder brother's house (*vale*), roots the whole group in the locality and gives it power (*sau*), a term which forms the name of the village and the *tikina*: Nasau, 'the *sau*'. Indeed, the mound (*'obu*) is the dwelling place of the group's oldest and most powerful origin spirit (*kalou vu*), a being responsible for the fertility of gardens, of men and women, for the success or not of undertakings and, generally speaking, for all life and death inside the group and beyond. They maintain with living people relations of a dream-like and emotional nature, which for the latter operate through the *loma*, the body's 'inner depths', the seat of the *yalo*, or as it is called today 'the soul' (Cayrol 2013).[7] Endowed with specific forms, human or animal, capable of assuming the features of the dead, the *kalou vu* are linked to plants, objects, stars or phenomena that differ from one group to another and give to each its own identity,[8] connected to the particular duty (*'avi*) they owe to the *'ui* Nasau or the *'ui* Nalawa. Those specific forms are the *icavu'i*. Some of them associated with the *'ako/lavo* generational distinction, as mentioned above, partially make up the most valorized form of address (*masumasu*).

The exogamous groups are composed of several lineages, supposed to be the children of siblings, ranked according to age seniority; the eldest member of the eldest lineage is said to be the direct descendant of the group's eldest ancestor and is the one drinking the kava cup intended for their[9] social unit during ceremonies. Standing at the head of their own lineage and their own group, they represent the ancestor and are said to direct their fellow members exactly as the first fish in a shoal gathers its fellows behind it while leading the way. The members of the group have specific duties to this kind of elder (or 'Elder').[10] The line of descent is not linked to an explicit geneal-ogy since the names of the deceased are very seldom remembered for more than two or three generations, but by a homonymic relationship.[11] The house of the eldest member of the eldest lineage, built above a mound, bears systematically the name of the original *'obu*, and this name will also be given to the house of their eldest child and grandchild, who will lead the lineage and group after them.

This homonymic relationship between this Elders' house and its *'obu* links them to the *kalou vu*, and concerns all the members of the group. For example, the sense given to people's dreams and emotions concerns mainly themselves and their close kin, but those of each Elder are thought to concern the whole group. The *'ui* is one of those Elders belonging to a group that is itself qualified as the eldest one and described as the oldest located in the region. Their *kalou vu* is said to be the most powerful of all, and the name Nasau given to the *tikina* is but the name of their own lineage and group. This is why, as Nasau people stress when talking of their female *'ui*, 'we try to make her happy (*marau*) so that we are too'.

To these groups, claiming to have a relatively ancient common origin, are also added, in most cases, other lineages that similarly recognize the status and position of the eldest lineage, related to the *'obu*, but which this time are clearly of foreign origin. These lineages are composed of former affines who have become 'siblings' (*'aci*) by virtue of settling in the locality, and with whom it is no longer possible to contract marriages. These lineages of foreign origin remain attached to their own origin spirits and possess different *icavu'i* ('emblems'). Nevertheless, they also maintain relations with the local *kalou vu*, whose power is predominant in the locality and supposed to protect them too.

The groups and lineages which compose them are named using generic terms that may vary according to the context: *yavusa* and *mataqali* for the groups, or set of lineages, *mataqali* and *tokatoka* for a lineage (cf. Turner 1986: 294). In Nasau village, where there are two large sets of lineages (Nasau and Nasauqaqa), each of these apart tends to be called *yavusa* but, when their members are in each others' presence, the chiefly Nasau *yavusa* to which the *'ui* belongs encompasses the Nasauqaqa *yavusa*, which thus becomes a *mataqali*.

Part of this ambiguity has to do with the fact that the terms *mataqali*, *yavus*a and *tokatoka* are not specific to Nasau. They stem from an official model of social organization 'invented' by the British colonial authorities. In the late nineteenth and early twentieth centuries, investigations in each region to discover the order of precedence of groups and to place under the Crown all unrecognized territories led to the widespread distribution of the official model. During these investigations, many Fijians attempted to understand and use a vocabulary that did not correspond to their own social organization, if only to answer the investigators' questions.[12] In certain cases, the old organization was entirely transformed while, in others, researchers nowadays are confronted by two systems that do not always correspond.[13]

In Nasau, the terms *tokatoka*, *mataqali* and *yavusa* are used daily; however, the lineages and sets of lineages have different names in ceremonial contexts. In these, a lineage's eldest member[14] is invited to drink the bowl of *yaqona* intended for his social unit with reference being made to his *bure*, to which is added the name of his house (*bure* plus name of the house), and this first expression is immediately followed by a second referring to the lineage's territory (*qele* 'soil' plus name of the house).[15] On the other hand, when lineages are grouped together, the twofold expression above changes to 'big house plus name of the house, *vanua* 'land' plus name of the house'. This shift is also apparent when Nasau and Nasauqaqa people are in each other's presence: the expression invoking the 'big house' and the *vanua* takes in all lineages to which the *'ui* is attached, including the Nasauqaqa. This shows well exactly how the various levels of the organization are linked by hierarchical relationships.

The Construction of the House and Big House

The ceremonial terms cited above are described as 'ancient' by Nasau people, and the reader will recall that, at birth, baby boys are associated with the *bure* and baby girls with the *vale*. It is clear that here masculine and feminine orders complement each other.

The term *bure* also refers to the old communal men's and bachelors' houses and is associated with *qele*, that is, more specifically, the soil of cemeteries and of gardens shared by a particular lineage. This is how it contrasts with the term *vanua*, which this time refers to the land as opposed to the river (*wai levu*) and to the country as a whole, as for example Nasau 'country' or *vanua*. Men who are born and die on their *bure*'s territory and who are buried there have a particularly close relationship with locality. Thus little boys are, as it were, rooted in their territory by the mounds, and Nasau people stress the fact that formerly the *bure* could also be called the 'mounds of brothers' houses'. By contrast, women are mobile. Born in these same territories, they have to leave them and, given exogamous marriage and virilocal residence, they are normally buried in their husband's *qele*. Moreover, women are associated with rivers, which used to be the means of travel in these inland regions, and where formerly girls' umbilical cords were placed so that they might catch a lot of fish. Those of boys were buried under a coconut palm or a large tree in the hope 'that they would climb high'.[16]

Generally, river fishing is practised by women. It is also they who lead the big ceremonial fishing parties organized on the occasion of the fiftieth and hundredth day of mourning for their husband. On these occasions, they use the paths of the spirits, who are said to go down the *'obu* everyday at sunrise and follow the course of the rivers downstream and go back upstream at sunset.

Associated with the gardens' soil, *qele* evokes masculinity in that it is shared between brothers of the same *bure*. Yams, planted at the top of the gardens, closely associated with men, are said to be *lu'u* in the earth, exactly like the body of a dead person, *vua* ('fruit'), when buried in a heap resembling a mound, covered with stones and then planted like a garden.

By contrast, taro, linked to women, are planted in little heaps of earth, called
buke'e, a term also used for pregnancy.[17]

The link between men and *bure*, through locality, is clear. *Vale* recalls
the ancient feminine houses that boys left for the group's *bure* at the time of
their initiation. So, is it possible to link the big house to women, daughters,
sisters and wives when we know that this is how the house of the eldest
member of the eldest lineage or the Elder is designated, referring to the
original mound? What is a *vale* (house) and what is a *vale levu* (big house)
for Nasau people?

Like humans, all houses (*vale*), have inner depths (*loma*) formed by the
people who live in them, a couple and their unmarried children, as well as
the wealth stocked there – mats (*masi*), whales' teeth (*tabua*) and so on –
that is necessary for ceremonial work. When talking about houses, men
often refer to those of chiefs, which generally possess an outside horizontal
pole over the top of the roof, the *doka*. The pole is associated with the chief's
own person. Rain falls off it and, like the chief, it is in direct contact with
atmospheric phenomena and the top of the universe. On the other hand,
the space in houses leading from the ground to the roof, held up by the
various posts inside, is linked with men. The lower part of the house and the
'ground', 'where rainwater accumulates', are connected to women, who are
said to complete the dwelling and make it 'safe'.

In this kind of representation, the mound (the height of which is more
or less important according to the status of the Elder) is not evoked. Even
so, it has still to be taken into account for it refers to the root in the
locality and to the presence of the *kalou vu*. Therefore men and women
occupy in the house a position between top and bottom, between what
is linked to the sky and what is rooted in the earth. The image of the tree
(*vunikau*), which is sometimes used by the Nasau people to invoke their
big house, easily comes to mind since a particular species of tree is one of
the most important *icavu'i* (emblems) of almost every group. Here, the
highest branches are associated with the youngest generations. This picture
of the *vanua* as a living and ever growing tree is of great importance since
the term *vu* evokes at once the Elders' origin spirits and the root, or more
precisely the lowest part, of a tree – that rising from the soil while rooting
underground. It is a growing process toward the two main directions: high
and low.

This high/low distinction runs lengthwise through each house (see
Figure 10.1). Indeed, every house in Nasau adopts a rectangular form and
has three doors, one on one of the shorter sides, the other two facing each
other toward the middle of the longest sides. The door on the shorter
wall opens on the lowest part (*ra*) of the house, while the doors on the
longest sides open on the higher part (*colo*) of the house. In everyday

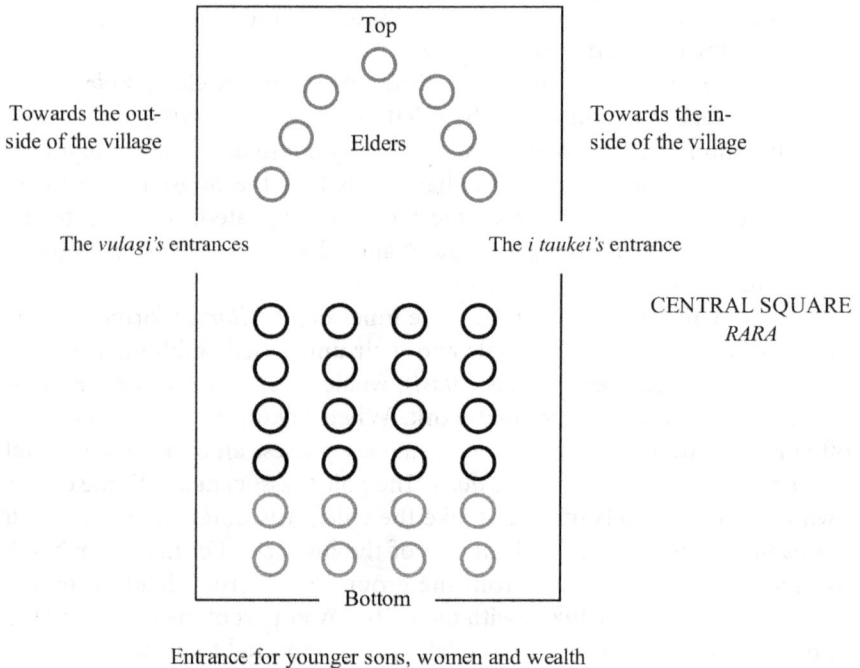

Figure 10.1: Spatial organization inside houses.

life, in a familial setting, the wife and children have to use the door on the shorter wall. Inside, the wife sits closest to the door, at the lowest end of the house, and has to serve the food from there during a meal. Directly outside this door and close by is the 'cooking house'. Meanwhile, the husband enters from one of the doors on the longest side to sit in a highest part of the house. He has to leave his seat to any higher-ranked or elder visitor or member of his family or social unit. It is according to this high/low axis that people sit during ceremonies and even informal kava drinking. Indeed during these ceremonies women and male non-elders have to use the door on the shorter wall. The latter sit ahead of the women, slightly higher (*colo*), but never beyond the doors on the longest sides of the house, because these are the crossing point the elders take in order to go and sit beyond them.[18] This way they sit in what is said to be the highest position. Thus the elders sit 'above', each one according to the relative seniority of their social unit, facing the *yaqona* bowl and the people sit below, at the bottom. During ceremonial kava drinking, said to be a 'rising', the elders drink one by one, according to their status, beginning with the highest-status person present. Facing the elders, in the lower part, sit the youth who serve the kava, and below them the younger men and, in the lowest part, the women. When wealth (*iyau*), whether it be termed male or female, is offered during the ceremony, the door on the shorter wall is the only permitted means of entry, and those making the presentation never take a position higher than that of the *yaqona* bowl. When kava roots are presented, they come and go with their 'head' facing the lowest part of the house, and are placed such that the space is, as it were, inverted. The elders sitting in the highest space are facing the roots (*vu*), the 'feet' of the kava.

This ceremonial high/low axis organizing the house and ceremonies is well known, but there is an additional axis of direction in the house, which must be mentioned (see Figure 10.1). Of the two doors facing each other at the top of the house, one opens out onto the centre of the village, the *rara* square, the other onto the outside of the village. The eldest *itaukei*, that is to say people from the locality, enter through the first of these, and the *vulagi* (lit. 'root of the sky'), a term used today to designate 'foreigners' but which formerly referred to affines, enter through the other. In other words, houses, which evoke the roots of the group in the locality, are mainly made of relationships linked to women, sisters and wives. Two ceremonies organized during weddings, the *'araboroboro* and the *tevutevu*, show the role played by women, and especially elder sisters (*ra'uka*) in the building of a new house (*vale*). Houses are built on the husband's territory and are destined for the young couple. In general, it is the eldest sister's job to organize and manage her brother's marriage. She is guided in this task by her paternal aunt (*ganei*), whose opinion is predominant in the choice of spouse. All knowledge concerning marriages is handed down from paternal aunt to niece, a fact that Nasau people stress.

The *'araboroboro*, translated as 'making the bottom of the pot', is a marriage ceremony apparently specific to Nasau.[19] The ceremony takes place outside, near the couple's future home. The women on the man's side of the *'araboroboro* sit on the ground in two rows facing each other, thus forming a rectangle that refers to the house. On one side are the women linked to the father of the groom, on the other side the women linked to his mother. On one of the short sides of this rectangle, corresponding to the highest in a house, the groom's eldest sister (*ra'uka*) comes and takes her place. All the women have their legs stretched out in front of them, covered by mats, made by women and part of the 'women's wealth', so they cannot be seen. The mat that is in immediate contact with the women's legs is of the same kind as those placed on the floor of a house.

From the other end of the space thus formed, the bride, who has remained standing, enters the rectangular space formed by the mats, followed in procession by the women from her side of the marriage (see

Figure 10.2: *'Araboroboro* ceremony, Nasukamai: the bride is about to enter the space formed by the women on the man's side of the marriage.

Figure 10.2). Everyone is careful to tread heavily on the legs under the mats. The bride, still followed by her procession, walks like this right across the circumscribed space to go and sit down on the lap of her husband's eldest sister, who puts her arms round her, thus not only welcoming her and protecting her as if she were a child, but also placing her at the highest part of the ceremonial space. The women following her do the same, but they find themselves sitting on the laps of those forming the long sides of the rectangle. This done, the whole gathering disperses. The ritual invites the bride into the space of a house whose foundations are already constituted by the women from her husband's locality, including the latter's sister.[20] Here, the brother–sister relationship acquires remarkable depth.

The *tevutevu* takes place after the building of the house destined to receive the new couple. Large amounts of goods are exchanged in front of the house between the 'woman's side' and the 'man's side'. Some of these will be redistributed, but a part of them will be used to fit out the young couple's house and provide them with the main articles of wealth necessary for various exchanges – an essential part of their dwelling's *loma*.

The newly-weds' house is decorated by the women who put pillows, mosquito nets, ornaments, blankets and sheets on the furniture brought. Mats are spread on the floor and *masi*, barkcloth, decorates the walls or beds, while crockery is put in the cupboard at the 'bottom' of the house. Once this has been done, all the women present gather together, and the oldest, the grandmothers, along with the eldest women, sit down in the top part of the house. For the time being, no man is allowed inside the house. Then a few men come in through the door on the shorter wall and take their places at the very bottom of the house.[21] There they prepare kava in a pottery bowl, not a wooden one as is usually the case for men, and offer it to the women sitting 'at the top', in a reversal of the usual hierarchy. When the kava has been drunk, the men depart, leaving the women alone inside the house. Some use elements of bedding or decoration to evoke the erect phallus. Others dress up as men and dance together, imitating flirtation or the sexual act, mocking men's behaviour.

As seen above, every group is linked to plants, animals, stars or even objects (*icavu'i*) that the *kalou vu* uses to manifest itself or show its power. One of them also linked to the *'ako/lavo* distinction (but not directly to the *masumasu*) is associated with people's genitals. Mothers therefore use the words 'yams', 'taro' or 'fish' to designate the genitals of their young children. It is expressly forbidden to use these terms in front of a brother, sister or maternal uncle, but women are allowed to use them between themselves, and especially between sisters in law, *dauve*, and cross-cousins, which gives rise to endless jokes, often made during weddings, and especially *tevutevu* ceremonies. The older women, sitting at the top, sing songs, called 'song of the *icavu'i*', about the grooms' *icavu'i*. They all have aspects in common: the emblems associated with people's genitals, presented in a particularly attractive way, meet each other while in motion, carried along by the wind or the flow of a river. There is much laughter, and the ceremony becomes a strictly feminine celebration.

These two ceremonies leave no doubt as to women's share in the composition of the bottom of the house and of its inner depths (*loma*), but women, through marriage, also play a role in the big house of the group.

Big Houses as Ceremonial Unities

We have seen how in the house (*vale*) the directional axis that organizes the inside, and thus defines the position of the people, refers to various distinctions and oppositions between the highest point and the lowest, women and men, elders and juniors, *itaukei* and *vulagi* (affines). We have also begun to highlight the role of some women, sisters or wives, in the making of the house, women through whom the affinal relationship begins. The fact that those relations have a great share in the composition of the house throws into question the *vale levu*, in which resides the Elder and which gives its name to the group and roots it in the locality through a homonymous relationship to the mound, linked to the original ancestor 'obu.

Apart from their names and the mounds on which they are sometimes built (which refer to the sites occupied by the *kalou vu*), the houses of the Elders are identical to all the others. The qualifier *levu* denotes greatness, an impressive aspect and multiplicity.

The big house, unlike the *bure*, may refer to sets of lineages, and therefore to society as a whole. Thus the house of the eldest of an eldest *bure*, associated as it is with the oldest mound of origin ('obu) in the locality, is characterized by a remarkable property of 'encompassment' or plasticity. This is evident at all important ceremonies (marriages, births, funerals and so on) where the houses of the eldest take on a ceremonial configuration which, even if it does not endure, is of the utmost importance.

On these occasions, wealth (mats, tapa, whales' teeth, garden produce and other items, including kava) is collected in every house (*vale*) in Nasau. To these goods are added those of the lineages who stand in an affinal relationship with the occupants of the house, through wives, sisters and married daughters. One of the 'ancient' names for a given household was 'doors of the house'. The wealth acquired from affines is said to follow 'the paths of wealth' which Nasau people say are the only ones enabling them to enter a territory other than their own. As soon as the goods have been presented, the affines are thanked in the name of their social unit. But, once it has been collected, all this wealth is carried to the house of the Elder, where it is added to the piles that have been similarly constituted in all the other houses of the group, until there is only one pile. During the ceremonial speeches accompanying the gifts, the different types of relations existing between the groups present are recalled, but when the pile is to be presented outside, it is placed exclusively in the name of the eldest's *bure* (which is none other than that of his house) and of the *qele* corresponding to it, or of the big house and its *vanua* where the wealth always ends up, thus forming even more substantial piles. On these occasions, the houses of the senior *bure*, and especially those of the eldest of the eldest *bure*, are very different from usual, and the 'big house' and the house that stands for the *vanua* undergo the same transformations. They appear to be larger, strengthened by all the people and wealth gathered together in one name, along with all their territories, which are likewise encompassed into one.

I noted above that for Nasau people, all fertility and success are due to the power of the *kalou vu*. The birth of children, the abundant produce of gardens, all the gendered processes of growth, are so many signs of good relations with the *kalou vu*. During marriage ceremonies, the *kalou vu* of all the participants are said to be present, so it is of the utmost importance that everyone in attendance should be without anger, rancour or jealousy, otherwise the young couple's offspring will be jeopardized. After the *solevu* – the ceremonies which conclude marriages, and during which new exchanges of the most important goods take place, in a competitive mode, between the woman's and the man's side – if everything has gone well, the bride's parents say that soon flies will come and accumulate inside the newly-weds' house, a reference to the faeces of the children to be born. As Nasau people stress, if this phrase is pronounced, the young couple will soon procreate.

The homonymy linking the house of the eldest of an eldest *bure* to the mound of origin (*'obu*) establishes a permanent relationship with the *kalou vu*. This house, which has become particularly imposing, thanks to the paths of wealth established through women, can now display the extent of its power (*sau*). The more descendants the group has, the more substantial its 'paths of wealth' will be. Thus, at all ceremonies, the eldest formulate wishes for life before drinking the bowl of kava given to them: '*Bula*, may your *kawa* be many', *kawa* designating both younger and older generations, both ascendants and descendants. I noted above the welcome that greets a new-born child, but birth also arouses ambiguous feelings. Joy is appropriate for a boy, although it is stressed that 'one loses' because on marriage he establishes his own household, whilst sadness is associated with the arrival of a baby girl thanks to whom, however, 'one gains'. Girls will have to leave their group and locality of origin when they marry, always experienced as a wrench by their close kin; even so, they give rise to a gain that comes from the ceremonial work of marriage and, above all, through the circulation of goods that favours wife-taking or maternal groups.

This building of the big house, not to say its growth, out of the plasticity of the house (*vale*) is the most common way of introducing affines into groups. This enables us to fully grasp the bases on which people, already related by marriage, can be incorporated into a new locality and a new 'big house' by becoming 'siblings' (*'aci*).

Two Major Kin Categories: 'Same' Kin and 'Close' Kin

The reception of *bure* of foreign origin, whose members were previously in an affinal relationship with those of the lineage receiving them, necessarily involves a radical transformation of all relations.

In the kinship terminology, the sex distinction between Ego's parents' siblings leads to a differentiation between two ensembles: persons of the same sex as father are *'ama*, and those of the same sex as mother are *'ina* (see Table 10.1). These terms, which also apply to spouses, are modified by an age distinction. Father's older brothers are *'ama levu*, and his younger ones *'ama lada*; mother's older and younger sisters are likewise differentiated, and these relative age qualifiers also apply to these persons' spouses. The sex distinction, however, is expressed differently on either side, the maternal uncle being called *gadina* and the paternal aunt *ganei*. No age distinction is marked here. The terms designating spouses are also expressed differently on either side; thus, the wife of a *gadina* is *nei*, a term which also forms *ganei*, while the husband of a *ganei* is *navugo*, a term for affines. Associated with a sex determination – *'agane* (male) or *yalewa* (female) – it also refers to the spouse's parents, to their spouses and to their siblings.

In ego's generation (G0), these distinctions continue: younger siblings are *'aci* and elder siblings are *'uka* or *ra'uka*. The distinction of seniority is relative to Ego when it concerns the direct siblings, and relative to Ego's parents when it concerns parallel cousins, who are younger or older according to their parents' own status. There is a difficulty here, however, in that the researcher is confronted by significant variants depending on the group's origin. Thus, the term *'aci* is sometimes only associated with same-sex siblings, those of opposite sex then being designated by the term *gane*, related to *ganei* and, perhaps, to *gadina*. On the other hand, the descendants of *ganei* and *gadina* are *makubu*, a category that is not modified by any distinction of age or sex. These same persons are sometimes called *'avale*, or more often *tavale*, a term in which the influence of Bau and of standard Fijian is usually acknowledged. Apart from this specific usage for Nasau, all siblings' spouses are *'avale* for a male Ego, while a female Ego employs this term only for her female siblings' husbands, her male siblings' wives being *dauve*. The spouses of *makubu* are all *karua*, 'thing two' for a female and male Ego. None of these affinal terms are modified by age distinctions.

Table 10.1: Nasau kinship terminology.

G+3	*kawa*
G+2	*'ubu 'agane – damai // 'ubu yalewa – tatai*
G+1	*'ama (levu – lada) – 'ina (levu – lada) – ganei // gadina – 'ina (levu – lada) – 'ama (levu – lada)*
G0	*'uka – ra'uka – 'aci – makubu // 'uka – ra'uka – 'aci – makubu*
	'avale – karua
G–1	*luve – na'u – na vasu vei yau*
G–2	*makubu*
G–3	*kawa*

Neither is this kind of distinction any longer in force in the generations below. A male or female Ego designates their children as *naluve*, but all descendants of siblings and of *makubu* of the same sex as Ego are, for a woman, *na'u*, and for a man they are *na vasu vei yau*[22]. On marriage, a male and female Ego adopt their spouse's perspective. A male Ego calls his wife's sisters' children *naluve*, and a female Ego calls those of her husband's brothers *na'u*, the descendants of siblings of the opposite sex to the spouse being *navuqo*. In some variants of the terminology, all descendants of opposite-sex siblings or *makubu* are also designated by this term, with the exception, for a man, of his 'true' *na vasu vei yau*.

In the generations below, the father's parents are, for both male and female Ego, *'ubu 'agane* and *damaï*, and the mother's are *'ubu yalewa* and *tataï*, the latter still being called by the 'ancient' term *makubu*, which also designates, with no sex distinction, all persons in the grandchildren's generation.[23] *'Ubu* alone can also be called *'uka* or *ra'uka*, referring here to seniority.

Nasau kinship terminology is almost identical on both sides, paternal and maternal. Consequently, it is not possible to attribute any particular prerogative to men. In addition, the two major kin categories created by the distinction or non-distinction of sex between siblings introduce noteworthy similarities or dissimilarities with Ego.

Indeed in Ego's generation (G0), a male or female Ego is like their *'aci*, and thus they all maintain identical status relations according to seniority with their own group of origin and *kalou vu* (see Table 10.2). The age distinction differentiates the *'uka* or the *ra'uka* from the other *'aci* and signals precedence. The age or seniority distinction is not marked by the cross-cousin's category (see Table 10.2). On both sides, paternal and

Table 10.2: Kinship terms marked or not marked by relative age and seniority on mother and father's side.

Generations	Terms marked by a relative age and seniority distinction on the mother // father's side	Terms with no age or sex distinction
G+2	*'ubu 'agane ('uka) // 'ubu yalewa (ra'uka)*	*damai // tatai (makubu)*
G+1	*'ama (levu – lada) – 'ina (levu – lada)*	*ganei // gadina*
G0	*'uka – ra'uka – 'aci*	*makubu*
G–1	*luve – na'u – na vasu vei yau*	

maternal, they maintain a different relation with Ego's group of origin and *kalou vu*. However, commenting on their relations with their cross-cousins (*makubu*), Nasau people emphasize that they are very close: 'We are the same'. Hence, they say, they could be siblings (*'aci*), although, out of respect, they do not use this term. From this point of view, these relations contrast with those linking Ego to the spouses of these *karua* persons, a term which appears to mark a notable degree of removal. For combined with *kawa*, the qualification *rua* ('two') is found in the generations above and below (cf. Turner 1991a: 193). Designating great-great-grandparents or great-great-grandchildren, this term encompasses the kinship terminology.

Fijian terminologies have generally been classified as Dravidian, based on the marriage of cross-cousins, and this feature would explain the existence of the joking relationships usual between those persons who would consider each other as potential spouses. The Fijian anthropologist Nayacakalou (1955, 1957), following Hocart, developed the idea of Fijian kinship terminologies as Dravidian. He worked mostly among his own people, where the marriage rules did indeed tend to give preference to unions with cross-cousins. Walter (1975) called into question the Dravidian generalization and showed – using documents from Rivers, Fison, Capell and Lester and his own study of Mualevu people in northern Lau – that not all Fijian kinship vocabularies present all the characteristics of marriage with cross-cousins. Thus, in Mualevu, though cross-cousins are indeed distinguished from siblings and parallel-cousins, there is a collateral term which marks a removal threshold beyond which marriages become possible. Mualevu people explain the necessity of this distance by referring to concepts of procreation: a child is formed from the blood of the father and mother, and marriage between first degree cross-cousins 'thickens' the 'blood', which should rather be diluted. The threshold marked by collaterality serves to fix a limit beyond which this thickening process no longer takes place.

In Nasau this type of gloss does not exist. A case of marriage between cross-cousins of this type is known, but it is considered an abnormality and, for some, such unions are forbidden even though in Nasau the joking relationship is also usual between cross-cousins who also consider each other as potential spouses. Moreover, it is also said that there is a tendency towards marriages between Ego and the descendants of their paternal grandmothers' brothers (from Ego's point of view a descendant of father's *gadina*) but on condition that there is no surviving memory of the former unions, thus creating a considerable distance.

In practice, marked genealogical amnesia makes the study of marriages in earlier generations difficult. It is, however, obvious that each *bure* gives specific orientations to its members' unions, thus creating privileged links with certain groups. These alliances tend to be renewed – and not always generation after generation – but, with the exception of rare marriages based on an exchange of sisters and the practice of sororate, spouses are nearly always chosen in a *bure* other than that initially in an affinal relationship to each other. Hence, the renewal of alliances takes place, at a distance, within the broader context of a 'big house'; this, moreover, increases the entrances to this same house, and thus to the 'paths of wealth' leading back to it. In Nasau kinship terminology, unlike a truly Dravidian type, only one term, *navugo*, may be characterized as affinal. Present in Ego's children's generation, it could be connected to this kind of distanced renewal.

But more can be said about marriages in Nasau through the *'ako/lavo* distinction. The latter present numerous difficulties.[24] Revealed by the first European observers and the first anthropologists to take an interest in the Fijian peoples of central Viti Levu, they did not become the specific object of later studies. The first authors noticed their connections with groups' different emblems (*icavuʻi*), and saw in these the remains of moiety systems. They noted that, although focused on group membership, they were more far-reaching. Thus, any *'ako* or *lavo* who met someone of the same generational category, whatever their origin, was in a *veiʻacini* (sibling) relationship with them, while the relationship between an *'ako* and a *lavo* was represented as that between *veiʻamani* and *veiluveni*, father and child. Likewise, the same authors observed that these distinctions came into effect in games or collective work, where each category competed with the other (see Hocart 1931, 1937: 547–48). According to some, they were also evident at circumcisions, where the circumciser had to be of a different generational category from the person circumcised (Brewster 1919: 314). Hocart stresses that the *'ako/lavo* distinction was important in the relationship between a paternal grandfather and his grandson, the latter taking the former's name, a feature also found in Nasau (Hocart 1931: 224; see also Turner 1991b).

This generational distinction continues to be important for Nasau people. They are still the most widely used words to address somebody, and they accompany a person throughout life, placing them in a *veiʻacini* or *veiʻamani–veiluveni* relation with those of the corresponding generational category. As I have shown, they partially make up the most respectful forms of address for Elders, the *masumasu*, even if today the ancient meanings of many of these expressions seem to be lost.

'Ako/lavo distinctions do not appear to constitute moieties even though they are linked to marriages. Indeed, Nasau people say that, in the past, one could never marry a person of the same generational category – which would have amounted to a marriage between *veiʻacini* – and today, when a spouse

Table 10.3: The *'ako/lavo* generational distinction and the *vei'acini* or *vei'amani–veiluveni* relationship among kin.

Generation	father's side		mother's side	
	Parents in a vei'acini relationship with Ego	Parents in a vei'amani / veiluveni relationship with Ego	Parents in a vei'acini relationship with Ego	Parents in a vei'amani – veiluveni relationship with Ego
G+2	*'ubu 'aqane*	*damai*	*'ubu yalewa*	*makubu*
G+1		*'ama – ganei*	*'ina – gadina*	
G0	*'aci – 'uka – ra 'uka*	*makubu*	*'aci – 'uka – ra 'uka*	*makubu*

comes from a region where these distinctions do not exist, they still adopt a different generational category from that of their spouse. Furthermore, the oldest men and women systematically use these distinctions to reconstruct kinship vocabulary during investigations concerning marriage. A consideration of the *'ako/lavo* generational distinction among the kinship terms (see Table 10.3) shows that Ego, male or female, is endowed with the same generational category as their siblings and parallel-cousins. In G0, they therefore have a *vei'acini* relationship, in which relative age distinctions operate. Ego's generational category is different, however, from that of their cross-cousins, where no distinction of relative age is marked; this relationship is of the *vei'amani–veiluveni* type. In the grandparental generation, Ego is in a *vei'acini* relationship with their paternal grandfather and maternal grandmother, all the *'ubu*, and often calls these grandparents *'uka*, 'my eldest siblings', unlike their maternal grandfather and paternal grandmother, who are called *tataï* and *damai* or *makubu*, terms to which no relative age or seniority qualification applies. Again, this relationship is of the *vei'amani–veiluveni* type. The only exception to this harmony is in Ego's parents' generation. A person's father and their father's siblings are in a *vei'amani–veiluveni* relationship with them, which corresponds perfectly with the latter's position in the kinship terminology, whereas their mother and her siblings, including the *gadina*, are – from the *'ako* and *lavo* point of view – their *vei'acini*. Therefore, from this point of view, there is an imbalance in the system: in Ego's parents' generation, paternal kin seem to be in a position of seniority with regard to maternal kin.

But marriage and fertility go hand in hand and, as we have seen already, the *icavu'i* play a great role there and this, once again, through women.

Indeed, it is women who, at marriages, sing the emblems related to the groups' fertility. In doing so, they evoke *icavu'i* that are not theirs, and in ritualized response those who are directly concerned throw water over the singers, aiming at their genitals (see Brewster 1922). Cross-cousins love to joke about those emblems that refer to the genitals, but only in the absence of the elders or a maternal uncle. During informal kava drinking, for example, large cups are served to cross-cousins, and reference is made to 'yam water' or 'prawn water' or any other emblems linked to their genitals; the bowls are usually placed as near as possible to that area of their bodies. The kava must be drunk in one swallow. The cup is then refilled and sent back to the person who gave it, according to the same rules, thus provoking abundant laughter among the whole gathering.

In others words, it seems that the reception of *bure* of foreign origin, whose members were previously in an affinal relationship with those of the lineage receiving them, necessarily involves a radical transformation of cross-cousin relations into sibling relations parallel with the transformation of *vei'amani–veiluveni* relations (focus on fertility) to *vei'acini* relations (based on locality). Moreso, unlike parallel-cousins, cross-cousins (see Figure 10.3) are also involved in the *vasu* position, which is included in the most respectful forms of address for the eldest, *vasu ki* (plus name of the mother's locality), that links a person to their mother's group. This position also refers to fertility.

Vasu and *Gadina*, 'True' Blood Lines and Relationship through Fertility

Marriage among indigenous Fijians inevitably refers to the relationship between a *vasu* and their *gadina*, maternal uncle. The relation between *vasu* and *gadina* is inherent to the brother/sister pair and to the latter's marriage. The sister's children belong to their father's group and to his territory; they are *vasu* to their maternal uncle (*gadina*), but also to the members of his *bure* and 'big house'.[25]

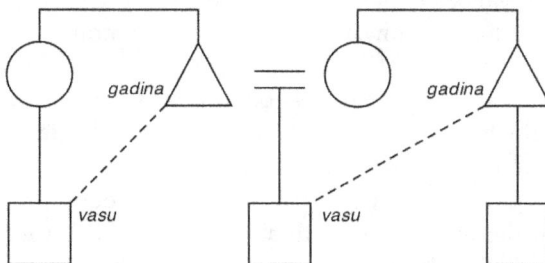

Figure 10.3: *Vasu* relations concerning cross-cousins.

As we have seen before in the kinship terminology, there is no specific term of address designating this position apart from *vasu vei yau*, 'the *vasu* connected to me', the term *vei* marking the relationship. I noted above the shallow depth of genealogical memory in Nasau. In direct contrast, the fact of a group being *vasu* to another is remembered over several generations, above all when the marriages at the root of this position concern the Elder whose unions ally groups of high status.

If, in their father's group, a person is related to locality and land, in their mother's group a person is linked according to wealth. A *vasu* can take home all the produce of their uncle's garden and all the goods of their uncle's locality, however valuable they may be. On the other hand, they have no prerogative over land. In Nasau, the village's brand new generator, although acquired with a lot of difficulty, thus changed hands, taken by a *vasu* attending a ceremony. The very next day, his *gadina* assembled the population of his village in order to organize the installation of the generator on the *vasu*'s territory and the electricity lines necessary for each household to benefit from it. Parallel to this, *vasu* are relied on when a meeting house (*vale ni soqo*) that concerns all the members of an ensemble of lineages is furnished they should provide all the crockery necessary for communal functions. This type of contribution is, moreover, particularly connected with maternal relatives during exchanges. In compensation, they are given mats, *masi* and *magi'i* (garden products).

The relationship between a *gadina* and his *vasu* is, like that linking a brother and sister, the most respectful and the one surrounded by the most prohibitions. A maternal uncle cannot carry his nephews on his back, the part of the body also connected with the spirits. A *vasu* cannot take part in a kava drinking ceremony if his maternal uncle is there, otherwise the latter will have to give up his place to him. On these occasions, if several *vasu* from the same locality are present, it is the descendant of this locality's eldest woman who drinks the first bowl.

Furthermore, the *vasu* relationship is a constituent element of the person through one of the two sorts of blood (*dra*) associated with it. Nasau people stress the resemblances between relatives by evoking blood. For example, if a little girl has marked physical features in common with her father or maternal uncle, it is said that the blood of one or other of them is the strongest (*kaukauwa*), and these parallels often refer to attributes of the *kalou vu*. Neither of the two sorts of blood seem to dominate the other; however, unlike the blood on the father's side, that on the mother's side is described as *bibi* ('heavy') and *dina* ('true').[26] The distinction between these two kinds of blood is not therefore to do with substance but with value, and all the ceremonies at which maternal relatives are present are hence considered to call for the most attention and effort, to be most difficult (*dredre*).

Most of these features are found throughout Fiji, but Nasau people also stress other points: the *kalou vu* maintain relationships of a different nature with the men and the women connected to them. To be more precise, their *sau* is passed differently to the one and the other from grandfathers. For men, these relations involve not only locality but also status, as mentioned above. Linked to the distinctions of age and seniority, they determine men's place in the order of precedence and the degree to which they may represent, in their own persons, different groups. For women, they concern above all procreation and fertility.

Everything happens as if groups' fertility was taken by women, when they marry, to their husbands' groups, thus benefiting the latter's descendants and, also, as if fertility and wealth were one and the same. The paths of wealth that come from women are also 'the paths of blood'. For a maternal uncle, his *vasu* are thus associated with the fertility stemming from his own group's *kalou vu*, and each group's descendants depend on his affines, as is also apparent in the rituals linking women to the constitution of houses.

Therefore, the relationship between a maternal uncle and his *vasu* is always a protective one. As Turner states when talking of Matailobau, in ancient times, if an attack on a village was planned, the *vasu* were warned so that they would not be present at the time of the attack. Today, a *gadina* comes and takes the knife which has wounded his *vasu* or the horse which has thrown him so that his life will not be endangered. If the health of an ill child gets worse, the paternal kin organize a ceremony to ask forgiveness (*soro*) of the maternal uncle, for this worsening could be due to some deterioration in relations between the two groups. Another point also deserves attention here. Relations with a locality's *kalou vu* and *vu*, normally on the side of life, can also bring illness or death between relatives, between a father and his son, for example, but never between a maternal uncle and his uterine nephews. The latter relationship, it is said, only exists on the side of life, and there are numerous examples illustrating this. Thus, in the village of Nasau, a health centre (*vale ni bula*) was built near a place marked by the presence of a *kalou vu*. Most of the population is reluctant to go there and, even more so, to spend the night there, apart from the *vasu*, who know that all they have to fear are the usual harmless jokes the spirits play on them. They are said thus to be manifesting their protective presence to the *vasu*.

Unlike the father's role, the protective relationship of a *gadina* towards his *vasu* is associated with a mother's role and relations with the body, as shown in certain examples given above. Thus at funerals, maternal kin position themselves near the body of the deceased and take care of it. The corpse cannot be buried on the father's land or, for a woman, on her husband's without permission from the deceased's maternal uncle. It is he who digs the grave and does the burying, helped by men belonging to the maternal group. This uncle is said to be the only one 'strong' enough for such an act, and the funeral represents the last opportunity for the *gadina* to surround his *vasu* with a mother's love. Similarly, it is stressed that the mother is at the beginning of life and the maternal uncle at the end. Brother and sister are thus placed in a relationship of continuity. As soon as the grave has been dug, the *gadina* goes to wash his hands in the river, an act which leads to a prohibition on fishing in a large part of it, according to the dead person's status. This prohibition will be lifted temporarily during the fiftieth day mourning ceremonies, and then definitively on the hundredth. The fact of not being able to fish at these times results in an extraordinary abundance of fish. During the ceremonial fishing organized at these two key moments of mourning, the first fish the men catch, surrounded by the women holding the nets, is called *kalou*; it is eaten alone by the maternal uncle who seems thus to ingest part of his dead *vasu*'s transformation and to complete a cycle. The pot in which this fish was cooked is taken away by the maternal uncle.[27]

The *vasu* position (*vasu ki*) which completes the respectful terms of address for Elders refers therefore to the mother's and the maternal uncle's group. This group is at the origin of the person's 'true' blood. Beyond the mother and maternal uncle, this relationship is maintained by the *kalou vu* of this group with the women born in it. This enables us to understand why, at kava ceremonies in which several *vasu* from the same locality take part, precedence is given to the son of the eldest of all the mothers. Otherwise, the maternal uncle, who has a closer relationship of locality with this group than the mother, and with its *kalou vu*, remains the referent in this relationship. A man's connection to the *sau* of the paternal *kalou vu* is, above all, a matter of status. Hence one is, as a descendant, a direct product of the relationship with the mother's *kalou vu*, who provide her fertility. The allusion to the maternal group in the most respectful terms of address for Elders refer therefore to part of the most fundamental relations constituting a person, just as much as to those which enable the paternal group, evoked by the *masumasu*, to endure.

Furthermore, regarding the constituting of a person, Nasau people's closeness to their cross-cousins is due to the fact that they all share the same components that are formed by similar relations (of fertility) to the same spirits. From this point of view, the relationship between a *vasu* and their *gadina* – and sex crossing, more generally – appears at once to provide both affines and affines turned into siblings. The marriage prohibition concerning affines turned into 'siblings' ensures that the two kinds of relations – those of status and seniority on the one hand, and of procreation and fertility on the other – are never mixed. Indeed the distinction between them appears to constitute the basis of the whole system. But we also have to understand the 'bula' ('life') relation expressed in the respectful form of address for the Elder and which passes through the paternal grandmother.

Life Relations from the Paternal Grandmother and the Naming of Persons

Although she attends all the ceremonies concerning her grandchildren, the paternal grandmother is not, so far as I know, the focus of a specific ritual, such as the 'araboroboro ceremony for eldest sisters, ra'uka. On the other hand, grandmothers play a noteworthy part in naming. To understand this, we must look again at the 'ako/lavo distinction which, as will become clear, gives remarkable coherence to Nasau terminology. Indeed, as Hocart observed, it is when they are linked to the naming of people, that the 'ako/lavo distinction is most notable (Hocart 1931).

At birth, children are said to be connected to their mother's group. They are *vulagi* (usually glossed as 'guest'), as are the members of this group, and a firstborn child is laid on mats brought by its *ganei*, at the top of its parents' house, on the side of the door through which the eldest among the affines enter. Nasau people say that, formerly, a child was always carried above the ground, passing from the arms of one woman to another, until its naming day, and that it was only when it had been named that it was put down on the ground. Today, naming always takes place on the fourth night after birth, at a ceremony called *vaka yaca* (from *yaca*, 'name'), during which the maternal spirits are thanked and the goods brought by the child's *ganei* (mats, tapa) are given to the maternal uncle, who is always present in the case of a firstborn child.

In any person's life cycle, this naming ceremony corresponds to the funeral ceremony, which takes place on the fourth day after death, and during which the deceased is summoned to take part in a last meal with their close kin before leaving them definitively. By contrast, the naming is the first of the rituals that integrate the child into its father's locality. This is followed by rituals that mark the first time the child is bathed in the river by the paternal grandmother, goes to its father's garden, has its hair cut (the hair is buried on its father's land) and, finally, is baptized. At all these ceremonies the maternal spirits are thanked, and the gifts brought by the *ganei* (mats, tapa) are presented to the maternal uncle.

Nasau men stress that, in ancient times, when there were fewer of them, the names given to children were those of the paternal locality's spirits, but that today this is no longer possible. Even so, its name links the child to its paternal *bure*, each of these groups having a stock of female and male names.[28] One of these names is given to the child who will be the only bearer of it in that generation, but as the stocks are limited, they are soon exhausted. Hence, the firstborn are given such names, as are most younger siblings, whilst the last-born children are given names from elsewhere, belonging to the maternal *bure* or taken from someone in the locality temporarily, such as a nurse, a teacher, an ethnologist. Moreover, the names of the paternal *bure* are distributed according to the child's status, and the systems of naming men and women have notable differences, female and male names not being of the same kind. It is at the heart of these differences that part of the meaning of the *bula* relation lies.

Firstly, the son of a *bure*'s eldest person will always have the same name as his paternal grandfather, in the third ascending generation. This name is systematically given to the eldest son of his immediate younger brother.[29] His younger siblings and his father's brother's younger children will have names taken from the second ascending generation. For women, the logic at work is only partly similar. For the eldest *bure*, the eldest daughter takes her paternal grandmother's name, while for the younger *bure*, the eldest daughter is given the name of the father's eldest sister (*ra'uka* or *ganei*), those of his other sisters – classificatory or not – being distributed among the younger or youngest daughters when possible, and according to birth order.[30] Hence, the paternal grandmother does play a role in naming but, unlike paternal grandfathers, she is more particularly associated with the level of social organization on which the *kalou vu* relation is the closest.

Names are essential components of a person; they establish homonymic, privileged relationships between those who share them: they have the same *loma*, deeper inside! Thus an Elder or a person in a senior position will address or refer to one who bears the same name as 'my name'. Moreover, as the names of the eldest, referring to grandfathers, grandmothers or the siblings of eldest fathers (*'ama levu*) can never be pronounced, children or young people who bear them are addressed or referred to using the expressions 'his/her grandfather', 'his/her father', 'his/her grandmother', which clearly evoke the homonyms in a position of seniority. These appellations change somewhat when a person has had a child: they are called father or mother of 'his/her grandfather', 'his/her grandmother' or 'his/her father'. Likewise for grandparents, who are then 'grandfather' or 'grandmother' of 'his/her grandfather', 'his/her grandmother' or 'his/her father', still based on an Elder man or woman's homonymic relationship.

The hierarchy operating is thus always discernable in the homonymic relationship. For, in a group of children, 'one's grandfather', for example, will always be distinguished from one's 'father', and even more so from those who have the names of younger siblings or names from outside the locality that can be spoken. It is the same for adults whose status is always marked by that of their eldest descendant's homonym. In respect of genealogical depth, and given the extent of genealogical amnesia here, especially for collateral kin, it is noteworthy that the names of a *bure*'s Elder are often the only ones remembered at the head of generations. On the male side, the names of the Elder tend to become absolute references, particularly in the case of eldest *bure*; thus a father can call his eldest son, when he has such a name, *yaca* ('name') directly.

This kind of name for an eldest son thus acquires special value which makes it virtually a title. Note too that his house, like that of his father and paternal grandfather, is named after the place where the mound of the very first ancestors present in the region stands. Here, with respect to 'the eldest', namesake relations seem therefore to make particular sense. I remarked above that, in the past, names referred to spirits, and their *sau* is said to follow the line of eldest, passing from a grandfather to his eldest grandson.[31] Taking into consideration both naming and generational distinctions, the system reveals itself to be even more coherent for these eldest sons. For, unlike those who have a 'father's' name, they are the only ones associated with the same *'ako/lavo* generational category as their namesake, their relationship being of the *vei'acini* kind.

Here the name relationship and generational category converge, thus placing these persons in the position of a perfect mirror image (see Figure 10.4). Likewise, the line of eldership so formed is the only one in the whole lineage that, in this logic, alternates the *'ako* and the *lavo*, which are associated in most cases with different emblems. The grandfather/grandson or *'ako/lavo* pair therefore acquires here an unrivalled completeness. This constitutes these eldest sons' very being, thus distinguishing them from all their younger brothers, who are not associated with the same elements, as they are in a *vei'amani–veiluveni* relation with their namesake.

Names play a major role here. Just as a chief must be in his rightful place, otherwise, it is said, he will die soon after his investiture, this type of eldest son must be worthy of his name and position. If such is not the case, he dies young and/or has no descendants. The list of names reveals an example of this kind in Nasau. The name of a deceased eldest son was given to a younger brother and will no longer be on the senior side, which suggests a debasement of the name. Thus homonymy with regard to male eldership in the lineage notably consolidates relations to locality and status, and it is these that are evoked by the part of the most respectful expressions for addressing Elders (the *masumasu*) referring to the paternal group. That this part, linked with one of the *icavu'i*, is impossible to change, even when it is a question of survival, shows their importance.

The system revealed for these eldest sons is not found with respect to eldest daughters of eldest *bure*; quite the contrary. An eldest daughter

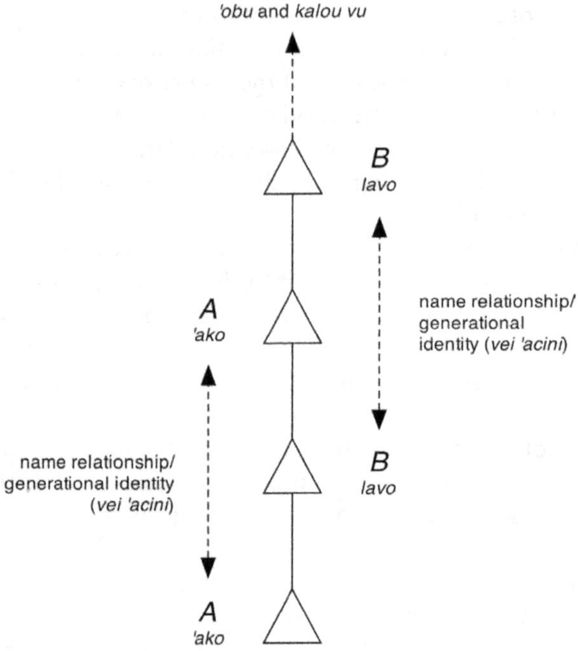

'obu and kalou vu

B
lavo

A
'ako

name relationship/
generational
identity (*vei 'acini*)

name relationship/
generational identity
(*vei 'acini*)

B
lavo

A
'ako

Figure 10.4: *'Ako/lavo* completeness.

and her paternal grandmother do not have the same generational category and, moreover, are never associated with the same emblems. A paternal grandmother is associated with those of her group of origin, and her granddaughter with those of her father's group. But this is also the case for all homonymic relations on the female side since neither do all women with the names of *ganei* have the same generational categoryas the latter (see Figure 10.5). In other words, the *vei'amani–veiluveni* are systematic here.

The role of grandmothers and their association with life (*bula*) is therefore not to be sought in the same sphere of coherence as that marking eldership on men's side and their connection with locality. The role of these women is different: they are the providers of female names in their husband's group, apart from those of the youngest who are too far removed from eldership to be taken into account here. These names, unlike male ones, although said to belong to the various *bure*, are always of foreign origin. They come from groups who stand as *bula* to one another, for no mother can directly hand down her name to her daughter. The only woman who passes on a name is the paternal grandmother, but her name is only handed down to her eldest granddaughter on the highest *bure* level. Therefore, these grandmothers are the conduits for female names, and which will thus increase the stock

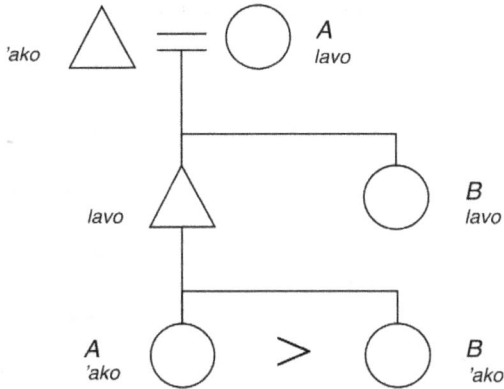

Figure 10.5: Relational category and naming on the female side.

attached to their husbands' *bure*. Female names are mobile, as are women, and their distribution systematically follows the alliances between groups. Moreover, their origin is long remembered. There is an anecdote worth recounting here to illustrate the strength of the connection associated with these names. One day, a girl at school in Suva came back to Nasau village saying that she and one of her new friends had the same name; her father or grandfather, after having at first thought this impossible, met this friend's parents and, together, they managed to establish that an ancient relationship existed between the two groups to which they belonged.

A *bure* needs women from another group in order to form the foundations of its houses, to endure from one generation to another, but also for the ʻako to succeed the *lavo* and vice versa. Therefore, women are once again clearly part of the perpetuation of generations, and Nasau people say that they keep the latter 'turning', with reference to the alternation of ʻako and *lavo*. With regard to eldership, women, once they have become grandmothers, by handing down their name to their eldest granddaughter, thus pass female names from one group to another. The reader will remember that naming is the very first ritual integrating the child, whatever its sex, into the paternal locality. Therefore, everything seems to indicate that these grandmothers also put into the hands of the men of their husband's group the most essential elements for the localization of girls, whose nature is different from that of boys.

There is an obvious parallel here: the wealth from the different houses through which affines enter circulates in the groups until it reaches the dwellings of the Elder, where it is collected in their name; taking the opposite route, women's names enter by way of marriage, through the house of the eldest of the eldest *bure*, to form and increase the groups' stock of female

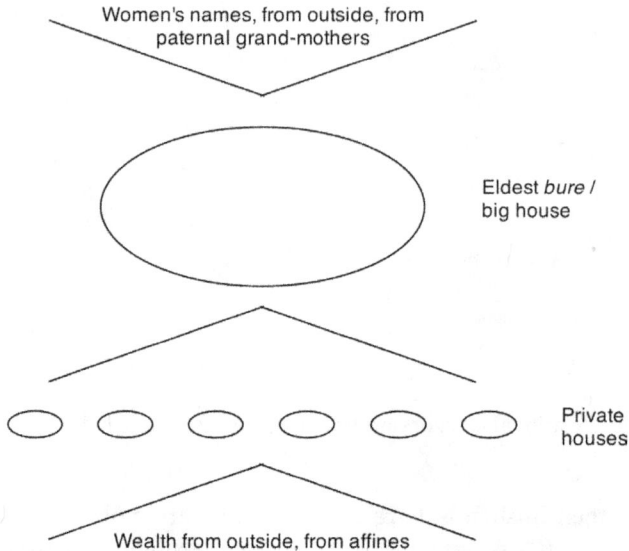

Figure 10.6: Paths of wealth and paths of women's names.

names (see Figure 10.6). It follows that the most valorized expressions, which in point of fact refer to the *bula* relation, are addressed only to these Elders. This relationship is their prerogative, and women's names and 'life' are thus singularly combined.

Other elements must also be taken into account in this *bula* relation. A careful look at what happens with the eldest of Elders *bure* reveals a specific configuration of names. From a homonymic point of view, over

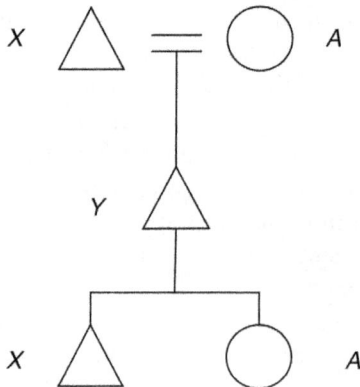

Figure 10.7: Naming transforms a marriage relationship into a brother–sister relationship.

three generations, a marriage relationship has been transformed into a brother–sister relationship (see Figure 10.7). This configuration of names alone contains the bases of the main locality, blood and life relations associated with absolute eldership. It is thus central to the coherence and renewal of Nasau social organization. The *bula* relation places said coherence, through paternal grandmothers and eldest daughters, on the side of these eldest men, formed by an extraordinary convergence of complementary relations.[32]

Conclusion

Since Annette Wiener's (1976) work, which brilliantly highlighted women's role in society – a topic which had been given very little consideration until then in anthropological studies in Oceania – many anthropologists, both men and women, have explored this issue. In Nasau, where distinctions, like identities, are of a deeply relational nature, neither of the sexes has pre-eminence over the other with regard to the long and complex work of forming and reproducing the *vanua*, whose source lies in the differentiated relations that men and women maintain with their origin spirits. Locality and status are for men, while mobility and fertility are for women, and each group depends on other groups for the renewal of relationships which form the basis of all life. Gender distinction alone is not sufficient for this renewal. Here it is completed by the distinction that makes the eldest – male and female – radically different from others. This difference lies in certain components of their being, in particular names, connected to specific relationships not shared by younger people.

Toren (1994b) points out how dualism in Gau captures the antitheses that she analyses in terms of the implications of balanced reciprocity versus tribute. This is possible, she argues because, 'given that all things go in pairs, a totality consists of a pair of pairs, which explains why, in Fiji, everything really goes in fours' (ibid.: 209). My own analysis here reveals how the number three mediates the movement from a pair (two), to a pair of pairs (four). Indeed, here the number three stands out. Thus, for Nasau people, the most respectful expressions for addressing Elders refer to three complementary relations, that of 'locality', 'true blood' and 'life', which link three distinct groups: the father's, mother's and paternal grandmother's. Likewise, a chief's house, which is an image of the *vanua*, is composed of three parts – the bottom, the top and the space above the roof – associated respectively with women, men and chiefs, the latter always being connected to absolute eldership but also to temporal depth. At kava ceremonies, three claps (*cobo*) mark the moment a chief drinks, two when it is his *mata ni vanua* (the 'face of the land'), who links the chief with *na lewe ni vanua,* the people (lit. 'the substance of the land') who are seated 'at the bottom'.[33] Three generations of the eldest demonstrate the coherence of the *vanua*. Many more such examples could be given. Value and temporal depth always go together. It makes sense then that three is also the figure on which transformations are based. The move from three to four is necessary if a ritual purpose is to be accomplished, taken to completion: a dead person leaves their close kin on the fourth night, a child also passes from the status of guest (*vulagi*) to that of one who belongs (*itaukei*, often glossed as 'owner') on the fourth night. All the major life-cycle ceremonies last for four nights.

I trust the reader will be able to see that there is a beautiful coherence here, evident at once in the transforming relations between Nasau people as they are lived day to day, and in the ritual observances in which these same relations inhere.

Notes

1. In Nasau's language the sound « t » is replace by a glottal stop, when this is not the case it means that the word is taken from the language of the Island of Bau.
2. In Fiji it is relatively rare, but far from exceptional, for a woman to hold such a title. Nasau people insist that the title of 'ui Nasau was accorded, by right, to the eldest woman of the eldest group of Nasau tikina (district).
3. *Icavu'i* refers to the totems or totemic emblems of a group. It is composed by *cavu*, a name of a group, the title by which the group is known, and, associated with the term *vanua*, to what gives a place meaning (Capell 1991: 28). The idea must be differentiated from *yaca*, which refers to the name of a person.
4. *Ki* is a term used to specify place, locality.
5. This chapter is based on fieldwork totalling a year conducted in Nasau, central eastern Viti Levu. Fieldwork was financed by the Centre National de la Recherche Scientifique, Paris, through funds obtained by ERASME (Équipe de Recherche d'Anthropologie sociale: Morphologie, Échanges), the French Embassy in Fiji and the Fonds Louis Dumont for research in the social sciences. My thanks go to these institutions, and to the people of Nasau, especially the late Marama na 'ui Nasau, Salau and her whole family, and to Paul Geraghty, who guided me in my first steps in the world of the 'ako and lavo.
6. On maps, Nasau village often goes by the name of Nadawa, the former place of residence of one of Nasau's constituent groups.
7. The term *loma* ('centre', 'middle') is also used as a prefix for states of consciousness or emotion.
8. Animals directly manifest the spirits' presence; as for plants, they are all signs of them. For example, a man who had received a visitor without being able

to offer him anything to eat sent his son to the bank of the river, where there grew a tree connected to the group. The child saw in the water under this tree an abnormal concentration of emblem fish, their scales shining in the sun. He was able to catch these fish to provide for his father's guest.

9. As mentioned earlier, the *'ui* can be a woman and this is why gender neutral pronouns are employed. However most of the eldest members of the eldest lineages are male. Those are the ones living on their group's territory. Their sisters leave the locality for their husband's because of exogamous marriages and virilocal residence.

10. We will designate the eldest member of the eldest lineage by « Elder », with a capital « E ».

11. Or namesake relationship.

12. These investigations were also at the root of conflicts as to the identity of groups at the head of different *vanua*. In Nasau, the group holding the right to the title of *'ui* was absent at the time of these inquiries, and the title was attributed to another group of equivalent status. I know of no real conflicts concerning the transmission of this title, which today has been restored to its former holders.

13. See Cappell and Lester (1941), France (1969) and especially Pigliasco's recent account of the matter (Pigliasco 2007: 161–69). Citing Groves (1963) and France (1969), Pigliasco reminds us that during the census of 1956, only 66 per cent of Fijians were able to say both to which *mataqali* and *yavusa* they were supposed to belong (Pigliasco 2007: 166).

14. Female *'ui* excepted, said eldest member is male. If an elder sister is to drink in lieu of her brother, the name of the house is always that of the original mound *'obu*, giving its name to the Elder's house.

15. Unlike other regions in Fiji, cups of kava are sent to their recipients once their social unit has been called out. Certain Elders, however, have titles that directly evoke the person themselves. Thus the female *'ui* Nasau drank her cup after she had been referred to as *Na Marama 'ui Nasau*, 'Dame *'ui Nasau'*. In this context of eldership, the entire group is represented by the titled person.

16. Note the association of men with what is 'above'. Today, the umbilical cords of girls are likely to be buried, but under smaller plants than those for boys and with sweet-smelling flowers.

17. The womb is also called *kete*. See also note 26.

18. These elders can also be Elders depending on the ceremonial context.

19. Mere Ratunabuabua, personal communication, 2008.

20. In the kinship terminology, all women are designated by the term *dauve*.

21. It appears that these men are above all on the woman's side.

22. It is worth noting that this term doesn't belong to the kinship terminology. It defines a position, that of the *vasu* in regard to the maternal uncle's, *gadina*.

23. This term is the only one that, along with *navugo*, does not mark generation. It occurs too in Ego's grandparents' generation, for the maternal grandfather alone, in the form of a sex-specific term. But it also appears in the form of a non-sex-specific term in Ego's generation to designate all cross-cousins, maternal and paternal and, again in the same form, it designates all Ego's grandchildren. Always positioned in an alternate generation, it seems to pull descent towards the maternal grandfather. Hocart (1931: 222) notes that, in Naitasiri, *makubu* designates the maternal grandfather, cross-cousins being *tavale*, but that, in Nakorosule, these two terms are used for cross-cousins, the first being familiar, the second respectful. The term *bu* (in *makubu* and *'ubu*) seems to be related to the increase in the number of Austronesian languages.

24. Hocart noted: 'Inquiry has failed to discover any practical consequence of these classes at the present day: they do little more than survive in the Highlander's love of etiquette' (Hocart 1931: 223).

25. This relationship was important in the development of twentieth-century anthropological theories. Its political aspect has been particularly emphasized for the realms of eastern Fiji.

26. In talking of conception, women evoke menstrual blood, which is differentiated from paternal or maternal blood; it gradually coagulates in contact with male semen, *wai ni 'aqane*, as in a bird's egg.

27. It will be remembered that the *'arabororo* is said 'to make the bottom of the pot', that the maternal relatives are relied on to bring crockery to the *vale ni soqo* and that, at *tevutevu*, women drink kava prepared in a pottery bowl, not a wooden one. During the funeral vigil, kava from the same type of bowl is also given to the women seated at the bottom of the deceased person's house, the body being placed 'at the top'. Again, at the meal that is part of the marriage ceremonies, the couple eat side by side, the bride near her maternal grandfather, and all the crockery used goes to the maternal kin. Women in general, and maternal kin in particular, appear to have a noteworthy relationship with pottery-like elements in ritual. The ritual preparation of kava in a wooden bowl (*tanoa*) is said to have been recently introduced; in the past, Nasau people drank this beverage from a hole dug in the ground. Thus today *tanoa* do not receive the same attention from Nasau people as they do elsewhere in Fiji. They are seldom hung on the walls of houses to keep them safe, and the legs of many of them are broken. I would suggest that earth is to pottery as men (paternal) are to women(maternal). Indeed one may surmise that maternal kin, and women in general, represent a form of fleshy container, while the 'inside', and the *yalo*, associated with the father's origin spirits, may be on the side of the paternal kin.

28. Here I refer to 'name' in the singular, but a composite Fijian name is always coupled with a Christian first name. See Turner (1991b) on names in Matailobau.

29. This practice protects these names, if the eldest should die. Younger siblings are also called *ba'i levu* (from *bati*, 'barrier', also 'teeth'), which designated the warriors in a chief's front line. In Nasau, they are responsible for watching over the house of the eldest, and are the only people allowed to stand up in it. At the funerals of the eldest or of chiefs, they watch over the body of the deceased, preventing anyone who is not a maternal kinsperson from approaching it. They also have the privilege of blowing the conch shell on the death of a chief, the only sign of sadness allowed. In the village of Nasau, it is the second group, sometimes encompassed by the one in which the title of *'ui* is handed down, which holds this position. In the context of lineages, it is not surprising that these younger siblings, so near the bodies and houses of the eldest, should be associated with their name. The youngest, as opposed to younger, siblings are the *ba'i lailai*, 'little ones'. They represent outer borders, and their names refer to the outside. At a more inclusive level, the role of *ba'i* is played by the affinal groups that are part of the locality: their places of residence in the villages are situated on the edge of the groups, forming so many borders between sets of lineages.

30. The naming of an eldest girl from Nasau, who had received the name of her paternal grandmother, had given rise to complaints among her *ganei*. As this little girl did not belong to an eldest *bure*, she should have had the name of a paternal aunt. At the same time, all her group were attaining a higher status because the eldest sibling of the eldest *bure* could not have children.

31. For the ceremonies accompanying circumcision, a grandson is isolated for a few days in his grandfather's house, not his father's. In this region of Fiji in the past, ceremonies may have included the taking of names. Early texts make reference to this, as well as to the associations made during these ceremonies, between the young circumcised boys and some of their emblems (e.g. Brewster 1922).

32. The real difficulty here is to understand how the discontinuity of *'ako* and *lavo* is linked to different emblems. The same *'obu* is related, generation after generation, to an eldest sibling with a different name and associated with a different emblem. Nasau people say that to begin with all Fijians were the same (*tauva'a*), then the first distinctions (*wasewase*) appeared with the *'ako* and *lavo*. Some groups of the Nasau region share one of their *masumasu*, but this is far from general. It is, however, the case for the two sets of lineages who live together in Nasau village: the *masumasu 'ako* of the one is identical to the *masumasu lavo* of the other. Yet, the majority of the wives of the members of the Nasauqaqa group, particularly on the side of the eldest, come from the different *bure* of the Nasau group, to which the *'ui* title is passed on; the second is in a position of seniority with respect to the first, who settled in the region more recently. One cannot today infer from this that these distinctions might have been linked to a form of dual organization, involving preferential choices for marriage.

33. For an approach to the *mata ni vanua*'s role in the kava ceremony, see Hooper (1982).

References

Brewster, A.B. 1919. 'Circumcision in Noikoro, Noemalu and Mboumbudho', *Journal of the Royal Anthropological Institute* 49: 309–16.

———— 1922. *The Hill Tribes of Fidji*. London: Seeley Service and Co.

Capell, A. 1991. *A New Fijian Dictionary*. Suva: Government Printer.

Capell, A., and R.H. Lester. 1941. 'Local Divisions and Movements in Fiji', *Oceania* 12(1): 21–48.

Cayrol, F. 2013. 'Une fin d'année sous tension. Entre cyclicités et relations entre personnes: une logique fidjienne des émotions', *Revue Hermès*, special issue, 65: 119–24.

———— forthcoming. 'Image touristique, image chrétienne: la cérémonie du *yaqona* (kava) mise en perspective (Fidji)' in *Image et patrimoine*, Paris, l'Harmattan.

Clunie, F. 1986. *Yalo i Viti: Shades of Viti*. Suva: Fiji Museum.

France, P. 1969. *The Charter of the Land: Custom and Colonization in Fiji*. Melbourne: Oxford University Press.

Gell, A. 1993. *Wrapping in Images. Tattooing in Polynesia*. Oxford: Oxford University Press.

Hocart, A.M. 1931. 'Alternate Generations in Fiji', *Man* 31: 222–24

———— 1937. 'Kinship Systems', *Anthropos* 32: 545–51.

Hooper, S. 1982. 'A Study of Valuables in the Chiefdom of Lau, Fiji', Ph.D. diss. Cambridge: University of Cambridge.

Groves, M. 1963. 'The nature of Fijian society', *Journal of the Polynesian Society* 72(3): 272–91.

Nayacakalou, R.R. 1955. 'The Fijian System of Kinship and Marriage, Part I', *Journal of the Polynesian Society* 64: 44–55.

———— 1957. 'The Fijian System of Kinship and Mariage, Part II', *Journal of the Polynesian Society* 66: 44–59.

Pigliasco, G.C. 2007. 'The Custodians of the Gift: Intangible Property and Commodification of the Fijian Firewalking Ceremony', Ph.D. diss. Manoa: University of Hawaii.

Toren C. 1988, 'Making the Present, Revealing the Past: The Mutability and Continuity of Tradition as Process', *Man* 23: 696–717.

———— 1994a. 'Transforming Love: Representing Fijian Hierarchy', in P. Harvey and P. Gow (eds), *Sex and Violence: Issues in Representation and Experience*. London: Routledge.

———— 1994b. '"All Things Go In Pairs, or the Shark Will Bite": The Antithetical Nature of Fijian Chiefshipship', *Oceania* 64: 197–216.

Turner, J.W. 1986 '"Owners of the Path": Cognatic Kinship Categories in Matailobau, Fiji', *Oceania* 56(4): 204–303.

_____1988 'A Sense of Place: Locus and Identity in Matailobau, Fiji', *Anthropos* 83(4–6): 421–31.

_____ 1991a. 'Weaving the Web of Kinship: Siblingship in Matailobau, Fiji', *Ethnology* 30(2): 183–97.

_____ 1991b. 'Some Reflexions on the Significance of Names in Matailobau, Fiji', *Journal of the Polynesian Society* 100(1): 7–24.

Walter, M.A.H. B. 1975. 'Kinship and Marriage in Mualevu: A Dravidian Variant in Fiji?' *Ethnology* 14: 173–80.

Weiner, A.B. 1976. *Women of Value, Men of Renown*. Austin: University of Texas Press.

11

How Ritual Articulates Kinship

◆●◆

Christina Toren

Yesterday afternoon a ceremonial reception in the village hall for all those who've returned from the *Bose ni Yasana* [Provincial Council] – first a *sevusevu* [ritual presentation of *yaqona* root] and then lunch is served. Afterwards we watch a DVD of the speeches and the *veiqaravi vakaturaga* [chiefly ceremonies, lit. attendance on one another in the chiefly way]. [. . ..] Watching the young children in the village hall as they watch the *veiqaravi*, I see how they name [and, in so doing, identify as specific kin] each person they know as he or she appears on the screen. [For example, the same man is variously named as *Momo* mother's brother or *Ratu* father and the same woman as *Bubu* grandmother or *Nei* father's sister]. [The children] *cobo* [clap ceremonially with cupped palms] and say *vinaka saka* ['thank you gentlemen and ladies'] in all the right places. They are attentive, even the smallest [aged four years old or so] being able to watch the proceedings for significant periods, though when the *veiqaravi* is over for the most part they disperse. The film is around two hours in length, but we're all fascinated – adults and children, me included.
—Fieldnotes, Gau, Fiji, 4 July 2007

This extract from my fieldnotes is intended to remind the reader of the high salience of ritual and ritualized behaviour not only for ethnographic analyses of kinship but, concomitantly, for those on whom these analyses bear. Indeed, one of the most interesting aspects of the present collection is its clear contribution to our knowledge of how ritual constitutes relations between people. Each chapter is replete with accounts of the ritualized behaviours appropriate to particular forms of relationship, of life-cycle rituals in which kinship is central, and of explanations for both ritual and ritualized behaviour. These observations are particularly pertinent to kinship as 'knowledge that counts', for ritual and ritualized behaviour are crucial to the process through which any one of us arrives at knowing what kinship consists in (cf. Nabobo-Baba 2006). In certain cases, ritual finds a relationship and gives it form, while in certain other crucial cases ritual brings relations into being. In other words, however we look at it – as relations found out or relations constituted – kinship is played out in ritual.

Virtually all the observations on ritual and ritualized behaviour in the present work are derived from adults whose experience and understanding became at once the object and the means of ethnographic analysis. This is a perfectly valid proceeding: we anthropologists tend to rely on adult informants. For this very reason, however, it is worth exploring here how these same adult informants came to know what they know – whether as ritual practice, everyday ritualized behaviour or exegesis of the meaning of ritual. This chapter therefore invites the reader to think about the fact that, in the course of growing up, children have to learn how 'to be' kin, and learning how to be kin entails making sense of the ritual and ritualized behaviours that specific kinship relations entail. Before turning to particular Pacific examples, here follows a brief excursion into a general theory of ritual.

Firstly, there is the observation made by Maurice Bloch (1986), in his historical analysis of Merina circumcision, that ritual practice is remarkable for its by and large unchanging nature over time. In other words, the details of ritual practice do not have to be written down in order to be remembered over extraordinarily long periods, passing from one generation to the next. This is because, as will become clear below, ritual practice is crucial to the intersubjective process of making sense of the peopled world or, in other words, of rendering the world meaningful. For all it is inevitably, and in every respect, intersubjective and historical, the learning process is just as inevitably autonomous. For any given person, rendering the world meaningful happens over time, meanings are never simply enshrined in language categories and 'received readymade' only then to be subject to 'empirical risks' as Sahlins (1985: ix) would have it; rather, meanings have to be constituted over time, and this goes both for meanings that are apparently 'given' in language categories and meanings that are derived from bodily practices entailed by both full-scale ritual performance and day-to-day ritualized behaviour. There are a number of excellent studies of how language is constituted intersubjectively (Bråten 1998; Rumsay 2003; Tomasello 2003) to which the reader is referred; the present discussion is confined to the micro-historical, intersubjective process through which any given person makes sense of ritual. The account here of how ritual and ritualized behaviour are rendered meaningful reiterates the theory I have proposed in previous works.[1]

Making Sense of Ritual

Firstly, ritual and ritualized behaviour are precisely a matter of what is done, when and how. Gilbert Lewis still provides the most useful definition:

> In all those instances where we would feel no doubt that we had observed ritual we could have noticed and will notice whether the people who perform it have explicit rules to guide them in what they do . . . What is always explicit about ritual and recognized by those who perform it, is that aspect of it which states who should do what and when. (Lewis 1980: 11)

As I have shown, this idea of ritual as behaviour that people say is governed by rules is of crucial importance to the process through which, over time, people constitute the meaning of ritual practice. For the most part, children are not taught 'the meaning' of ritual or ritualized behaviour, though in the case of certain life-cycle ceremonies, such as weddings, their meaning is likely to be alluded to in passing; also, where people are concerned to maintain a knowledge of their traditions, children in the late stages of primary school and later may well be taught them in school, which is the case in certain Fijian schools. Even in such cases, however, allusions to the 'meaning' aspect of ritual practice are likely to be cursory – 'this ceremony asks for a woman in marriage', or 'this ceremony shows our respect for chiefs', 'this is what you do when someone dies', or merely 'it is traditional to perform this ceremony'. Furthermore, it is usually the case that children have already learned at home, and learned well, the rules of many a ritualized practice – that is to say, who should do what and when and how – long before they arrive at the point of being able to name it, let alone to attribute to it any explicit meaning. The process is described in general terms below, but first it is important for the reader to understand that ritual and ritualized behaviour are not to be taken for granted as 'symbolic'.

As adults and anthropologists, we tend to privilege our own ideas over those of children; in so doing, we have taken for granted that for everyone ritual must stand for something other than itself, and that this something is carried by the material symbols, the behaviour (including the language used and so forth) that are prescribed for a given ritual act. My various studies show, however, that the idea of ritual as symbolic in this sense is an artefact of a developmental process whose eventual outcome inevitably conceals the nature of the process itself from those who are its products – that is, from adults (meaning pretty much anyone above the age of twelve or thirteen). Such meaning as is ascribed to any given ritualized behaviour by ourselves and others lies not so much in the ritual process itself, but in the very developmental process through which we make meaning out of ritual (see Toren 1990, 1993, 1999a, 1999b, 2006, 2007, 2011). This is a process that in its nature is always unfinished, and always – more or less radically – transforming, for meaning is always capable of further elaboration.

Adults are usually capable of ascribing a meaning to ritualized behaviours, but from a child's point of view that meaning cannot be obvious; it does not declare itself. For the child, the significance of the behaviour may be simply that 'this is how you do X'. So, for example, Pauwels (this volume) observed in Lakeba (as I have done for Gau) that as soon as a child could stand up and walk it was taught to sit down when others were sitting in the same room; indeed, this was the very first injunction given to the child. Thus by the age of four or so, a child who grows up in a village in the Lau islands or in the islands of Lomaiviti (central Fiji) is likely to know that on entering a house or room where others are seated, they should immediately crouch or sit down on the floor, or if passing among those present, walk on their knees. For the child, the significance of this behaviour may be simply that the child's father or mother or other adult had instructed them what to do, but otherwise the behaviour carries no necessary extra meaning. In other words, there is no necessary idea for the child that this arbitrary act and others like it are symbolic of something else, that they have meaning beyond themselves. Of course, prescriptive injunctions from parents, people a child loves or fears or those in authority have a significant emotional dimension (which no doubt informs too the infant's and young child's voluntary imitation of others), but the crucial thing here is that the symbolic meaning of the prescribed or imitated behaviour is not intrinsic to it. Rather, what the child comes to know is that there is usually 'a right way' to do things, that it is considered proper or correct to observe this or that mode of behaviour, which may itself be rendered explicit in the form of 'a rule'. In the case of these Fijian village children, the rule of modifying one's body posture when entering a room or passing among others has already become second nature by the point where, at a somewhat older age (six or seven or so) these same children are able to explain its meaning as 'respectful' (*vakarokoroko*).

The reader will be surely familiar with the fact that children are routinely on the receiving end of injunctions from adults concerning their behaviour, especially in respect of 'the rules' of what to do and what to say and how. 'Say please'. 'Don't interrupt'. 'Eat with your mouth closed'. 'Don't run in the house'. What is striking about these injunctions by adults to children – in any given case, anywhere in the world – is that from the child's point of view these behavioural rules have no transparent purpose when stated outside the simple doing of them; that is to say, they have no intrinsic instrumental end. Rather, they are learned as something one does, apparently for its own sake, under certain circumstances. It should be noted, too, how pervasive these behaviours are. With very little effort, the reader will be able to think of an impressive list of prescriptive injunctions by adults to children concerning greeting behaviour, physical deportment, and eating and drinking – to say nothing of all the other domains where behaviour is under close scrutiny (in church, for instance). The rules rendered explicit in these injunctions by adults to children constitute the ritualized aspect of the behaviours to which they refer.

In anthropological texts, 'ritual' refers usually to discrete ceremonies. 'Ritualized behaviour' is used here to refer more widely to behaviours that are pervasive in daily life, so taken for granted that their ritual quality is rarely recognized. Most if not all behaviours have a ritualized aspect – that is to say, an aspect that can be rendered explicit as 'a rule'. Any given child, anywhere in the world, is likely to have learned numerous rules of behaviour a number of years before they are able to say what these rules might mean. The idea that behaviour is and should be meaningful is important here; indeed, this idea is itself necessary if the child is to render ritualized behaviour meaningful. That the child should come to seek out a meaning for a prescribed behaviour makes phenomenological sense in that they already have extensive experience of the gestural or paralinguistic dimension of communication (see Tomasello 2003: esp. 1–42).

Elsewhere I have suggested that the following steps might be general in the cognitive developmental process of rendering ritualized behaviours meaningful (Toren 1993). First, the child performs a behaviour for its own sake – either because it has been told to or because it identifies (in the loosest possible sense) with those others whom it sees performing that same behaviour. This performance is usually described as 'imitation' and is prevalent in children up to age six or seven, informing their play as well as the other activities of daily life. Second, where the behaviour is prescribed by injunctions, its prescriptive quality forces the child over time (roughly, age six to nine) to become aware that this particular behaviour has a meaning beyond itself, that it is symbolic of something else. Third, at around age nine, the child begins to work out what it is that the behaviour is symbolic of, to constitute its deeper significance – for example, to understand that a particular style of speaking goes along with a particular style of physical deportment and that both may be meaningful in a particular way, that they may, for instance, differentiate 'people like us' from 'people not like us'. So, for instance, a Fijian village child from a chiefly clan may come to understand that quiet and dignified manners, proper greeting behaviour and general deportment may evince chiefliness (*i vakarau vakaturaga*), an idea that, as Nabobo Baba (this volume) makes clear, is of continuing significance to Fijians. Finally, around age eleven, the child arrives at an understanding that behaviour that it first understood as having no extra significance, as being merely 'the way you do X', is actually principled – that is to say necessary. It is at this point, at the point where a behaviour has been rendered fully meaningful, that it becomes intrinsically coercive: the behaviour can be rendered explicit as 'a rule' because its meaning aspect has come to be understood as the reason for the behaviour itself. For example, that modification of one's bodily comportment is symbolic not only of ones acknowledgement of an other's status, but also, more subtly, of one's own.

The nature of ritual and ritualized behaviour is such that it demands that we seek out its deeper meaning; that is, if one must behave in a certain way, this implies that the behaviour itself has significance, that there is a meaning there to be found. It has to be emphasized, however, that most ritualized behaviours are already second nature to the child, long before the deeper meanings of the behaviours are found out and made explicit. Knowing 'what to do, and when and how to do it' is crucial to the process by which the meaning of ritual and ritualized behaviours is constituted over time, and it is this process itself that ultimately renders the behaviour mandatory, a rule. Once one has arrived at the meaning of a rule that has for so long governed one's behaviour – for instance, 'it is respectful to' – it becomes necessary to see that same rule imposed on others by means of both injunctions and the example provided by one's own proper behaviour.

Necessity is at once the outcome of the learning process and its necessary condition. Indeed, one can argue not only that ritual is best defined as 'behaviour said to be governed by explicit rules', but also that the very idea of 'the rule' is the ultimate product of ritual and ritualized behaviour. The efficacy of ritual is precisely that it produces explicit behavioural rules.

Acknowledging Kinship

It will be apparent to the reader of this volume of essays that the ritualized behaviour that acknowledges kin at once signals who they are and, at least in part, the nature of the relation between them. Take, for example, 'avoidance relationships'. Avoidance between brother and sister, in most Pacific cases, becomes mandatory by puberty and, following as it does on an early child-hood in which the same relationship was intimate and loving, evinces its deeper significance precisely in acknowledgement of the behavioural mod-ifications required by the presence of the cross-sex sibling. Likewise, and in most of the cases presented here, the strict avoidance between mother's brother and sister's child comes into effect at puberty or during adolescence, following a childhood in which, should they live in the same village, the sister's child – especially if he is a boy – is often an indulged favourite with mother's brothers, especially in the immediate family. In eastern and central Fiji, the rule of avoidance between mother's brother and sister's child, for all it may derive from the superior status of the sister in respect of her brother, devolves on the younger party, who must leave a room when their mother's brother enters it, or at the very least, seat themselves at a significant distance and in an inferior position. The relationship combines the licence appropriate to the superior status of the mother's brother's child as *vasu* to the mother's people – their right to 'take without asking' – with the extreme respect, avoidance and obedience that is properly shown by a real or classificatory son-in-law or daughter-in-law to the father-in-law. It should be noted here, however, that the respect accorded the mother's brother is nowadays likely to co-vary at once with the ages of both parties to the relationship and with their rank, as is evident in the examples that follow.

> Maciu volunteers the fact that he does not observe the *tabu* on speaking with certain of his *momo* [mother's brothers]. He stands in this same relationship to two somewhat older men of his own commoner clan and he jokes and talks with them; with the much older son of the paramount chief [also his *momo* but a member of the chiefly clan] he has talked only when they've been alone together; with the head of another chiefly clan he has never once spoken a word and if he were to enter the house, Maciu would immediately have to leave it. I ask whether this was so when he was little and he says no, because then he didn't know, it's been so ever since he's been 13 or 14 and *yalo matua* – of mature understanding.
> —Fieldnotes, Gau, 1 July 2007

In this connection, it is interesting to consider briefly here the ritualized behaviour that is enshrined in the Dravidian terminology that obtains in eastern and central Fiji. Within generations, relationships are designated by fully reciprocal terms, for example, *veitacini*, 'taci to one another' (same-sex siblings), *veiganeni*, 'gane to one another' (opposite-sex siblings), *veitavaleni*, 'tavale to one another' (same-sex cross-cousins) or *veidavolani*, 'davola to one another' (opposite-sex cross-cousins).[2] Across generations, the base term designates the senior party to the relationship, for example, *veitinani* and *veitamani* refer respectively to the relation between a mother (*tina*) and her children and a father (*tama*) and his children.[3] But in the case of a child and its parents' opposite-sex siblings – its mother's brothers and father's sisters – the term *veivugoni*, 'vugo to one another', is again fully reciprocal. This Dravidian terminology is used in reference and address within and across villages and chiefdoms, and routinely extended to take in previously unknown people.[4] It entails that one marries ones kin – that is to say, one whom one can call cross-cousin.[5]

The very idea of the clan as a clan is constituted in exogamy, and in eastern and central Fiji it is cross-cousins who bring the clan (*mataqali*) into being. The corollary of this is that between clans, hierarchy can and does become an openly contested issue, and cross-cousinship (a competitive, joking relationship between equals) is made to play against siblingship (always hierarchical) in such a way as to leave the issue always unresolved (see Toren 1994, 2000). Any given person lives this tension in the transformations that take place over time in the relation between any child and its parents' opposite-sex siblings. Both within and across sex, a child is often a great favourite with its real mother's brothers and real father's sisters – much indulged, affectionately teased and generally allowed great liberties; if the marriage is endogamous to the village, this may be especially true for a boy with his mother's brothers. But at some point in the child's mid to late teens, this relation is abruptly transformed into the strictest of all cross-generational relations. Respect, avoidance and obedience are all enjoined on the junior party in relation to the mother's brother. At the same time, it is this relationship that allows the junior party as *vasu* to take without asking anything they want from the mother's people, and more particularly, from men of the mother's clan – that is, from mother's real and classificatory brothers. In other words, the *vasu* position combines the licence allowed cross-cousins with the extreme avoidance and respect that is characteristic of relations between brother and sister, and it is this binding of antithesis that allows the term *veivugoni* to be fully reciprocal, where other terms for cross-generational relations name the senior party.[6]

Lévi-Strauss argued in 1945 that in the 'atom of kinship' constituted in the relations between brother, sister, father and son, relations between men and women in the senior generation will stand in correlative opposition to relations between men across generations (Lévi-Strauss 1977: 46). In Fiji, this should mean, for example, that reserve between brother and sister is opposed to familiarity between husband and wife, just as reserve between father and son is opposed to familiarity between mother's brother and sister's child, but as we have seen this set of oppositions does not, in fact, obtain as such. Nevertheless, when we take the point of view of a male Ego as a child who becomes a young person who becomes an adult, we can see that at any given point in this process Lévi-Strauss's thesis holds; for example, the father's sternness with the young child contrasts with the playful familiarity of the mother's brother; while a gradual relaxation in the relation between father and son over time contrasts with increasing avoidance between mother's brother and sister's child. It does not follow, however, that fathers and sons are precisely familiar with one another. In Lau, Simonne Pauwels tells me, those classified as father and son barely speak to each other, and the son avoids speaking in their father's presence even when his father is old. In Gau, familiarity was, and is, likely to vary as a function of the closeness of the relationship, and of relative age and rank. The relations between a male Ego and his father's sisters undergo a somewhat less pronounced and elaborated change in contradistinction to the relation between him and his mother.

Ritual Distinctions Enshrined in Kinship Terminology

It is not surprising, then, to find that the distinctions that are brought into being in ritual and ritualized behaviour maybe enshrined in kinship terminology. Thus Völkel's linguistic analysis of Tongan terminology (this volume) shows that the grammatical marker of alienable or inalienable seems to be based on the idea of control over birth that is ascribed to the mother and the father's sister, an idea that is fully explained by Douaire-Marsaudon's in-depth ethnographic analysis (this volume) of how the politico-economic prerogatives of the Tongan *fahu* are a product of the ritualization of the superiority of the father's sister (*mehekitanga*).

Or look at the ritualized behaviour in which, as Hoëm (this volume) describes for Tokelau, people who are taking part in any community-wide endeavour virtually always do so by 'making sides', such that one side may be ranged against the other. This is also the case in many a Fijian *vanua* (land, place, country, chiefdom) where people may, for example, compete as those who are 'land' against those who are 'sea' (this very often being the case in the *vanua* of Sawaieke in Gau, where I did fieldwork) in respect of raising money, for instance. These 'sides' become visible precisely in ritual where they occupy different *vakatunuloa* (temporary shelters) built especially to house them for that particular occasion. Note, however, that the distinction between 'land' people and 'sea' people is laid down in childhood in the ritualized behaviour whereby, when they are eating together on some community occasion, children learn that those classified as 'sea' must not eat fish, while those classified as 'land' must not eat pig or other land meats such as river shrimp. In the case of Gau, the distinction between 'land' and 'sea' also distinguishes commoner clans from chiefly clans, and is pervasive in day-to-day life.

Indeed, for central Fiji at least, the ritualization of 'making sides' is given in the term *veiqaravi*, lit. 'facing each other' or 'attendance on one another', which carries within itself the antithetical tension between balanced reciprocal exchange across houses and tribute to chiefs. *Veiqaravi* may denote ceremonies such as those alluded to in the extract from my fieldnotes that begins this chapter; it may also denote the actual disposition of houses 'facing each other' in the space of a village, the ritual obligations owed by one clan to another, the balanced exchange relation between people classified as 'land' and 'sea' or the tributary ceremonies proper to attendance on a high chief.[7] Moreover, Cayrol (this volume) provides a far-reaching analysis at once of social organization, kinship terminology and ritual in Nasau, Fiji, in which the making of sides evinces itself over and over again in different forms. Indeed, it seems that the propensity for what Hoëm calls 'sidedness' is likely to be pervasive among Pacific peoples and, where it is found, will certainly be a feature of children's experience, such that by the time they are adults it is 'natural' to 'make sides' in any collective endeavour in the name of the community.

The reader will be able to discern, in respect of any of the day-to-day ritualized behaviours or full-blown rituals described in the preceding chapters, that adults deem it essential ritually to observe kinship in all its specificity of relationship. This observance of ritual is freighted with the emotions that characterize relationships, and inform the 'meaning' that adults ascribe to any given ritualized behaviour and, perforce, the process in which children constitute those meanings for themselves. Thus the necessity that is the outcome of the process of rendering ritual meaningful over time, from infancy through to adulthood and into old age, is a product of the history of its constitution. Elsewhere I have described this process in detail in respect of the constitution in ritual of Fijian chiefship which, my analysis shows, ultimately rests on the effective removal in marriage of sisters (especially those who are the eldest in their sibling set) from their sphere of influence in their natal group, and the concomitant subordination of in-marrying wives to their husbands (Toren 1990: 31–49, 234–44; 1994). Note, however, that the father's sister's curse in respect of their mother's brother's children remains powerful, and in the present work Pauwels and Cayrol demonstrate conclusively the continuing superiority in ritual of the female eldest of a sibling set over her brothers. To say that the sister is superior in ritual is, in short, for her to be superior as a function of the meanings that can be made by any given brother and sister over time. In this connection, it is worth reiterating Pauwels' observation (this volume) that, for the Fijians of the Lau Islands: 'To have no sister or no brother is to be *daku lala* ("with an empty back"), or without back-up so to speak. That is why parents without a daughter or a son take in somebody else's child, so that their children can learn how to be cross-sex siblings. After a few years, the child will return to its parents'.

The Exigency of the Rule

The many subtleties of meaning to be derived from the observance of ritual and ritualized behaviour – that is to say, from observance of 'the rules' – are evident in the essays collected here. It is the exigency of ritual as rule which, among Truku people of Taiwan, makes the *powda gaya* practices which any household must observe at once evince and constitute their relations to one another as kin. At the same time, as Ching-Hsiu Lin shows (this volume), the relatively recent monetization of exchange relations has given rise to a situation in which the fulfilment of ritual obligations between kin across households is producing a clear social stratification where before there was equality. That ritual and ritualized behaviour are central to the continuity and transformation of kinship over time is clear in all the essays. Thus Bonnemère's ethnographic analysis (this volume) makes the ritual cycle for male initiation among the Ankave-Anga of Papua New Guinea central to her argument that 'being a maternal uncle is the status that is the most valued in Ankave men's lives'. Her careful analysis suggests that 'the rules' regulating, for example, consumption of certain foods by both a woman and her brother during the period of her pregnancy, are considered to be of the utmost importance. Thus: 'Having a sister who bears a child is not, however, a sufficient condition for a man to become a maternal uncle; he has also to be endowed with a specific capacity that is acquired gradually through ritual'.

Or take Tcherkézoff's insightful analysis (this volume) of the ritual constitution of 'the community' in meetings that exclude in-marrying wives from influence, and thus in effect make village exogamy prescriptive in Samoa. This is a beautiful example of how ritual brings into being the very meanings it is said to express: a woman who makes the mistake of marrying in her own village cannot be comfortable in any of the regular village meetings where her status as 'wife' is at odds with her status as 'a village daughter'. As Tcherkézoff's account shows, in the ritualized and very visible meetings of any group that is called *nuu* – in its broadest sense 'the community': 'The husbands partially disappear from the scene, but the wives stand out clearly. The husbands are assimilated, but not the wives. The husbands blend into a system that refers to titles (either as a *matai* chief or as one of a group of servants that is said to be "the way to become a chief"). Wives are identified only in terms of their husbands.' The concomitant significant relationship is, of course, that between brother and sister, where the requirement to respect the sister resides in her special relation in ritual to the origin gods and ancestors, which, as Tcherkézoff tells us, 'used to be ritually condensed in the ceremonial virgin figures, but is more or less deemed to be the purview of all female kin'.

That ritual continues to carry deep meanings from the past into the present is particularly evident in examples like this from Samoa, and in Hulkenberg's fascinating account of how barkcloth (*masi*) figures in the ceremonial exchanges that find out kin relations between Fijians overseas and give them particular form. Her analysis, like others here, shows how the relation between people and their ancestral gods takes on a transformed and transforming presence in contemporary ritual where, given the dominance of Christian practice and doctrine in the lives of many Pacific people, the observer might have supposed that they had long ceased to be acknowledged.

Over and over again, in the pages of this volume, the reader will have found accounts of kinship rituals and the ritualized observance of kinship in 'the rules' of behaviour that are said to be proper to these same relationships. In each case, it is important to bear in mind, first, that ritual and ritualized behaviour are remarkable for their endurance over time and, second, that, from the point of view of any person who encounters them as a child, the meaning of ritual and ritualized behaviour is not given, but is rather constituted over time in an intersubjective, microhistorical process whose outcome renders mandatory the behaviour that ritual prescribes. The constituting process is one in which transformation and continuity are aspects of one another, in which connection it is worth noting the potentially transforming efficacy of other dimensions of day-to-day experience – school education away from home, urban living, television and other media, and evangelical religion, for instance. To the extent that adults relax their injunctions to children to 'follow the rules' of ritual and ritualized behaviour, these same children are more or less likely to arrive at ideas of what to do, how and when that will differ more or less significantly from those of their parents – an observation that is apparent in the examples from my fieldwork that bring this chapter to its end.

Gunu ti. Afternoon tea at home. Behaviour of Kitione – now 32 months old. He's with us for tea and, once the cloth is cleared away, for *yaqona* [kava, the serving and drinking of which is always ritualized, however informal the occasion]. He stomps about the room, sitting in the laps of those he favours, from various young men to the highest status chief of the commoner clans [his great-grandfather] who has come to drink *yaqona* in our house on account of my birthday. [Kitione's familiarity with his old grandfather is to be expected.] More interesting is that he is tremendously self-confident and I notice that no one tells him to sit down and be quiet. He is at ease with so many people that it's quite remarkable – happy to throw himself down on the floor and rest his head on the thigh of almost any one of the dozen or so men who are already there. Incidentally, at tea I notice for the first time that the children do not seem to be walking *lolou* [their bodies bent over in the posture of respect that is proper when moving amongst others who are seated on the floor] and that, in general, they are not being told to sit down and be quiet so much as they used to be [even six years ago]. [. . .] So far as I can tell, neither are they respecting the doorways, entering only by the common entrance as they should. At least in my house, they'll come in by any entrance that's open, though today Seini (aged about 14), who comes *takitaki* with a celebratory dish from her mother, asks my permission before she makes use of the *katuba e vanua* (land door) to exit my house and take the dish up to the house where

we eat. She has come up to the *darava e wai* (sea door) [to be used only by the owners of the house and certain very high-ranking others] and stays outside until I ask her to come in, [when she very properly uses the common entrance].
—Fieldnotes, Gau, 22 July 2007

Notes

1. To my knowledge, Toren (1990) remains the only full-length study of the process in and through which people make sense over time of 'the meaning' of ritual and ritualized behaviour and, in this particular Fijian case, in so doing constitute the idea that hierarchy is to be taken for granted as a principle of social relations.
2. *Tavale* used to apply only to male cross-cousins, *dauve* to female cross-cousins and *davola* to opposite-sex cross-cousins. Today there is a strong tendency for *tavale* to be used in all cases indiscriminately.
3. This accords with the way the terms are used by a third party; when used by Ego, *veitinani* and *veitamani* refer respectively to their relations with mother (*tina*) and father (*tama*), while *veiluveni* designates Ego's relation to those they call child (*luve*).
4. Thus a young man from a distant island who was employed for some months in Sawaieke country as a surveyor was known by a particular senior man to be his *vugo*. Once this single relation was known, the young man needed only to notice what any other person called his *vugo* to know what he should call the new person.
5. Even if the parties to a proposed marriage fall into a category with whom marriage is forbidden (*veitabui*), it is often possible to find a genealogical route whereby the couple can be called cross-cousins, after the fact as it were. One can marry someone to whom no easy genealogical connection can be traced; the marriage brings into being the relations between the man's side and the woman's side that would have obtained had they been known to be cross-cousins before marriage.
6. Cf. Lévi-Strauss's discussion of how, for the Lele, the system of relations in the atom of kinship changes as a function of 'succeeding phases of individual life' (Lévi-Strauss 1978: 100).
7. For an extended analysis of the transformation in ritual of balanced reciprocity into tribute, see Toren (1990, 1994).

References

Bloch, M. 1986. *From Blessing to Violence: History and Ideology in the Circumcision Ritual of the Merina of Madagascar*. Cambridge: Cambridge University Press.

Bråten, S. (ed). 1998. *Intersubjective Communication and Emotion in Early Ontogeny*. Cambridge: Cambridge University Press.

Lévi-Strauss, Claude. 1978 [1973] 'Reflections on the Atom of Kinship', in *Structural Anthropology II*. Harmondsworth, UK: Penguin (Peregrine) Books.

Lewis, G. 1980. *Day of Shining Red: An Essay on Understanding Ritual*. Cambridge: Cambridge University Press.

Nabobo-Baba, U. 2006. *Knowing and Learning: An Indigenous Fijian Approach*. Suva: Institute of Pacific Studies, University of the South Pacific.

Rumsay, A. 2003. 'Language Desire and the Ontogenesis of Intersubjectivity', *Language and Communication* 23(2): 169–87.

Sahlins, M. 1985 *Islands of History*. London: Tavistock.

Tomasello, M. 2003.*Constructing a Language*. Cambridge, MA: Harvard University Press.

Toren, C. 1990. *Making Sense of Hierarchy: Cognition as Social Process in Fiji*. London: Athlone Press.

———— 1993. 'Sign into Symbol, Symbol as Sign: Cognitive Aspects of a Social Process', in P.Boyer (ed.), *Cognitive Aspects of Religious Symbolism*. Cambridge: Cambridge University Press.

———— 1994. '"All Things Go in Pairs or the Sharks Will Bite": The Antithetical Nature of Fijian Chiefship', *Oceania* 64(3): 197–216.

———— 1999a. *Mind, Materiality and History: Explorations in Fijian Ethnography*. London: Routledge.

———— 1999b. 'Compassion For One Another: Constituting Kinship as Intentionality in Fiji', *Journal of the Royal Anthropological Institute* 5: 229–46.

———— 2000. 'Why Fijian Chiefs Have to Be Elected'm in J. de Pina Cabral and A. Pedroso de Lima (eds)', *Elites: Choice, Leadership and Succession*. London: Berg.

———— 2006. 'The Effectiveness of Ritual', in F. Cannell (ed.), *The Anthropology of Christianity*. Durham, NC: Duke University Press.

———— 2007. 'Sunday Lunch in Fiji: Continuity and Transformation in Ideas of the Household', *American Anthropologist* 109(2): 285–95.

———— 2011. 'The Stuff of Imagination: What We Can Learn from Fijian Children's Ideas about Their Lives as Adults', *Social Analysis* 55(1): 23–47.

Notes on Contributors

————— ◆●◆ —————

Pascale Bonnemère is Senior Researcher at the Centre National de la Recherche Scientifique, France, and currently director of the Centre de Recherche et Documentation en Océanie CREDO (AMU-CNRS-EHESS), Marseilles. She is the author of *Le pandanus rouge: corps, différence des sexes et parenté chez les Ankave-Anga, Papouasie-Nouvelle-Guinée* (1996), *Fruits d'Océanie* (1999) and co-author of *Drumming to Forget: Ordinary Life and Ceremonies among a Papua New Guinea Group of Forest-Dwellers* (2007), and the editor of *Women as Unseen Characters* (2004) and co-editor of *Ce que le genre fait aux personnes* (2008). Her latest book, *Agir pour un autre* (2015) offers a new analysis of the Ankave ritual cycle that takes in all participants, including women.

Françoise Cayrol is a member of the Centre des Nouvelles Etudes sur le Pacifique, has worked at the Ecole des Hautes Etudes en Science Sociales, Paris, and the Museum of New Caledonia, and currently works at the University of New Caledonia. She has conducted fieldwork in Viti-Levu, Fiji; her research interests include the relationship between age, gender, status, kinship and ceremonial forms that are specific to the societies of central Fiji. She is currently also researching the Fijian diaspora, and the role of community associations among the descendants of Fijians, Japanese, Javanese and people from Wallis and Futuna in New Caledonia.

Françoise Douaire-Marsaudon is director of research at the Centre National de la Recherche Scientifique, France, a member of the Centre de Recherche et Documentation en Océanie CREDO (AMU-CNRS-EHESS), Marseilles. Her research interests include the (trans)formation of political systems in Polynesia and their relationship to the construction of the person, processes of Christianization and relations between memory and history. Her publications include *Les premiers fruits: Parenté, identité sexuelle et pouvoirs en Polynésie occidentale (Tonga, Wallis et Futuna)* (1998) and the co-edited volume *The Changing South Pacific: Identities and Transformations* (2005).

Ingjerd Hoëm is Professor in the Department of Social Anthropology, University of Oslo. She has conducted fieldwork in Tokelau and in Tokelau communities in New Zealand regularly since the mid 1980s. She has published widely on aspects of life in the Pacific, and her publications include *A Way with Words* (1995), *Theatre and Political Process: Staging Identities in Tokelau and New Zealand* (2004) and the forthcoming book *Languages of Government in Conflict*, which deals with international politics relating to Tokelau.

Jara Hulkenberg is Honorary Research Fellow at the Centre for Pacific Studies, University of St Andrews, and Lecturer in Pacific Studies at the Oceania Centre for Arts and Pacific Studies, University of the South Pacific. Her current research examines how and why Fijians in the UK live life 'in the Fijian way', how kinship and complex hierarchical relations are played out in the day-to-day fulfilment of ritual obligations centred on life-cycle and religious events, and how ceremonies create transnational spaces that connect Fijians globally. She is the author of the forthcoming monograph *Masi: Cloth of the Vanua*.

Ching-Hsiu Lin is Assistant Professor at the Department of Public and Cultural Affairs, National Taitung University, Taiwan. His main field of research is the interplay between various forms of property and social change among indigenous societies in Taiwan. His publications focus on current issues among different indigenous groups in Taiwan, including indigenous knowledge and water management in Bunun society, as well as the impacts of privatization on gender relations in Truku society.

Unaisi Nabobo-Baba has worked as a teacher, teacher trainer, researcher at various institutions in Fiji and in the wider Pacific region (Micronesia, Polynesia, Melanesia, New Zealand and Australia). She is currently Associate Professor in Education and Chair of the University of Guam's Institutional Research Review Board. She is author of *Knowing and Learning: An Indigenous Fijian Approach* (2006) and numerous articles, including the *Fijian Vanua Research Framework* (2008).

Simonne Pauwels is Researcher at the Centre National de la Recherche Scientifique, France, and a member of the Centre de Recherche et Documentation en Océanie CREDO (AMU-CNRS-EHESS), Marseilles. She has done research in the Tanimbar archipelago, Eastern Indonesia, and is currently working in Fiji in Lakeba and Taveuni on land issues, siblingship, chiefship, relationships between village- and city-dwellers, and *balolo*, (sea worms, Eunice viridis) as a representation of what comes from outside. Her publications include *Metanleru, un voilier prédateur: Renommée et fertilité dans l'île de Selaru* (2009) and the co-edited volume *D'un nom à l'autre en Asie du Sud-Est: Approches ethnologiques* (1999).

Serge Tcherkézoff is Professor of Anthropology and Pacific Studies at the Ecole des Hautes Etudes en Sciences Sociales, at the Australian National University (visiting; he coordinates an EHESS program hosted by ANU and supported by the French Embassy), and (part-time) at the University of Canterbury, New Zealand. He is a member of Centre de Recherche et Documentation en Océanie CREDO (AMU-CNRS-EHESS), Marseilles. Drawing on fieldwork in Samoa during the 1980s and 1990s, his research involves an ethnohistorical critique of European narratives about Polynesia. His recent publications include *First Contacts in Polynesia: The Samoan Case* (2008) and the co-edited volume *Oceanic Encounters: Exchange, Desire, Violence* (2009).

Christina Toren is Professor of Anthropology and Founding Director of the Centre for Pacific Studies at the University of St Andrews. Her publications include *Making Sense of Hierarchy: Cognition as Social Process in Fiji* (1990) *Mind, Materiality and History: Explorations in Fijian Ethnography* (1999) and two co-edited volumes, *Culture Wars* (2009) and *The Challenge of Epistemology* (2012).

Svenja Völkel is Assistant Professor of Linguistic Typology at the University of Mainz, Germany, and she has also worked as Associate Lecturer and Researcher in Social Anthropology at the University of Heidelberg. Since 2002, she has conducted fieldwork in Tonga with an interdisciplinary focus. Her research interests include ethnolinguistics, cognitive anthropology, language typology and language contact. Her publications include *Social Structure, Space and Possession in Tongan Culture and Language* (2010).

Index

◆●◆

www.ingramcontent.com/pod-product-compliance
Lightning Source LLC
Chambersburg PA
CBHW060031030426
42334CB00019B/2270